# CREATIVE
# SELLING

# CREATIVE SELLING

**H. WEBSTER JOHNSON**

Professor Emeritus of Marketing
Wayne State University

**A.J. FARIA**
Chairman
Department of Marketing
University of Windsor

**4th EDITION**

Published by
**SOUTH-WESTERN PUBLISHING CO.**

S93

CINCINNATI        WEST CHICAGO, IL
DALLAS        LIVERMORE, CA

# PREFACE

The basic principles of selling are as sound and reliable today as they have been through the decades. However, the mastery of basic selling skills continues to grow in importance with advances in technology. While *Creative Selling* perpetuates the seasoned principles, this edition relates them to contemporary situations that are fresh and stimulating. The path to a successful selling career is carefully laid with language that is easy to understand and actual selling experiences that act as the mortar to enforce important concepts and make the path safe and easy to travel.

## DESIGN

This book will appeal to a wide range of readers. It has been designed for the
- community college student who is preparing for a career in marketing or sales
- business college student seeking the background necessary for a career in sales
- mature student in adult education classes
- beginning salesperson looking for a thorough grounding in selling fundamentals
- experienced salesperson who wishes to sharpen selling skills
- sales manager and university student wishing to supplement a business knowledge with a more precise insight into the selling function
- many others considering a career in selling

## CONTENT

*Creative Selling* provides a direct approach. For every topic covered, many examples are provided. There will never be any doubt as to what is intended. The authors have benefited from comments, suggestions, and examples provided by the many thousands of teachers, students, and salespeople who have used this book in the 20-plus years since the first edition was published in 1966. This fourth edition retains the best of the earlier editions yet adds significant new material.

## Organization

The book is divided into five sections for clear and logical coverage of the material. The Introduction provides a broad overview of selling. Topics covered include the role of selling in the economy and in the business firm; different types of selling jobs; and the rewards, challenges, and satisfactions offered by a career in selling.

Part 1, which includes three chapters, presents the background information that is necessary for a successful sales career. The issues presented range from the personal qualities needed in selling—such as appearance, personality, vocabulary, and dress—to the type of customer, industry, company, and product information needed by every salesperson. A simple diagram illustrating the relationships among the characteristics needed for sales success is presented in the opening chapter of Part 1 and is built upon in the following chapters.

Part 2 focuses on the most important person in the selling process, the customer. The two chapters in this part of the book thoroughly review the internal motivations and external forces that influence buying behavior. A knowledge of this material is essential for all salespeople.

Part 3, with six chapters, is the longest section of the book. Each chapter examines in detail one phase of the selling process, beginning with finding and qualifying customers through the topics of gathering customer information, making the sales appointment, capturing your customer's attention, making the presentation, demonstrating your offering in a creative fashion, handling objections, and closing the sale. Again, a diagram representing the stages of the selling process leading to the successful completion of a sale is presented in the opening chapter of Part 3 and continues through the final chapter.

The final part of the book includes two chapters that cover the important topics of how to use your selling skills effectively and how to manage your time, territory, and financial resources.

The book is logically organized to move the reader from an introduction to selling, through the stages of the selling process, to the management of a territory.

## Learning Aids and Special Features

Many features are included within this book to enhance the learning environment it provides. Each section of the book contains part openers that summarize what has been covered and what material is coming up in the next chapters. This links the various topics presented. Diagrams that are presented early in the book are continued as new material is added, to provide additional clarity.

Within each chapter is a feature referred to as **Tips** (theory-in-practice). These **Tips** present interesting and creative examples of how the sales concepts presented in the chapters can be put into practice. Also included within all chapters are numerous figures and tables that support the text discussions.

The text also includes end-of-chapter materials. There is a total of 140 end-of-chapter questions that review the chapter material; 42 sales challenges that present interesting problem-solving assignments based on the material most recently covered; and 31 cases. Many of the cases offer the opportunity to engage in role-playing exercises. The final case at the end of the book presents an interesting territory-planning situation. This case can be tried over and over to see if the reader can improve upon his/her solution.

## INSTRUCTOR MATERIAL

A detailed Teacher's Manual is available to all instructors using *Creative Selling*. This manual describes the purpose of each chapter in the text, provides teaching suggestions, and includes solutions for all end-of-chapter questions, sales challenges, and cases. The Teacher's Manual also includes 420 multiple choice questions that can be used for examination purposes.

## ACKNOWLEDGMENTS

The authors would like to thank the many thousands of teachers, students, business executives, and salespeople who have used earlier editions of this book over the past 20 years. Your continued support has made this new edition possible. We would also like to thank our colleagues, business associates, friends, acquaintances, and others who have offered helpful suggestions for this edition. Special thanks are extended to Susanne Patterson for typing the bulk of the manuscript. Finally, we would like to thank our wives, Josephine Johnson and Barbara Faria, for their continuing support.

## ABOUT THE AUTHORS

H. Webster Johnson, Professor Emeritus of Marketing at Wayne State University, received his A.B. and M.B.A. from the University of Michigan, and his Ph.D. from Ohio State University. He has taught marketing and related subjects at a number of universities. Dr. Johnson has conducted marketing research studies for various companies; supervised studies for several cities, particularly relating to retailing and wholesaling; taught sales courses in college; and presented numerous specialized selling courses for varied organizations. Dr. Johnson has published five books, had a number of articles published in professional magazines, prepared reports for business firms, and conducted research for the Federal Government. The American Marketing Association, as well as other marketing associations, has benefited from his active participation over a long period.

A. J. Faria, chairman of the Marketing Department at the University of Windsor, received his Ph.D. from Michigan State University. Dr. Faria has taught at Georgia Southern College, Wayne State University, and Michigan State University and has worked in marketing and sales with Chrysler Corporation, the Sunshine Biscuit Company, Tulsa Oil Company, and Davidson Bros. Wholesaling, Inc. Dr. Faria has served as a consultant to more than two dozen major business firms, has conducted many sales seminars and sales training programs, and has authored four books and more than 60 journal articles and conference papers.

# CONTENTS

# PART FOUR   INCREASING YOUR SALES EFFECTIVENESS

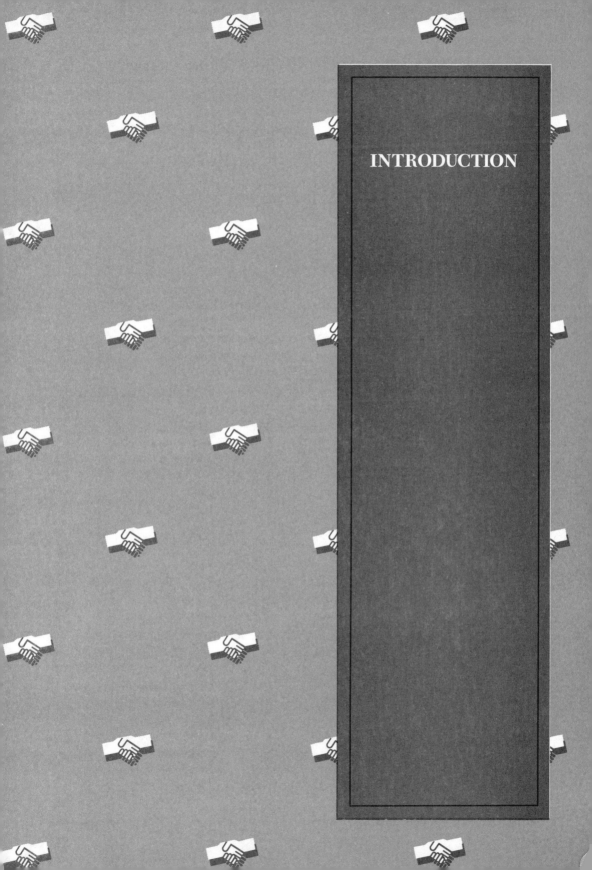

# INTRODUCTION

# 1

# YOUR CAREER IN SELLING

Benjamin Feldman, an agent for the New York Life Insurance Company, has a motto. This motto is "I want to be the best." When you consider that Ben Feldman has sold more than $83 million of life insurance in one year, more than $1 billion of insurance over his career, and has averaged more than $1 million per year in earnings for the past ten years, who would quarrel with his motto?

Ben Feldman's goal is to be the best. What is your goal? Have you thought about setting goals for yourself? Perhaps you have a simple or short-term goal, such as to break 100 on the golf course or bowl a 600 series. What about your career goals? These are far more important.

Your career, along with your family, will occupy the largest part of your time. As such, the selection of the right career is one of the most important decisions that you will make.

The right job should not only provide an adequate income to satisfy your family's needs but should also provide personal satisfaction and pleasure. Have you considered the possibility that these goals can be achieved through a career in selling?

## WHAT IS SELLING?

Whether or not we recognize it as such, each of us has selling experience. As a child you may have persuaded your parents to buy you something you badly wanted. On many occasions you may have persuaded your parents to let you stay up to watch a TV program you wanted to see. Another time you may have influenced a classmate or a special person to go to a movie with you. You may have talked a group of people into a beach outing, picnic, or volley ball game. Maybe you've sold something that you were tired of to a friend, or traded items with friends for something of theirs. You may have taken part in a garage sale.

These are all examples of sales, or sales-like situations. Selling involves more than just the exchange of a product for money. Candidates for political office must sell themselves to the voters. A minister must sell principles and ideas to the congregation. You may have to sell a new concept or way of doing business to your boss. Everyone can benefit from a knowledge of selling principles.

Selling is the process of matching needs and wants with the means of satisfying those needs and wants. In many cases this is quite simple. A salesperson approaches a customer looking at a particular shoe on display at the front of a shoe store. "May I help you?" the salesperson inquires. "Do you have this shoe in size 9?" asks the customer. The salesperson has the customer take a seat, retrieves a size 9 shoe from the back room, and helps the customer try it on. The shoe fits and a sale is made. The entire transaction may have taken five minutes.

This type of sales transaction, where the customer knows exactly what is wanted and the salesperson simply responds to the customer's request, occurs millions of times every day. On the other hand, there are some sales that take much time, effort, and persuasion to complete.

A computer salesperson may have to visit a potential business customer many times over several months. The salesperson may need to talk with the firm's representatives from personnel, purchasing, marketing, production, and finance to determine the company's needs. There may be a need to make numerous demonstrations, work out many details, or convince a committee that the computer system being offered is better than competitive systems. This type of sale also occurs many times every day and can be very rewarding. Kim Kelley, a computer salesperson for Honeywell, earned a commission of $81,000 on one such sale.[1]

Selling encompasses a variety of situations from very simple to very complex. The modern salesperson calls on a wide range of people engaged in a wide range of activities. Today's customers are more sophisticated and knowledgeable. A salesper-

---

[1] "Honeywell's Kim Kelley Closes in 'Big Ticket' Computer Deal," *The Wall Street Journal*, January 22, 1974, pp. 1-2.

**Illustration 1-1   Some selling situations require repeated sales contacts and detailed product demonstrations.**

son must understand a customer's needs thoroughly and must be a combination problem solver and marketing expert. Today's salesperson must have knowledge and creativity.

What then is selling? Selling is a person-to-person process that promotes an exchange of goods, services, or ideas. Selling is the process of bringing potential benefits or need-satisfying solutions to the attention of those who can profit from them.

# IS SELLING A GOOD CAREER CHOICE?

A career in selling can be rewarding in many ways. It is a means of achieving status and fulfillment. When you become a salesperson, you take the first step toward a position of authority. As a salesperson you will be dealing with people, satisfying needs, and solving urgent problems. Over time you will develop considerable knowledge of people, products, and business practices.

Selling can be the start of an interesting career. Through selling you can advance to positions of greater authority. As you advance, your authority and responsibilities will increase. You will grow in confidence as your business experience expands. More and more, studies show that the highest positions in business are being filled by men and women who started in sales.

## Good Financial Rewards

Careers in selling can be very rewarding financially. At the start of a selling career you can expect to earn approximately the same amount as you would in many other starting jobs. If you are successful, your income will rise faster than in other jobs. Importantly, you have the satisfaction of knowing that what you earn depends solely on your own efforts. To earn more, you only have to sell more. There is no ceiling to how much you can earn. Tables 1-1 and 1-2 provide some indication of earnings potential.

### Table 1-1

| Average Sales Incomes | | |
|---|---|---|
| | Consumer Goods | Industrial Goods |
| Sales Trainee | $21,300 | $24,800 |
| Regular Salesperson | 29,200 | 34,100 |
| Senior Salesperson | 39,200 | 42,600 |
| Sales Supervisor | 47,900 | 49,800 |

Source: "Salespeople's Annual Compensation," Sales & Marketing Management, (February 17, 1986), p. 56.

**Table 1-2**

## Sales Income By Industry

### Consumer Goods

| | |
|---|---|
| Appliances (household) | $31,000 |
| Drugs & medicines | 40,000 |
| Food products | 27,000 |
| Health-care products & services | 34,300 |
| Housewares | 31,500 |
| Tools & hardware | 33,000 |

### Industrial Goods

| | |
|---|---|
| Automotive parts & accessories | $30,500 |
| Auto & trucks | 29,500 |
| Building materials | 35,000 |
| Chemicals | 33,000 |
| Computer products & services | 50,000 |
| Electrical equipment & supplies | 48,000 |
| Electronics | 40,000 |
| Fabricated metal products | 35,000 |
| General machinery | 39,000 |
| Instruments & allied products | 34,300 |
| Iron & steel | 30,000 |
| Nonferrous metals | 32,000 |
| Office machinery & equip. | 36,000 |
| Paper & allied products | 31,200 |
| Petroleum & petro. products | 30,000 |
| Printing | 40,000 |
| Publishing | 30,000 |
| Rubber, plastics, & leather | 35,000 |
| Textile & apparel | 31,000 |
| Transportation equipment | 35,000 |

### Services

| | |
|---|---|
| Service industries | $31,000 |
| Transportation | 32,500 |

Source: "Sales Compensation," Sales & Marketing Management, (February 18, 1985), p. 62.

Nick DiBari retired from Comdisco, a computer software company, in November 1983 at the age of 38. From 1971 to 1983, Nick DiBari earned more than $7 million in commissions, an average of nearly $600,000 per year. In 1983 alone, Nick DiBari earned $1,258,956.[2] Enormous single-year commission earnings have also been achieved by Irving Rousso of Russ Togs, Inc. ($796,000); David Tracy of Fieldcrest Mills, Inc. ($288,577); Richard Barrie of Faberge ($282,585); and Robert Lair of Cessna Aircraft Co. ($242,749).[3]

Joe Girard is listed in the *Guinness Book of World Records* as the world's best salesperson. During his career, Joe Girard sold more than 13,000 cars and trucks, earning millions of dollars in commissions. In a single year, Joe Girard sold as many as 1,426 vehicles.[4]

Now that Joe Girard has retired, Debra Schepper may be on her way to replacing him as the world's best salesperson. Ms. Schepper was recently honored as the top Toyota salesperson in the United States, having sold more than 1,300 cars in a single year.[5] Clearly, the potential for top salespeople is unlimited. According to the U.S. Bureau of Labor Statistics, more salespeople earn over $500,000 per year than people in any other profession.

### Selling Leads to Positions of Authority

The high visibility of sales jobs makes them excellent positions from which to advance to jobs of even higher responsibility and authority. Many company presidents, including those for American Hospital Supply, Goodyear, Hershey Foods, Sunbeam, Procter & Gamble International, Xerox, IBM, and Monsanto, among others, began their careers in sales. Not all salespeople will become company presidents, of course, but if you have the ambition to reach the top, selling is a good place to start.

The reasons generally cited for the advancement of salespeople are that sales jobs involve the mainstream of business

---

[2]"What Made Supersalesman Nick DiBari Call It Quits?," *Sales & Marketing Management*, April 2, 1984, pp. 43–49.

[3]"Willy Loman, Eat Your Heart Out," *Dun's Review*, December 1980, pp. 68–72.

[4]Joseph Mastrangelo, "Super Salesman Was Once a Loser," *The Detroit News*, April 23, 1978, Sec. B, p. 3.

[5]"Tops in Sales," *The Detroit News*, August 6, 1984, Sec. C, p. 2.

operations; sales jobs provide a broad view of the company, its products, and its customers; and sales jobs provide experience in dealing with people. In selling, you can often write your own program for advancement.

A salesperson's first promotion is normally to a position of branch, district, or territorial sales management. Opportunities, however, are not limited to sales management positions. Other areas of business activity such as advertising, sales promotion, public relations, product management, buying, research, personnel, credits and collections, and merchandising could benefit from a person with sales experience. Your progress will depend on your ability and desires.

## Job Security and Opportunities

A glance at the classified section of any major newspaper generally shows more listings for sales jobs than for other positions. In 1890 there were only 264,380 salespeople in the United States.[6] The U.S. Department of Labor estimates that there are more than six million people currently employed in sales jobs. This figure does not include millions more employed in part-time sales positions. This represents a growth in sales jobs during the twentieth century that is nearly seven times the overall population growth. Furthermore, the Bureau of Labor Statistics indicates that more than 300,000 sales openings will occur each year during the remainder of the twentieth century.[7]

A good salesperson is rarely without a job. Security in selling is based on the salesperson's ability to produce business. No other employee group is less subject to layoffs, unlike other professions that generally follow the swings of the business cycle.

When Braniff International ceased operations in 1982, Norm Neelley, a Boeing 727 captain earning $77,000 per year, found himself unemployed. Where, at age 45, could Norm find a job that would match his captain's salary? Within a few days Norm Neelley accepted a sales job with Bell Chemical of Dallas. After

---

[6]Carroll D. Wright, "American Labor," *One Hundred Years of Commerce*, edited by Charencey M. Depew (New York: D. O. Haynes & Co., 1895), p. 12.

[7]*Occupational Projections and Training Data, 1983 Edition*, Bulletin 2052, U.S. Department of Labor, Bureau of Labor Statistics, September 1983, p. 44.

only six weeks, Norm had opened 21 new accounts for Bell, won the praise of his superior, and predicted that he would soon be earning more than he had as an airline pilot.[8]

When teaching jobs became scarce, Jerry Atkinson, a 38-year-old high school history teacher, needed a new job. Jerry found a sales job with the J. Wilbur Co. of Kansas City, a firm that sells promotional advertising items. Jerry Atkinson is now enjoying his career more than ever before and, compared with his teaching job, has far greater earnings potential.[9]

Selling offers many career opportunities for women. It is estimated that more than two million women are currently employed in sales jobs. There are over 100,000 women working as real estate agents alone. Women are increasingly sought for sales positions with computer manufacturers, media companies, publishers, pharmaceutical manufacturers, and others. Wife-and-husband teams are popular in fields like real estate sales.

Geraldine Young is a 34-year-old former home economics teacher whose ambitions were greater than what could be achieved teaching high school. Ms. Young decided to try a career as an industrial sales representative. She convinced several companies to let her handle their industrial tools as their representative in the New York City area. Within seven years, Geraldine Young has built up an industrial distributorship with yearly sales of $1.5 million.[10]

## Exciting and Challenging Work

If you enjoy traveling, facing new challenges, meeting new people, and being your own boss, selling is the job for you. Compared with other jobs, selling provides much freedom. A salesperson is not confined to a desk from nine to five. As long as the job is done, salespeople are often given considerable decision-making authority within their territories.

Make no mistake—selling is not easy. If you are looking for an easy way to get ahead, selling is not the job for you. If you are confident of your abilities, however, selling is a means of

---

[8]Keith McAllister, "Eight Who Switched to Selling—Thanks to Hard Times," *Sales & Marketing Management*, September 13, 1982, pp. 47–49.

[9]*Ibid.*, pp. 47–49.

[10]Betty Gibson, "How a Black Woman Made it in Industrial Distribution," *Sales & Marketing Management*, July 2, 1984, pp. 49–52.

showing your real worth. Aiding customers in their buying decisions, watching their mental and emotional processes, and observing their buying habits and behavior add great variety to your job.

### Selling Provides Mobility

Opportunities in selling exist everywhere. A good salesperson is not confined to a limited geographic area. As the number of sales jobs continues to increase, good salespeople find their mobility increasing. A salesperson's mobility applies to career opportunities as well. Selling skills developed while working for one business firm are readily transferable to other businesses.

### Selling Contributes to Society

With selling, you enjoy the feeling of doing something worthwhile. Some people express themselves in club, charitable, church, or civic activities. In selling, you have an additional means of expressing yourself by selling products and services that will enrich the lives of others. Think about how society has been enriched by modern technology, developed in laboratories, but brought to you through the efforts of salespeople.

Invention and technology develop thousands of new products each year, but selling brings them to people. Every sale made to the satisfaction of buyer and seller provides an opportunity to be of service to all concerned. Think about the more than 13,000 new cars and trucks Joe Girard sold over his sales career. Think about the pride the owners felt as each new car was driven home for the first time. Think about the jobs provided for those who build and service the 13,000 cars and trucks. Good salespeople take pride in contributing to the well-being of customers and businesses.

### Selling Contributes to Self-Development

A salesperson cannot stand still. A sales career encourages self-development. Salespeople must constantly monitor changing products, technology, and customers. Those in selling must read, listen, and constantly adapt their selling techniques. You will learn to keep your eyes and ears open and to profit from the know-how of others.

**Illustration 1-2** A good salesperson monitors current events that affect both business and personal life.

This constant adjustment—being ever responsive to customer needs—helps you to develop as a salesperson. You learn to conform with the conventional but remain original and persuasive on important issues. You learn to express your views in a way that gains agreement without antagonizing. You make friends by being friendly; gain sales by serving the best interests of your customers; and gain success through a constructive, balanced, and planned application of selling principles.

### Selling Provides Individual Responsibility

One universal characteristic of selling is the individual's responsibility for getting the job done. It is generally not possible nor desirable to provide a high level of supervision to salespeople. As a salesperson, you must be willing to accept responsibility for getting your job done. You must be willing to work without supervision. If you require day-to-day supervision, a selling career is not for you.

# SELLING AND THE MARKETING PROCESS

You've heard the phrase "The customer is always right." Although the customer may not *always* be right, a business firm must always cater to the needs of its customers. A business firm can only be successful if it achieves repeat sales to customers over time. To get repeat sales, a business firm must satisfy the needs of its customers. If current customers are not happy, they will deal with other firms in the future.

Marketing is the combination of all those business activities that are concerned with understanding and satisfying consumer needs and wants. Marketing includes product planning and development activities that bring about new products and improve existing products; promotional activities that communicate information about products and services to customers; distribution activities that deliver products to places where consumers can see and acquire them easily; and, finally, pricing and packaging activities that make the product appealing in the marketplace. Selling is an important part of this marketing process.

## The Business Firm

Marketing, production, and finance are the most basic activities of a business firm. A business must be able to finance its operations, produce something of value, and sell its output. If the firm falters in any of these basic areas, its chances for long-run success are poor.

Figure 1-1 shows how marketing performs two important functions within a business firm. Marketing must (1) obtain demand for the business firm, and (2) service the demand obtained. To obtain demand, marketing activities such as advertising, sales promotion, product planning, pricing, and packaging are performed. To service demand, activities such as warehousing, inventory management, credit, transportation, installation, and order processing are performed.

Selling contributes to both obtaining and servicing demand. Personal selling, along with advertising and sales promotional activities, is a very effective and direct method of obtaining demand. As well, part of the responsibility of salespeople is to see that demand is serviced properly. This is accomplished by ensuring that shipments of products to customers are made on

**Figure 1-1**

## THE BUSINESS FIRM AND MARKETING FUNCTIONS

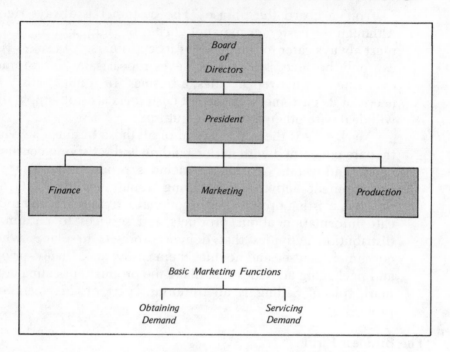

time, and that the shipments arrive with the right products in the right quantities. If shipments are not on time or not correct, the salesperson will initiate corrective action so that a customer is not lost.

### The Marketing Mix

The top marketing executives of every business firm must make a number of decisions concerning what products and services the firm will offer, what prices will be charged, how the firm will communicate with its potential customers, and how and where the firm will make its products and services available. The combination of these decisions is referred to as the firm's *marketing mix*. The elements of the marketing mix are sometimes referred to as the **four P's** of marketing: (1) **product**, (2) **price**, (3) **place**, and (4) **promotion**.

In developing a business firm's marketing mix, each element must fit with the others in such a fashion that the best overall marketing program is developed. As shown in Figure 1-2, this process might be compared with the fitting together of the pieces of a jigsaw puzzle. Each piece must complement the others to achieve the most effective marketing program.

Just as we have identified the elements of the firm's marketing mix, so can we identify a promotional submix that includes all those activities comprising the promotion piece of the marketing mix puzzle. The promotion submix is made up of advertising, personal selling, sales promotion, and publicity. Advertising is nonpersonal communication through media such as television, radio, newspapers, magazines, and billboards. Sales promotional activities involve such things as in-store displays, shows and exhibits, contests, coupons, demonstrations, and similar activities. Publicity involves any not-paid-for communication that the business firm receives, such as a newspaper or radio announcement that the business has contributed to a local civic project.

**Figure 1–2**

## THE MARKETING MIX AND PROMOTION SUBMIX

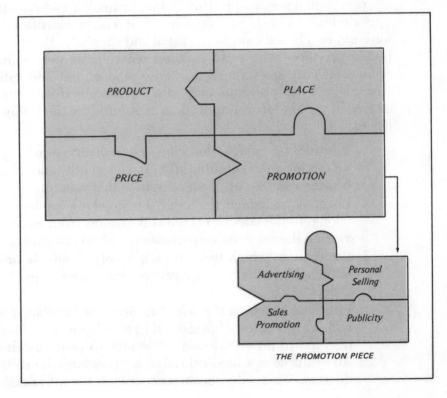

Each element of the promotional piece must be fitted together in the same fashion as the overall marketing program. Advertising and personal selling, for example, should be planned so as to complement one another. Advertising may be used to pave the way for salespeople by introducing the company and its products before the salesperson calls on a potential customer. The importance of this form of introduction is illustrated in Figure 1–3.

In a similar fashion, advertising messages that contain mail-in information requests can be used to develop leads for follow-up by salespeople.

Selling, as can be seen, plays an important role in the marketing process of the business firm. It is an essential part of the promotional element of the marketing mix and is instrumental in obtaining and servicing demand for the business firm.

## TYPES OF SELLING JOBS

Sales positions may be classified in many ways. Selling does not represent a single opportunity but, instead, a wide range of opportunities. The U.S. Department of Labor classifies sales jobs into two broad categories: retail and specialty. Retail salespeople are those who work in stores where customers come to them. Specialty salespeople are those who go out and call on customers. Sales positions may also be described in terms of degree of selling effort required, as suggested by the following listing.

1. **Positions in which the sales job consists primarily of delivering merchandise.** Milk, baked goods, and heating oil are examples of products sold in this manner.
2. **Positions in which the sales job involves inside order-taking.** Retail sales clerks who take orders from customers visiting the store are resrepresentative of this category.
3. **Positions in which the sales job involves outside order-taking.** The salesperson visits regular accounts and takes orders.
4. **Positions in which the sales job involves building good-will.** This type of job, referred to as missionary selling, is devoted to providing sales assistance to your customers. An example is a medical detail salesperson who calls on doctors. This salesperson encourages the physician to

**Figure 1-3**

## COORDINATING ADVERTISING AND PERSONAL SELLING ACTIVITIES

"*I don't know who you are.*

*I don't know your company.*

*I don't know your company's product.*

*I don't know what your company stands for.*

*I don't know your company's customers.*

*I don't know your company's record.*

*I don't know your company's reputation.*

*Now—what was it you wanted to sell me?*"

**MORAL:** Sales start **before** your salesman calls—with business publication advertising.

**McGRAW-HILL MAGAZINES**
BUSINESS • PROFESSIONAL • TECHNICAL

*Photo courtesy of McGraw-Hill Publication Co.*

**Advertising paves the way for the sales approach.**

prescribe products from the company the salesperson represents.

5. **Positions that require technical knowledge.** This involves selling sophisticated products, such as computers, which must be adapted to special customer requirements.
6. **Positions that require the creative selling of tangible products.** This involves the dual tasks of identifying a customer need and then selling the customer a specific product. Household appliances, aluminum siding, and many other products are sold this way.
7. **Positions that require the creative selling of intangibles.** This is often difficult selling as there is no physical product that can be shown or demonstrated. Advertising space and insurance are examples of intangibles.

Beyond these, sales positions may also be described in terms of the nature of the selling effort required and the type of business the salesperson represents. In terms of selling effort, salespeople may be classified as order-takers, order-getters, or support salespeople. By type of business, the salesperson might be employed by a retail, wholesale, manufacturing, or service business.

## Order-Taker Selling

Order-taking involves the routine completion of sales to regular or repeat customers. Once an account becomes a regular customer of a business firm, routine follow-up is necessary to keep the customer. Often order-taking salespeople have a regular route to follow. The job requires explaining details, making adjustments, handling complaints, negotiating prices and terms of sale, and keeping customers informed of new developments.

Manufacturers, wholesalers, retailers, and service firms all employ order-takers. Nabisco Brands, a multi-billion dollar manufacturer of snack foods and related products, employs a large sales force of order-takers. The typical Nabisco salesperson will call on ten to fifteen customers per day, generally supermarkets. On each call, the salesperson will straighten the Nabisco products on the store shelves, check for out-of-stocks, do some dusting and rearranging, and write up an order. From time to time, the Nabisco salesperson will attempt to get point-of-purchase advertising into the store, set up end-of-aisle displays, and encourage the retailer to engage in cooperative advertising programs with Nabisco.

## Order-Getter Selling

Order-getter salespeople aggressively seek out new business for their companies. The order-getter locates new prospects, opens new accounts, identifies new opportunities, and builds new relationships. Order-getters work for manufacturers, wholesalers, retailers, and service businesses. As the order-getting job is normally more difficult than order-taking, the order-getter normally earns more.

Order-getters may sell anything from computers and Boeing 747s to encyclopedias and cosmetics. The selling process may range from more than a year for a $25 million airplane to less than ten minutes for an Avon product. Although the bulk of order-getting selling takes place with face-to-face contacts, a growing amount is occurring through telephone sales.

## Support Selling

Support salespeople do not get orders themselves; instead, they help the order-getting salespeople. Most support salespeople work for manufacturers. Support salespeople are often referred to as missionary salespeople or technical specialists.

Missionary selling is not tied directly to a specific sale. Rather, it is intended to create interest and goodwill. The medical detail salesperson, one type of missionary seller, calls on doctors. The medical detailers do not sell—they describe products, their advantages, uses, research conducted, and they leave samples. It is hoped that doctors will prescribe these products for their patients and that druggists will buy and stock the products.

The technical specialist (or sales engineer) is highly trained. This person is often more concerned with answering technical questions and solving customer problems than with completing a sale. The technical specialist often will accompany an order-getting salesperson to talk with the customer's engineers. Once the technical issues have been resolved, the order-getter can complete the sale.

## Retail Selling

Many products purchased at retail stores require little sales assistance. The customer selects the product from the shelf and takes it to a sales clerk for payment. The sales clerk handles the customer's payment and places the product in a bag. A retail sales job of this nature requires little skill and provides little financial compensation.

Many retail selling jobs require a great deal of skill and offer very good earnings potential. Think of the knowledge required when selling products like major appliances, photographic equipment, personal computers, and televisions and stereos, to mention but a few. Customers will naturally ask questions and a salesperson must have good product knowledge to complete sales. For many retail selling jobs, considerable training is required. In some cases, special training such as the American Gem Society certificate program must be completed to qualify for a retail selling position.

**Illustration 1-3 Retail selling often requires a great deal of knowledge in order to be effective.**

Bea Cupp works in the household appliance department of the Sears, Roebuck & Co. Department Store in the Fairlane Shopping Center in Dearborn, Michigan. Ms. Cupp has been working for Sears for nearly twenty years and has developed many loyal customers who come to her when they have a need for a new appliance. Bea also closes many sales to walk-in customers that she meets for the first time. On average, Bea works more than 40 hours per week, in addition to attending sales staff meetings and training sessions. Bea is paid a commission on gross sales and earned more than $25,000 last year.

## Wholesale Selling

According to the Bureau of Labor Statistics, approximately 700,000 salespeople are employed by wholesalers. The customers these salespeople call on include manufacturers, institutions such as hospitals and schools, retailers, various branches of the government, and other wholesalers. As the typical wholesaler sells thousands of products, a broad product knowledge is essential for the wholesale salesperson.

Wholesale selling involves both inside and outside work. Many regular customers may be routinely contacted by telephone to determine their product needs. The wholesale salesperson also maintains regular contact with current accounts and calls on potential new customers to open new accounts. As can be seen, there are both order-taking and order-getting aspects to this salesperson's job.

## Selling for Manufacturers

Manufacturers employ many salespeople. These salespeople may call on other manufacturers, wholesalers, retailers, institutions, or service businesses. A manufacturer's salesperson generally has a territory to cover and is responsible for servicing existing accounts and pioneering new accounts within the territory. Depending on the territory size, this job may require extensive travel and periods away from home.

The job of a manufacturer's salesperson may be relatively routine, such as a salesperson for Procter & Gamble who makes regular calls on existing accounts. The job can also be very complex. Imagine the selling effort required for major industrial equipment, computers, and airplanes. However, the rewards for these jobs are great.

## Selling Services

Many salespeople sell services rather than products. Selling services involves areas such as banking, hospitals, car rental and leasing, accommodations and recreation, insurance, advertising space, investment counseling, and much more. These services are required by both households and businesses.

## Other Selling Jobs

As indicated, selling involves a wide range of opportunities. In addition to the sales jobs already identified, other sales opportunities exist in door-to-door selling (Avon employs more than 100,000 salespeople), party-plan selling (such as Tupperware), and mail-order selling. Some salespeople are self-employed. They may serve as manufacturer's representatives or brokers, representing a number of business firms in a particular geographic area.

Some door-to-door and party-plan salespeople earn extremely good commissions. The top Avon representatives earn more than $50,000 per year; the top Amway representatives (there are more than one million worldwide) earn over $100,000 per year; and Linda Tardiff of UndercoverWear (which uses the party plan) earned more than $250,000 in commissions in 1983.[11] These earnings are achieved, for the most part, by people who started on a part-time basis.

There are many additional sales jobs with which you are probably familiar. The purpose here is not to provide a complete listing of all sales jobs but to show the variety of sales positions that are available.


## CREATIVITY IN SELLING

Behind every successful product and company is an efficient, well-organized sales force. Consider the achievements of firms such as Encyclopedia Britannica, Avon Products, IBM, Singer, General Electric, Texas Instruments, and Procter & Gamble; then consider the contributions made by their sales forces. Good selling skills can stimulate entire economies. As stated by former President Lyndon Johnson, "Our salesmen and women are the creative organizers of the free market so vital to the growth, prosperity, and well-being of our nation."[12]

Although much selling work is routine, long-run successful selling requires creative efforts. Creative selling establishes

---

[11]Rayna Skolnik, "Naughty is Nice for UndercoverWear," *Sales & Marketing Management,* August 13, 1984, pp. 41–44.

[12]Speech given to Sales & Marketing Executives International, New York, February 20, 1964.

markets where they never existed. Creative selling discovers latent demand and converts it to active demand. A creative salesperson analyzes products and markets, identifies needs, and shows customers how their needs can be satisfied.

### Stimulating Creativity

Everyone possesses creative potential. Creative potential, however, is not the same as creativity. Actual creativity only comes about as the result of hard work.

As a salesperson, the starting point to stimulate your creative potential is preparation. This preparation involves knowing your company, your products, and thoroughly understanding your customers.

*Professional Insurance Agents*

**Illustration 1-4   A creative salesperson analyzes each customer's particular needs.**

The greater your understanding of your products, the better able you will be to visualize opportunities where your products can be put to use. The better your understanding of your customers, the better you will be able to identify needs that you can satisfy.

**Illustration 1-5** The creative salesperson must be able to adapt to different selling situations.

*Professional Insurance Agents*

*Tip\* The owner of a small chain of three supermarkets needed a new register for one of the stores. Terry Dickinson, a salesperson for a business machine company, was called in. During their discussion, an employee of the supermarket interrupted to inform the owner of a stock-out for a popular selling product. The owner was noticeably irritated and complained about the frequency of stock-outs at the three stores. Terry asked some additional questions and took many notes. At the end of the discussion, Terry made no attempt to close a sale but told the store owner that she would be back the following morning.*

*The next morning, Terry was back to make a complete presentation about one of her company's advanced POS (point-of-sale) machines. This machine served as a cash register, credit-checking, and inventory-updating machine. Supported with testimonials from satisfied retailers, Terry explained how the machine can help to reduce credit and bad check losses. The main emphasis, however, was on how the machine helps to reduce stock-outs through continuous monitoring of inventory levels. The store owner was thoroughly impressed and decided to*

---

\*TIPs (theories in practice) are short examples that will appear throughout the book to illustrate various concepts or ideas.

**24** Introduction

*switch the cash registers at all three supermarkets to the new POS machines. By being thoroughly familiar with her firm's products and her customer's needs, and by using a little creativity, Terry was able to convert a small sale for one cash register into a large order for POS machines.*

## THE ROAD TO SUCCESSFUL SELLING

When successful salespeople are asked why they like selling, they invariably give the same replies. Here are a few: The challenges offered by the job, the freedom to manage themselves, the financial rewards, job security and mobility, the opportunity to deal directly with people, and membership in an elite group of professionals. Do these reasons sound good to you? If so, the following chapters will intensify your interest. Whether you are a young person just starting your career, an experienced person looking for greater achievements, or a successful salesperson who desires to improve current selling techniques, the material in this book is for you.

## QUESTIONS

1. What motto would you like to live by? Explain.
2. What is the most recent sale you have made? Briefly explain the circumstances.
3. What is a thorough but concise definition of selling?
4. Are incomes from sales as described in this chapter higher or lower than you anticipated?
5. Why are sales jobs a good starting position for top management jobs?
6. What do career opportunities in selling look like over the next ten to twenty years?
7. What do you think motivates people like Nick DiBari, Joe Girard, and Ben Feldman?
8  What are the major elements of the marketing mix? Where does selling fit in the marketing mix?
9. What are the major differences between order-taker selling and order-getter selling?
10. Is product knowledge most important for retail selling, wholesale selling, or selling for manufacturers? Explain your answer.

# SALES CHALLENGES

1. Interview a store manager or buyer. Question this individual about the various sales representatives that call at the store. Do they use different sales styles? Are any unusual or highly creative presentations used? Ask the manager or buyer to describe the most and least successful salesperson calling at the store. Write a short report describing what you learned from this experience.
2. Explain on one page why you would consider yourself as more of an order-taker or order-getter type. Give an example from your background illustrating your answer.
3. A customer enters the sporting goods department of a large store and approaches the nearest salesperson.

**Salesperson:** Hello, may I help you?

**Customer:** I'd like to see the beginner's golf-club set that was advertised for $89.95 in the newspaper.

**Salesperson:** They're right over here. (The salesperson leads the customer to the golf-club display and watches the customer examine the clubs.)

**Customer:** I notice that the set doesn't include a putter.

**Salesperson:** That's correct. The putter has to be purchased separately.

**Customer:** Does a bag come with the set?

**Salesperson:** No, the bag has to be purchased separately.

**Customer:** Thank you. I'll have to think about it for a while. Maybe I'll stop back later.

How would you rate the effort made by this salesperson? Rewrite this scenario explaining how you would respond if you were the salesperson.

# CASES

## 1-1 Going from Order-Taker to Order-Getter

Harry Kopko has been working at the order desk of Imco Plumbing Products for the past six years. In this job, Harry answers customers' questions about Imco's products, terms of sale, and delivery schedules. Harry also takes fill-in orders that are telephoned to Imco by established customers. Harry works from 8:30 a.m. to 4:30 p.m. each day. Harry has been with Imco for a total of eight years. He is 34 years old, is married with two children, and earns a salary of $19,000 per year.

A job on Imco's sales force has just become available because a salesperson quit unexpectedly to go to work for another company. Because of Harry's experience on the order desk, he has been offered the job. Accepting the job would mean relocating to a city approximately 350 miles from where Harry and his family currently reside. Harry and his wife both have relatives near their present home, and Harry's oldest child is in the third grade.

The job Harry has been offered would involve calling on retail accounts. Harry would service accounts presently stocking Imco products (primarily hardware stores, home centers, department stores, building supply outlets, and discount stores) as well as call on new outlets to encourage them to consider the Imco line. The travel involved in the job would require Harry to spend about one night per week away from home. Harry would be provided with a company car (which he does not now receive), an expense account, and would receive a base salary of $12,000 plus a commission on sales. The salespeople can also earn a bonus each year for meeting the quota established for them. Harry knows that the average salesperson earns commissions of approximately $14,000 per year and bonuses totalling another $2,000.

1. What are the major issues that Harry should consider before accepting or rejecting the job offer?
2. What questions should Harry ask before making a decision?
3. If you were in Harry's position, what would your decision be? Why?

## 1-2  Decisions, Decisions

Barbara Hemeli is in her last term at Almont State University. She is a marketing major with a good grade-point average. Barbara has been active in a number of campus organizations and has been secretary/treasurer of the Student Marketing Club for two years.

Barbara is considering a job offer from a large food products manufacturer. The company's products are distributed primarily through supermarkets. The job Barbara has been offered involves service selling to supermarkets and certain smaller retailers in a medium-sized eastern city. Barbara would be expected to keep the customers' stores adequately stocked, set up displays, coordinate retailer advertising with that of her company, and help out with store openings.

The starting salary for the job would be $1,200 per month for a six-month trial period. After this, the method of compensation would be half salary and half commission. Barbara was told that the average salesperson for the company earned $18,000 in their second year and more in later years. If Barbara's work is satisfactory, she was told that she could choose to stay in sales, move into sales management when openings occurred, or move into management training in other areas of the firm. Examples were cited of several young people who had quickly progressed from sales jobs like hers to management positions at salaries in the $30,000 range.

1. Do these facts fit your conception of a sales job? How do they differ?
2. Would you like to have this job? Why or why not?
3. What other information should Barbara have before making a decision?

# PART ONE

## PREPARATION FOR SELLING

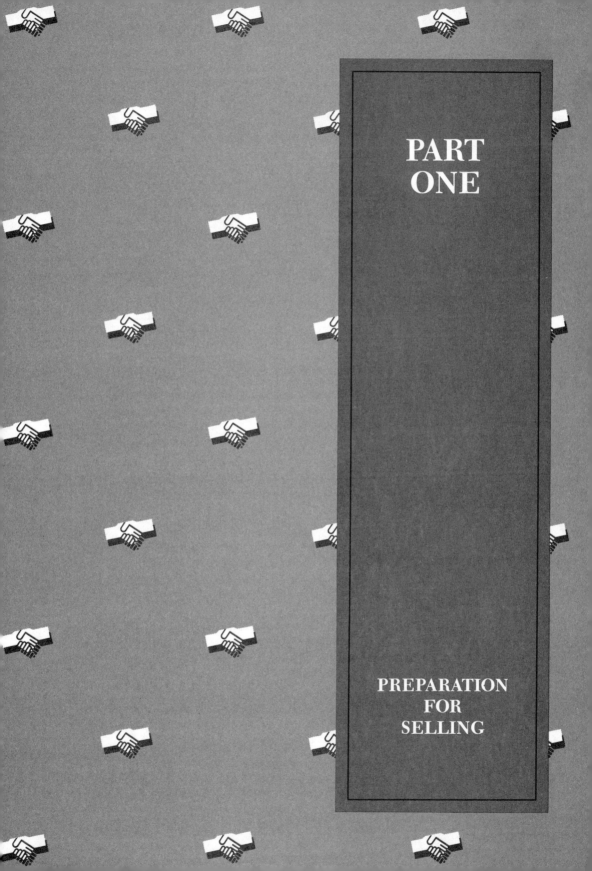

The opening chapters of this book provide background material on selling and sales careers. The chapter you have just completed, Chapter 1, describes the many types of sales jobs and the rewards that a career in selling can bring. Chapter 2 focuses on the personal characteristics and qualities that are needed to achieve sales success. You can identify the qualities you now possess for sales success and will learn how to develop others. Chapter 3 discusses the most important person in the business life of the salesperson, your customer. Customer types, buying motives, and determining appropriate customer appeals are covered. Important background knowledge for the salesperson is presented in Chapter 4. This chapter covers the wide variety of industry, company, and product knowledge that each salesperson must have before attempting to call on potential customers.

# 2

# YOUR APPEARANCE, PERSONALITY, AND ATTITUDE

Eddie, a young jockey just beginning his career, lost his first race. He also lost his first 10, and then his first 20 races. But he kept trying. Eddie had no winners in his first 100 races, or his first 200. Most people would have become discouraged and quit, but Eddie kept trying even though he lost his next 50 races. Finally, after 250 straight losses, Eddie won his first race. His perseverance paid off.

Would you have given up rather than persevere through 250 straight losses? Fortunately, Eddie Arcaro didn't, and he went on to become one of the most famous jockeys in racing history. He was the leading money winner through many years of his career and eventually became a millionaire. There are many qualities needed to be successful in a sales career. The perseverance shown by Eddie Arcaro is one of the most important. Do you possess this kind of perseverance?

Perhaps you are considering a career in sales, or you are striving to advance in your present sales career. Take a look at yourself. Are you prepared to mold yourself to succeed in selling? Are you willing to undergo the discipline required to achieve success? Are you able to develop the attributes that will make you a successful salesperson?

## THE COMPLETE SALESPERSON = SALES SUCCESS

It takes a complete salesperson to achieve sales success. The elements that make up a complete salesperson are shown in Figure 2-1. A complete salesperson possesses (1) good personal characteristics, (2) thorough knowledge and understanding, and (3) good selling techniques. If you lack strength in any of these three areas, your chances for selling success are diminished.

**Figure 2–1**

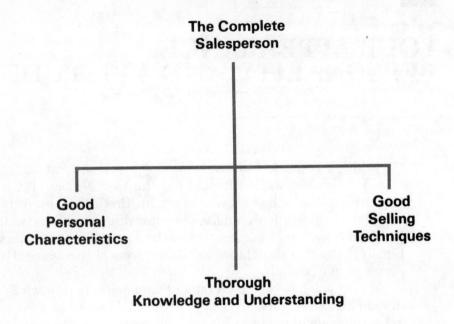

THE FORMULA FOR SALES SUCCESS

The Complete
Salesperson

Good
Personal
Characteristics

Good
Selling
Techniques

Thorough
Knowledge and Understanding

How do you measure up to the complete salesperson? As you read through the chapters of this book, measure yourself against this formula for sales success. This chapter begins the success formula with an examination of personal characteristics.

## YOUR APPEARANCE

Consider your appearance. What do others see when they look at you? To be objective, you must view yourself as a customer would. This is often referred to as your looking-glass self. A mirror reflects your appearance exactly as it is. Your reflection in a mirror is exactly how you appear to a customer. Examine your appearance in light of the following headings.

### Outward Appearance

First impressions are very important. The first thing a customer sees is your outward appearance—your clothing, grooming, and facial expression. In *Contact: The First Four Minutes,* Dr. Leonard Zunin describes these outward features as your *surface language.*[1] Just as your voice communicates, your surface language communicates. A good first appearance is important in making a sale.

Appropriateness is the key to the way you should dress. Your clothing should be suitable for the selling situation and for the type of customer you are calling on. A feed salesperson calling on farmers would probably dress quite differently from a medical detail salesperson calling on physicians.

**Illustration 2-1 The type of sales situation indicates the appropriate style of dress.**

*Tip   Susanne Patterson is a recent college graduate working for a major textbook publisher. She is bright, friendly, and knowledgeable. Susanne is aware of the importance of a good outward appearance. Although Susanne's sales territories are college campuses where students generally dress in a casual style, Susanne's customers are college professors who generally dress conservatively. Therefore, while on the job, Susanne dresses in a conservative, business-like fashion. Although new with the publishing company, Susanne has already created a good impression among her customers.*

Three excellent books are available that describe appropriate dress for many different business and selling situations. These are *Dress for Success, The Woman's Dress for Success Book,* and *Live for Success.* The author of these books, John T. Molloy, is a successful consultant to business firms on appropriate dress and writes a daily, syndicated newspaper column.

---

[1]Leonard Zunin, *Contact: The First Four Minutes* (New York: Nash Publishing, 1972).

An examination of one or more of these books could be very helpful.[2]

Your grooming is also important. Fragrances, hair style, and make-up should be appropriate. At the normal distance between you and a customer, the customer can not only see and hear you, but can smell you. Therefore, if you wonder whether you need a shower or a change of clothing, you probably do.

A salesperson communicates continuously, even when nothing is said. Frowns and smiles communicate a great deal. A ready smile is an important contributor to your outward appearance. This creates a friendly atmosphere to which your customer will respond instinctively. Remember, just as you watch your customers' facial expressions as clues to their thoughts, they are watching your expressions as clues to your thoughts.

**Illustration 2–2  A ready smile contributes greatly to a sales-person's appearance.**

---

[2]John T. Molloy, *Dress for Success* (New York: Warner Books, 1975), John T. Molloy, *The Woman's Dress for Success Book* (New York: Warner Books, 1977), and John T. Molloy, *Live For Success* (New York: Morrow Books, 1981).

Finally, do not walk into your customer's office with a cigarette, cigar, or pipe in your mouth. If the customer dislikes smoking, you can lose a sale before your presentation even begins. The sales performance of a real estate agent improved considerably when it was suggested to him that he stop smoking cigars while showing homes to potential customers.

## Voice and Speech Habits

Immediately after seeing you, your customer will hear your voice. In some cases this may occur simultaneously. A good speaking voice and speech habits will enhance your sales presentation while a poor voice and speech habits will detract from it. Your voice is your primary means of communication. In telephone selling, your voice is even more important because your customer can't see your facial expressions, hand gestures, and other movements.

A good selling voice should be warm and friendly. Lower voice tones generally sound warmer than high tones. Although you can't change your voice, you can control your volume, pitch, and articulation. Here are three suggestions to make your voice more pleasing: (1) don't talk too fast or too slow, (2) avoid a speech pattern that is dull and monotonous, and (3) avoid extremes of loudness and softness.

Certain speech habits can also detract from your sales effectiveness. Mumbling, mispronouncing words, and using slang can be irritating to your customers. A simple way to discover whether you suffer from any voice or speech problems is to record your voice. Many salespeople are surprised to hear how they sound. If you have some common voice problem, do not despair. Voice training can do wonders and speech clinics are able to correct most speech defects.

## Mannerisms

Many people have little habits that are annoying to others. You can probably think of a friend or acquaintance who has a habit that is annoying. Continuously tapping your fingers on a table top, removing and replacing glasses, or playing with a pen or pencil are examples of mannerisms that customers may find annoying. If sufficiently annoyed or distracted, your customer may cut your sales presentation short. Be conscious of your behavior patterns. Ask your family and friends if you have consistent, noticeable mannerisms that may distract or bother them. Once discovered, make a real effort to correct them.

## Manners

Good manners are slowly becoming a rare commodity and, as you know, the rarer something is, the more valuable it becomes. Although good manners may not close a sale for you, they will certainly never lose a sale. Over time, good manners will enhance your image in the eyes of your customers. Here are some simple do's and don'ts to put into practice: (1) never visit your customer without an appointment, (2) never take more of your customer's time than is necessary, and (3) always thank your customer for his or her time and purchases. Simple things such as offering a friendly "Good morning," or "Have a nice day," make your customer feel good and don't cost you anything. Selling can be thought of as the art of pleasing people, and this begins with the way you treat them.

## Health

It is easier to maintain a good overall appearance if you are in good health. The many activities of a sales job require stamina and can be exhausting. Exercise, a balanced diet, and adequate rest are important considerations for a salesperson.

*Photo courtesy Bonne Belle*

**Illustration 2-3  Good health is important to sales success.**

# PERSONALITY TRAITS TO CULTIVATE

Think about any five people that you know. Each one is different. Not only is their outward appearance different, but each has a unique way of behaving and responding. The combination of attributes that characterize each person as a distinct individual is their personality. Certain personality traits are helpful to a successful sales career. These traits should be cultivated. As you read through the following list of desirable personality traits, evaluate yourself against each one.

## Perseverance

Perseverance is a combination of determination and persistence. This is a must if you are to succeed in selling. Research shows that it takes an average of five sales calls to complete a sale. If you give up too easily and accept the first "no" as final, you won't complete many sales. Trying a little harder, attempting one more close, or giving one more demonstration is often all that is needed to change a "no" to a "yes."

Perseverance takes courage. It is easy to become discouraged in the face of refusals; giving up, however, will never lead to success. Would anyone have ever heard of Eddie Arcaro if he lacked perseverance?

With perseverance you will keep going even when sales are slow. The determination you show today will pave the way for sales in the future. How many salespeople give up after only half trying? Perseverance can be cultivated. Do not leave jobs half finished. Establish goals for yourself and work to accomplish them.

## Enthusiasm

Your enthusiasm can be the difference between making and losing a sale. After all, if you are not enthusiastic about your product or service, why should your customer be? Enthusiasm stimulates people to act. Would you be more likely to respond positively to a friend who excitedly says, "Let's go see that new movie, I've heard it's really good!," or one who says with a yawn, "There's nothing else to do, why don't we go see that new movie?"

Enthusiasm is contagious. To make a sale, arouse your customer's enthusiasm. A high level of enthusiasm in your sales presentation will, in turn, affect your customer favorably. Enthusiasm comes from a sincere belief in your company and the products or services you are offering. In response to a survey, sales managers rated enthusiasm as the most important characteristic for a salesperson to possess.[3]

## Dependability

Can a customer count on what you say? Customer confidence is the foundation for repeat sales. Customers must be able to rely on what you tell them. Your product does not have to be of the highest quality or meet the highest performance standards, as long as it lives up to what you say it will do. Similarly, your delivery service does not have to be the fastest, as long as the customer receives deliveries as promised.

Dependability can be cultivated. Do not make promises that you can't keep just to make a sale. A buyer once made this comment about a salesman: "In all the years I've dealt with Ray, he never let me down. I always knew that I could depend on whatever he told me." If your customers say this about you, there is no doubt that you possess the quality of dependability.

## Honesty and Sincerity

Closely associated with dependability are honesty and sincerity. Honesty is a trait that is reflected in how straightforward you are with your customers. Be honest, even if it means losing a sale. Don't make claims about your company's products or its ability to deliver that you know aren't true. Being truthful about what can and cannot be done may result in a short-term loss, but this will be more than made up in long-term gains as your customers realize that you can be trusted.

Honesty is a prerequisite for sincerity. A sincere salesperson is one who takes an active interest in a customer's needs and problems. Sincerity is shown by being thoughtful, helpful, and anxious to please. Your sincerity will gain the appreciation of your customers and will lead to many signed orders.

*Tip    Robert Gordon works for H. B. McManus Chemicals and sells to customers in the pharmaceutical industry. Bob is in the process of talking to Yoko Nguyen, a buyer*

---

[3]William J. Stanton and Richard H. Buskirk, *Management of the Sales Force* (Homewood, Illinois: Richard D. Irwin, Inc., 1983), p. 99.

*for a leading firm. Bob realizes that if a sale is to be made, he will have to promise a quick delivery. After consulting his production and shipping departments, Bob learns that a quick delivery is not likely because of the backlog of orders. Bob, therefore, sacrifices the sale and informs Ms. Nguyen that McManus Chemicals will not be able to deliver when needed. Ms. Nguyen informs Bob that she appreciates his honesty. Although Bob has lost this sale, he has established the trust on which future sales will be based.*

## Character

Would you buy anything from a person of doubtful character? Of course not, and neither would your customers. Building a good reputation is important. If you possess the qualities of dependability and honesty, it is likely that you have a good reputation.

Character is closely related to integrity. Integrity is shown through a frankness and openness of operation, in scrupulously fulfilling obligations and promises, and in doing more than is expected. A salesperson with character can be expected to carry out duties even when unobserved and unrewarded.

*Courtesy of Cray Research, Inc.*

**Illustration 2-4   Success in selling often requires long hours and extra effort.**

## Empathy

Empathy is the ability to see things through the eyes of others, to put yourself in someone else's shoes. The more clearly you understand the feelings, needs, and problems of your customers, the better you can satisfy them. Empathy is closely related to interest. An interested salesperson constantly thinks in terms of customer benefits. Customers will appreciate your interest and thoughtfulness and will respond accordingly.

## Respect

Most customers will earn and deserve your respect, but even when this is not so, proper respect should be shown to all customers. You may not agree with your customers nor enjoy their company, but all are entitled to respect. Your respect shows your appreciation and sound judgment. Your customers will notice this and show a greater appreciation for you.

## Sociability

Many people believe that to be successful in selling you have to be extremely outgoing, always ready with a joke and witty conversation. This is not true. In fact, this type of behavior may be viewed as too aggressive by some customers. Nevertheless, it is important that you enjoy meeting people and feel comfortable in their presence.

If you feel that you are introverted, try to be more outgoing. Smile when you meet new people. Be the first to hold out your hand, to offer a cheerful greeting, and to make a pleasant remark. Strike up conversations with new acquaintances. Spend your leisure time reading so that you feel comfortable discussing a variety of current topics. As is true of other traits, a more outgoing nature can be cultivated.

## Cheerfulness

Selling to a customer who is in a good mood is much easier than selling to a customer who is in a bad mood. A smile and a friendly attitude are contagious. A cheerful smile and greeting will help to put your customers in a good mood. Furthermore, your cheerful attitude will improve your outlook, so that when problems are encountered, they will seem less formidable.

A cheerful salesperson is not one who has solved every problem, but is one who is unafraid to face problems and solve them one at a time. If you are cheerful within, it will appear in your attitude and zest for life. Your optimism will spread to those around you. Always leave your troubles at home or in the office. Never burden your customers with your problems.

## Assertiveness

As a salesperson, you must remain in control of the sales situation. This does not mean that you should be overbearing or too aggressive. However, you should not be afraid to show initiative. You can remain in control by showing your customers that you know what you are talking about. If your customers have confidence in your knowledge and abilities, they will listen to what you have to say and heed your advice.

## Self-Confidence

Self-confidence is a belief in yourself that makes others believe in you. Self-confidence grows with experience. As your successes increase, so will your confidence in yourself. When you have tried and succeeded, you develop a confidence that will show as you carry out new assignments. You will have a feeling of knowing what to do and when to do it. Your confidence will create loyalties in your customers. As you inspire confidence in your customers, they will welcome and appreciate your advice.

How do you develop self-confidence if you don't have it? Start each day with a positive attitude. Before each sales call, tell yourself that you know you can complete this sale. Set little goals for yourself. As you achieve each goal, your self-confidence will grow. As your belief in yourself and your abilities grows, set higher goals. With enough self-confidence, you will be amazed at what you can achieve.

## Poise

Poise is an aura or feeling that you convey to your customers. It is a result of your self-confidence and your control of the situation. Poise comes from hard work, thorough preparation, detailed knowledge about your offerings, and confidence in your abilities. When you are poised, you are in control of yourself and your feelings. Without poise, some customers and sales situations may prove unnerving. With poise, these situations are easily handled.

*As Sandra Mills entered the office of a buyer she was calling on for the first time, she was greeted by a harsh, "What do you want? I hope you're not going to waste too much of my time!" The rudeness of the buyer would have unnerved many salespeople. Sandra, however, remained in control of her feelings. "All I would like," Sandra simply replied, "is the same consideration you would expect if you were in my shoes." Sandra's calmness impressed the buyer. Thirty minutes later, she walked out with a sale.*

## Mental Ability

Mental ability involves a combination of intelligence and the skill to think quickly. High intelligence is helpful in many selling situations but is not needed in every sales job to be successful. Hard work, an attention to detail, and the cultivation of good selling skills, can make the salesperson of average intelligence more effective than a brilliant but less conscientious salesperson.

Being able to think quickly is often referred to as mental agility. Agile thinking requires having facts available and being able to use them when needed. Mental agility enables you to think of ways in which your company's products and services can be used to solve customer problems. If you often find yourself asking the question, "Why didn't I think of that during the sales presentation?"—you probably lack mental agility. To acquire mental agility, you must prepare. The best preparation is a thorough knowledge of your company, customers, and products.

## Imagination

Imagination is the salesperson's ability to bring some creativity into the selling process. Any salesperson can take orders, follow directions, and carry out routine work. To be really successful, however, a salesperson must be imaginative. Imagination allows you to see problems through the eyes of your customers and devise new ways of solving those problems. You will envision new uses for products and new ways of displaying them to make the products more attractive.

The imaginative salesperson assesses new developments and adapts them to fit customers' needs. Imagination requires a combination of mental ability, alertness, careful thinking, intensive application, and initiative.

# PERSONALITY TRAITS TO OVERCOME

The previous section discussed traits that can be helpful to achieve sales success. These should be cultivated. On the other hand, you may possess certain negative traits that can hinder your sales success. You must work to overcome these traits.

## Not Listening

Salespeople often feel that to be in control of the sales situation, they must do the talking. They mistakenly equate talking with assertiveness. Although talking is necessary to present facts to customers, listening is equally (if not more) important. If a salesperson is to respond to a customer's needs and problems, the customer must have an opportunity to do some talking. Listen to what the customer is saying. This is the only way in which you can understand and respond to your customer's needs.

## Being Critical

Criticizing others or spreading gossip will not gain the trust of your customers. The person who criticizes others when talking to you, probably criticizes you when talking to others. Being critical will only serve to put your customers on guard when talking to you. Everyone has faults but no one wants those faults discussed by other people.

## Being Argumentative

Winning an argument with your customer but losing the sale is not the route to sales success. Even arguments over issues unrelated to your sales presentation, such as politics or football games, may cause hard feelings that result in a lost customer. If a customer says something that you disagree with, don't immediately jump on the defensive. Analyze what has been said. Use poise and tact. Respond calmly and logically—not with criticisms. Your calm response will generally soften your customer's position.

## Poor Humor

Although humor can be used effectively in a sales presentation, poor attempts at humor can kill a sale. A salesperson may believe that a clever response to a customer's question is smart, but the customer may not agree. Similarly, jokes that are critical of a particular ethnic group or religion, or that are off-color, may be offensive to your customer.

## Laziness

Salespeople have much freedom in their jobs. There is no one supervising their actions day-in and day-out. This may make it tempting to sleep in, end the day early, or spend the afternoon watching a movie. The salesperson who follows this course of action, however, will not be successful. Selling is hard work.

## Impatience

Sales success takes time and effort. Your selling techniques will improve and your customer understanding will grow with experience. Do not become discouraged if sales success is not immediately forthcoming. You will not be earning the huge commissions spoken of in the previous chapter in your first year. Nick DiBari earned more than $1 million in commissions in his thirteenth year with Comdisco, not in his first year. Many things take time to mature—selling abilities, large earnings, and promotions to higher positions. Don't cut your career short because of impatience.

## YOUR ATTITUDE

If you have a good appearance and good personality traits, you are off to a good start toward sales success. Additional ingredients that you will need are good knowledge and understanding and good selling techniques. These will be discussed in later chapters. Even with all of these positive factors, however, one more ingredient is necessary. This is a positive attitude.

A positive attitude will bring all of your other qualities together. Appearance, personality, knowledge, and skills are not enough. A positive attitude is the activating ingredient that, when combined with your other talents, produces sales success.

Psychologists say that a positive attitude is one of the most important qualities to individual success. To be successful, you must have a positive attitude toward life in general and your work in particular. This is particularly true in selling, where your success depends entirely on your own efforts.

A positive attitude is a combination of enthusiasm, determination, and self-confidence. With these attributes, there is no limit to the success you can achieve. Enthusiasm is one of the most important personality traits of successful salespeople. Enthusiasm is contagious; it makes people want to buy. How do you develop enthusiasm? Frank Bettger, a highly successful salesperson, stated it this way, "To become enthusiastic—act enthusiastic."[4] Start today! Act enthusiastic about every aspect of your life and work. "Force yourself to act enthusiastic, and you'll become enthusiastic!"[5]

You are the only one who can honestly rate your attitude in light of the basic personality traits and qualities that we have discussed. Reflect for a few minutes and answer each of the following questions.

|  | Yes | No |
|---|---|---|
| • Do you wake up each morning looking forward to the new day? | ____ | ____ |
| • Do you take on new projects enthusiastically? | ____ | ____ |
| • Do you look forward to new challenges? | ____ | ____ |
| • Do you enjoy meeting people? | ____ | ____ |
| • Do you take a sincere interest in other people? | ____ | ____ |
| • Are you willing to put the interests of others ahead of your own? | ____ | ____ |
| • Are you willing to put in longer work hours, starting the day early and working late? | ____ | ____ |

If you answered "yes" to each of these questions, you have the positive attitude necessary for sales success. If you answered "no" to some or all of these questions, it will be necessary for you to examine your attitude. Since all of us fall short of perfection, certain changes may be essential. Can you adjust your attitude to one that is appropriate for sales success? Leading psychologists and successful people in all walks of life claim that you can change if you really want to.

---

[4]Frank Bettger, *How I Raised Myself from a Failure to Success in Selling* (New York: Prentice-Hall, Inc., 1949), p. 11.

[5]*Ibid.*, p. 11.

You have a self-image, a mental image of the type of person you are. This image is often filled with negative, as well as positive thoughts. If the negative thoughts can be eliminated, and positive ones substituted, it follows that your positive attitude can change your personality for the better.

## DEVELOPING YOUR SALES PROFILE

Before your sales knowledge and skills can be put to use, you must have the right appearance, personality, and attitude. Each of these can be developed. The following simple guidelines can help you develop the right sales profile.

### Realize There Is Room for Improvement

Everyone could use improvement in some aspect of their sales profile. You must understand where you most need improvement and you must have a strong desire to improve. Ask yourself these questions: How much do I want to succeed? Where do I most need improvement? Am I willing to work hard to achieve the right sales profile?

### Assess Your Current Sales Profile

Take a close look at yourself. If you are to improve, you must know where you stand now and which areas need improvement. Use the checklist shown in Figure 2-2. First, go through the checklist and rate yourself. Second, have several people who know you well rate you. Compare the results. Are there any differences between how you see yourself and how others see you? In which areas do you need improvement?

### Develop a Plan for Improvement

After evaluating yourself and taking a look at how others evaluated you, how did you score? Higher than expected? Lower? Were you surprised at your score? Encouraged? Discouraged? What is your next step? To develop a winning sales profile, you must realize the need for improvement and have a strong desire to improve. Then you must develop a plan for improvement.

Self-development is not easy, but the potential rewards are great. It is important that you don't become discouraged. Just

**Figure 2-2**

## CHECKLIST FOR SELF-DEVELOPMENT

Rate yourself honestly on these qualities. Do not worry if you are low on some. That is to be expected and will give you a chance to improve. For each trait listed below, give yourself 4 points for an A, 3 points for a B, 2 points for a C, and 1 point for a D.

| SALES TRAITS | RATINGS | | | |
|---|---|---|---|---|
| | A<br>Out-<br>standing | B<br>Good | C<br>Average | D<br>Need Im-<br>provement |
| Appearance | ____ | ____ | ____ | ____ |
| Personality | ____ | ____ | ____ | ____ |
| Sociability | ____ | ____ | ____ | ____ |
| Dependability | ____ | ____ | ____ | ____ |
| Honesty | ____ | ____ | ____ | ____ |
| Sincerity | ____ | ____ | ____ | ____ |
| Loyalty | ____ | ____ | ____ | ____ |
| Integrity | ____ | ____ | ____ | ____ |
| Assertiveness | ____ | ____ | ____ | ____ |
| Attitude | ____ | ____ | ____ | ____ |
| Maturity | ____ | ____ | ____ | ____ |
| Character | ____ | ____ | ____ | ____ |
| Intelligence | ____ | ____ | ____ | ____ |
| Mental Agility | ____ | ____ | ____ | ____ |
| Courage | ____ | ____ | ____ | ____ |
| Cheerfulness | ____ | ____ | ____ | ____ |
| Poise | ____ | ____ | ____ | ____ |
| Respect | ____ | ____ | ____ | ____ |
| Imagination | ____ | ____ | ____ | ____ |
| Initiative | ____ | ____ | ____ | ____ |
| Empathy | ____ | ____ | ____ | ____ |
| Interest | ____ | ____ | ____ | ____ |
| Self-Confidence | ____ | ____ | ____ | ____ |
| Perseverance | ____ | ____ | ____ | ____ |
| Enthusiasm | ____ | ____ | ____ | ____ |
| TOTAL | ____ | ____ | ____ | ____ |

**HERE IS YOUR GRADE**

| | |
|---|---|
| Less than 50 | **Not good enough** |
| 50 - 68 | **Room for improvement** |
| 69 - 86 | **Could be a bit better** |
| Greater than 86 | **Excellent** |

like you, successful salespeople possess the qualities we have discussed in varying degrees. Everyone is strong in some areas, weak in others. Your job is to overcome your weak points. Set up a program for improvement and follow it rigorously. Carry a list with you of those traits you want to improve . Review it often.

## START WITH GOAL SETTING

The first step in formulating a proper sales profile is to establish goals. Force yourself to think about where you would like to be next year, in five years, in ten years, and in twenty years. Complete the exercise shown in Figure 2–3 to the best of your ability. Be specific and realistic in your short- and long-term goals.

**Figure 2–3**

### WHAT ARE YOUR GOALS?

|  | What Do You Want to Be Doing (job)? | How Much Do You Want to Be Earning? | How Will You Get There? |
|---|---|---|---|
| Next Year |  |  |  |
| In Five Years |  |  |  |
| In Ten Years |  |  |  |
| In Twenty Years |  |  |  |

Now that you have been forced to think about your goals, are you willing to exert the effort needed to achieve these goals? Most people would like to achieve high earnings and a position of status. However, not everyone is willing to work hard enough to achieve such goals. You must decide whether you're willing to work hard enough. If not, you probably don't have the proper sales profile for success in a selling career.

## GET STARTED NOW

A number of important characteristics have been presented in this chapter. None of them will be useful unless you begin working now. Do not be afraid to think big. Believe in yourself and have faith in your abilities. With self-confidence and hard work you will succeed. If you believe in yourself and have the proper sales attitude, you will put confidence and enthusiasm into everything you do.

## QUESTIONS

1. What elements contribute to making the complete salesperson? Give an example of each.
2. What elements contribute to a salesperson's overall appearance? Which of these are easiest to change? Which are most difficult?
3. Do you agree with the following statement made by a successful salesperson, "You are judged by the words you use and the clothes you wear"? Explain your answer.
4. Describe what is meant by personality. Is there such a thing as the right sales personality? Explain.
5. Must a salesperson be aggressive and outgoing to be successful? Explain.
6. How might a salesperson develop better listening habits?
7. The following statement was made by a sales manager to one of the authors of this book: "If a salesperson hasn't made it inside of a year, he or she might as well forget it!" Do you agree or disagree? Explain.
8. What is meant by mental agility? Why is this important to salespeople?
9. Why would Frank Bettger, a very successful salesperson, state, "Enthusiasm is based on belief; belief, in turn, is based on knowledge"?
10. Why is goal setting important? What does a salesperson accomplish by setting goals?

## SALES CHALLENGES

1. You are the manager of the sporting goods department of the J. C. Nickel Department Store, a major retail store located in a large metropolitan area. You must hire another salesperson for your department. As a first step you are going to place an advertisement for the position in the local newspaper to attract applicants. Write the advertisement that you would

put in the paper. As you don't want to spend more than you have to on the advertisement, justify the inclusion of all information you have put in the ad.

2. You have just walked into the middle of the following conversation:

**Harry:** I've been in sales for most of my life, over 35 years, and it's personality that separates the winners from the losers.

**Sharon:** I don't agree. It's integrity that makes the difference. If your customers know they can trust you, they're going to buy from you.

**Paul:** You're both wrong. It's plain, old-fashioned hard work. The person who puts out the most effort will be the most successful.

Your three co-workers turn to you looking for a resolution to their disagreement. How would you respond?

3. For one day, keep a diary of all the nonverbal messages you receive. How much can you tell about people simply from observation? Based on what you have observed, how can nonverbal communication be used by salespeople?

## CASES

### 2-1 Developing a Program for Sales Success

Tim Filipic and Barbara Oakes were engaged in conversation over dinner at Franco's Italian Restaurant. Barbara is a secretary in the business department of a small community college. Tim is a salesperson for Home Entertainment, a large retailer that sells televisions, stereos, personal computers, video recorders, tape players, radios, and a wide range of related products. Tim was talking about his progress (or lack of progress) at Home Entertainment.

**Tim:** I'm just not performing up to par. I've been working at Home Entertainment for two years, and my sales aren't much better than when I started. Come to think of it, they're not much better than when I worked at Video World out at the mall.

**Barbara:** Why don't you take a sales course at the college? Remember, I gave you a copy of their spring schedule?

**Tim:** I don't know. The tuition is kind of high, and I hate to give up two nights a week.

**Barbara:** Some of the courses are offered on Saturday mornings.

Tim: Are you kidding? Saturday mornings! Besides, I have to work some Saturdays.

Barbara: What about the books on selling I told you I saw in the college bookstore?

Tim: I've never gotten much out of reading. I don't think a book can teach me how to sell.

Barbara: With all of the videotape equipment you have at the store, why don't you record your sales presentation so you can see what it looks like? I understand they do that in some of the sales classes at the college.

Tim: That won't work. Making a presentation in front of a camera isn't the same as making a presentation to a customer.

Barbara: You said one of the salespeople at your store, Marc Schumacher, was very successful. Why don't you ask him for advice?

Tim: He's successful because he's good looking and has a nice voice. Besides, why should he help me? If I start taking customers away from him, he'll lose commissions.

Barbara: I'm tired of listening to you complain and not do anything about it. I'm going to talk to Professor Gayle Field about you. She teaches some of the sales classes at the college. I'll see what she can suggest.

1. From the dialogue, what are some of Tim's problems?
2. If you were Professor Field, what sort of program would you outline for Tim?
3. Can Tim develop into a successful salesperson?

## 2-2 Filling Two Sales Vacancies

The Midwest Drug Company, a full-line drug wholesaler located in Brentwood, a city of 500,000 people, employs 18 salespeople. Each year the sales manager replaces about three salespeople. Some quit; some are fired. New sales trainees usually advance to the sales force after 6 to 12 months of training.

Two of the company's salespeople have just resigned to take better positions, and two sales trainees in the firm have been assigned to the territories left vacant. The sales manager must now hire two people to become trainees for future sales positions. To get applicants for the two trainee positions, the sales manager ran an advertisement in the Sunday edition of *The Brentwood Journal*. Twenty-one applications were received by mail. After a short examination, 16 applicants were rejected as not suitable; five applicants were interviewed and the following information was recorded for each.

## Jack Keane

Jack Keane, 21 years old, recently graduated from the business school of Brentwood University. He is single and lives with his parents. His grades in college were average. He was active in school affairs, belonged to a fraternity, and had many college friends. He is 5 feet 10 inches tall, weighs 165 pounds, and has light hair and blue eyes. He makes a nice appearance and speaks well.

Jack is a church member and sings in the choir. As a youth, he was active in the Boy Scouts. He enjoys sports and regularly attended social activities in school. He never tried out for any athletic teams while in school.

During high school he worked at various summer jobs, such as mowing lawns, delivering circulars, and caddying at a golf club. When he entered college, he worked at the post office during each Christmas vacation. One summer, he was a counselor at a YMCA camp. The second summer, he did manual labor for a cement contractor. The third summer he sold encyclopedias door-to-door. Jack is very interested in a sales career and will accept a starting salary of $1,000 per month while in the training program.

## Oscar Lindman

Oscar Lindman is 24 years old, married, and has a two-year-old child. He owns a modest home in a suburb of Brentwood. His wife takes care of the home and has no outside employment.

Oscar's grades in high school were average. He played on the high school football team but was not an outstanding player. He met his wife when both were students and they married three years after high school graduation. Shortly after graduation, Oscar got a job driving a delivery truck for a local department store. A year later, he became a salesperson in the automotive section of this store. He enjoyed selling, but not in a retail store.

When Oscar was 21 years old, he left the store and became a salesperson for an automotive jobber. His income increased each year, and he was happy with his work. Three years after he was hired, the owner died and the business was liquidated. Oscar was out of a job.

He applied for the position of sales trainee with Midwest because he believes the job will soon lead to one similar to his former position. Oscar could have gone to work for another automotive jobber in Arcadia, but that would have required selling his home and moving to Arcadia, 300 miles away. Both Oscar and his wife prefer living in Brentwood. On checking references, it was determined that Oscar had been fairly successful in selling and had built up a friendly clientele. Oscar wants $1,400 per month as a starting salary.

## Elizabeth Cosky

Elizabeth Cosky is 28 years old, married, and has no children. Elizabeth and her husband own a very nice home in one of Brentwood's suburbs. They each have their own car.

Elizabeth graduated with above-average grades from a very good high school. Although she did not go to college immediately, she has taken night courses at a local community college. In high school, Elizabeth was active in many school activities. She currently remains very active in a number of social, church, and community organizations.

After graduating from high school, Elizabeth's first job was in the credit department of a furniture store. After three years, Elizabeth accepted a higher paying job in the personnel department of a large manufacturer. She has been with this company for almost eight years. During the past two years, Elizabeth has started selling jewelry on a part-time basis. She has achieved modest success in selling to friends, relatives, and co-workers. Elizabeth has also taken the initiative to set up demonstrations at party-type get-togethers in people's homes.

Elizabeth has applied for the job of sales trainee because her part-time selling made her realize that she would enjoy a sales career. She likes meeting people and the challenge of a sales job. All references checked gave Elizabeth a high rating. Elizabeth is willing to accept $1,500 per month to start, less than she is making now.

## Sam Perkins

Sam Perkins, age 35, is single. He drives a big car, is well dressed, and gives the impression of being a free spender. He had lived at home with his parents until he was 30 years old. He then moved to Brentwood, where he took a sales analysis job for a local manufacturing firm. Sam has an apartment, plays golf in the summer, and skis in the winter. He usually spends his vacations in Florida in January. Sam is friendly, well-liked, and generous. His job performance is satisfactory. He is six feet tall, weighs 190 pounds, and has a pleasant voice.

Sam graduated from a small liberal arts college. After graduation he went to work for the Tidewater Company, a manufacturer of pumps. He worked at a number of jobs in the office of this company; when he left he was supervisor of the adjustment department. Sam left Tidewater and his hometown when he realized he was in a rut. Life was pleasant, but he was getting nowhere. When he took the job at the large pharmaceutical house in Brentwood as sales analyst, he soon became acquainted with the activities of the sales department.

After several years at various desk jobs, he concluded that ultimately he would like to be in sales administration. To get this type of job, he would have to do some selling. He had suggested to the sales manager that he would like to sell, but the sales manager told him that he would be far more successful working in the sales department in the office.

Determined to gain selling experience, Sam applied for the job of sales trainee at Midwest. When interviewed, he stated frankly that he knew he could sell and was willing to start out as a sales trainee, a lesser job than his current position. His present salary is $24,000 per year, but he is willing to start as a trainee at $1,600 per month. He stated he was confident that in five years he would be in a sales administrative position with the Midwest Drug Company.

## Eva Laval

Eva Laval, age 40, is married and has three children. She owns a home in Brentwood, and drives a medium-priced car.

Eva completed high school and started to work right after graduation. Her first job was as a stock clerk in a supermarket. After one year, she became a cashier. Six months later, she became head of the produce department, and a year later she was made assistant manager. In spite of her retail background, Eva did not like working in a grocery store and concluded that her future would be limited there. When a friend invited her to work for a drug wholesaler, she was glad to leave.

After a year's experience in the warehouse and office of the drug wholesaler, she became a salesperson with her own territory. Her success as a salesperson, although not outstanding, was sufficient to give her an increasing income each year. Six months ago the owner of the firm retired, leaving the management to three of his children. Immediately, dissension arose. The new owners were constantly bickering with one another. Morale declined, and sales suffered. Because of the turmoil created, Eva decided she would have to seek another job.

When she saw the advertisement for a sales trainee in wholesale drugs, she applied. When interviewed for the position, she stated frankly the reason for wanting to change. She said she would be willing to start at $1,600 per month, even though she was now making more than $1,900. She said that she anticipated a very short training period. She felt that within six months she would be out in her own territory. She was convinced that she would be above her former income within a year. She said that she would be glad to work for the Midwest Drug Company since it had a fine reputation. The sales manager of Midwest Drug knew of Eva and knew she had a reputation as a steady salesperson and a consistent producer.

1. Develop a chart rating each of the five applicant's on the basis of the qualities discussed in this chapter.
2. Which two applicants should be hired? Why?
3. Write a letter that you would send to the three applicants not hired.

# 3

# YOUR MARKET AND
# CUSTOMERS

It was Monday morning and Joe Amort, a salesperson for Spartan Industrial Supply, was making his first call of the week. Joe was calling on Aaron Roberts of the Stanton Machine Tool Company. Before entering his office, Joe looked at his customer file. Among the assorted entries, he noticed the comment, "avid golfer." Joe made his entrance, greeted Mr. Roberts pleasantly, then said, "With the great weather this past weekend, I'll bet you got in several rounds of golf." This brought a big smile to Mr. Roberts' face as he began describing a particularly good round on Saturday morning.

One of the first steps in the selling process is getting to know your customers. Customers are somewhat predictable as a group, but as individuals they have different temperaments and characteristics. Selling requires an individual approach to the needs, problems, and habits of each customer. Although you will never be able to understand fully what motivates each of your customers, a firm base of customer understanding can be established by learning fundamental facts applicable to most people.

## UNDERSTANDING MARKET DIFFERENCES

Steve Gilboe had been successfully selling insurance to professionals (doctors, dentists, corporate executives, etc.) for many years. Steve's manager suggested to him that along with his professional business, he should consider other markets where the company's insurance programs have been successfully sold by other salespeople.

After several months, Steve found that he was not achieving the same success in the nonprofessional market that he enjoyed in the professional market. One day, while making a call at the home of a machine operator, the prospect interrupted Steve's presentation with the question, "Steve, what the heck are you talking about?" This question jolted Steve into realizing that, even though he was talking to someone who needed insurance, he was talking about issues the prospect didn't understand. Steve had been making the same presentation he normally made to his professional customers—people who were earning more than $200,000 per year.

Steve's mistake is common among salespeople who do not realize that their customers are individuals with different needs, interests, and values. Thus, Steve will have to develop a new approach to be successful in the nonprofessional market; but among professional customers, Steve will continue to use the approach that has been successful in the past. This suggests that there are similar groups of customers who can be approached in the same fashion, while different approaches are needed for other groups.

## Identifying Market Segments

Business firms have long recognized the existence of market segments. Market segments are groups of customers with similar characteristics. Because customers within a particular market segment possess some similarity, it is hoped that they can be approached in basically the same way. Thus, while the auto companies are selling cars to over 170,000,000 adults across the country, they are not producing millions of different models to suit the particular tastes of each customer. Instead, they are producing a few dozen separate makes and models geared to a few dozen major market segments.

As a salesperson, you can use the same approach. Although each of your customers will be different in some way, they will also possess some characteristics in common. By grouping your customers in a logical and meaningful fashion, you will be able to identify groups of customers who have common interests and needs, and can be approached in a common fashion.

## Segmentation Approaches

There are many ways in which a market can be segmented. At a very general level, markets can be divided as follows:

1.  Consumer markets
2.  Retailer markets

**Illustration 3-1   A sales approach should be developed to suit each market.**

3. Wholesaler markets
4. Manufacturing markets
5. Service markets
6. Institutional markets
7. Farming markets
8. Government markets
9. Foreign markets

Although each of the nine listed groups represents a market segment, each group is still very broad and can be segmented further. For example, the retailer market can be further segmented by characteristics such as size (small, moderate, or large establishments); ownership (independents or chain organizations); location (neighborhood, central business district, or shopping center); price and service (high margin-full service or low margin-limited service); and product offerings (drug stores, hardware stores, department stores, supermarkets, sporting goods, etc.). In a similar fashion, each of the other general groups can be further subdivided.

The consumer market represents the largest number of buyers of the above groups and can be subdivided many ways. Some examples are shown in Table 3–1.

Segmenting the market can be thought of as a step-by-step process. The market can be segmented first in broad or general terms and then into finer and finer segments. This process will

**Table 3–1**

| Major Consumer Segmentation Variables | |
| --- | --- |
| **VARIABLE** | **TYPICAL EXAMPLES** |
| A. Geographic | 1. Region of the country<br>2. Population density<br>3. Climate |
| B. Demographic | 1. Age<br>2. Sex<br>3. Life cycle stage<br>4. Income<br>5. Occupation<br>6. Education<br>7. Nationality<br>8. Race<br>9. Social class<br>10. Religion |
| C. Psychographic | 1. Life style<br>2. Personality<br>3. Benefits sought<br>4. Usage rate<br>5. Loyalty |

stop when you have identified groups of customers who are similar enough that the same sales approach would be appropriate for all customers in that group. Your challenge would then be to develop a different selling approach for each group of customers, or market segment.

## WHAT TO KNOW ABOUT YOUR CUSTOMERS

It is important to maintain adequate information about your customers. In the example given at the beginning of this chapter, Joe Amort was able to begin his sales call on a positive note by bringing up a topic of special interest to his customer. After getting his customer in a positive mood, Joe was able to start his sales presentation with an attentive and happy customer. Joe was successful because he possessed appropriate information about his customer.

Most salespeople would be expected to know their customers' names and some general facts about each customer. Many other facts, however, that might be even more useful are often ignored or forgotten. This is a mistake.

What information should you have about your customers? Many customer facts are available. The type and variety of information you need depend on the products you are selling and the customers you contact.

### Facts of a Business Nature

When calling on purchasing agents or buyers for business firms, you should have certain information about each buyer's firm.

**Name and Address of Company.** This information may seem obvious, and most salespeople certainly would be expected to have this information. However, keep in mind that many companies have similar names. Also, many companies have multiple addresses, and many office buildings have multiple business tenants.

**Type of Business.** What type of business are you contacting? Is it a refiner of raw materials, a parts producer, or an assembler of components? Is it an industrial distributor, consumer goods wholesaler, or retailer? Does the company buy parts for assembly or fabricate its own parts? Is the company's business labor-intensive or automated? What services does the company require? Is the business seasonal? The answers to these questions will give you an idea of whether the company can use what you have to sell and in which fashion your offerings can best be put to use.

**Customer Markets.**   To whom does your customer sell? The more you know about the markets your customer services, the more help you can provide to that customer. After all, the better your customer's performance, the more your customer will need to buy from you.

**Volume of Business.**   The information gathered under Type of Business, as previously discussed, should indicate whether your customer's firm has a need for your goods or services. Beyond this, you should also assess the extent and nature of the need. What volume might you expect to sell to the customer? How frequently? In what grades, sizes, colors, etc., might the customer be interested? Keep in mind, the absolute size of customer firms isn't always an indication of their buying potential. It is their size in combination with the nature of their business.

*Tip*   *Vince Schendon sells abrasives for metal finishing work. Vince spent many hours trying to sell to the purchasing agent of a large firm (over 1,000 employees) only to find that the firm made little use of abrasives as most of the firm's casting work required little grinding. This experience taught Vince that the nature of the firm's operations, not its size alone, was the important factor in determining sales potential. Having learned from this, Vince found a small plumbing fixtures firm (fewer than 80 employees) located close to the large firm. The small firm used more abrasives than the larger firm, since all of its products required thorough finishing work. The plumbing fixtures firm has become a good volume customer for Vince.*

**Company Credit Rating.**   It is important to know the credit rating of your customers. Much time and effort can be wasted making a sales presentation to a customer who is financially insecure and may be unable to pay. One industrial sales representative learned this lesson the hard way. Considerable time and energy was spent to close a sale to a new account only to have the sale voided by the representative's credit department because of the poor credit rating of the customer.

**Company Organization and Policies.** Be familiar with the organizational structure of your customer's firm. Know who reports to whom; especially know where buying authority rests. In some situations key buying responsibility is not in the purchasing department. The key buying influence may be in engineering or production, with purchasing responsible only for approving a purchase order.

Some companies may have specific policies you must follow. For example, some purchasing departments will only allow salespeople to make calls on certain days of the week and/or during specific periods of the day. Some companies may require that your firm be approved at the head office as an acceptable supply source before buyers for the company can purchase from you. Perhaps the company has specific policies with regard to delivery schedules that suppliers must meet if you are to sell to them.

**Past Sales History.** You should maintain a transaction history for the customer company. Each time that a sale is made, record all of the details of the transaction. What products were purchased? In what volumes? What were the terms-of-sale and delivery arrangements? What has been the customer's purchase frequency? Have you had a long, successful relationship with this company, or have past sales been intermittent and difficult to achieve? Your transaction file on the customer company should give you insight into the needs of the customer and how to better service the customer in the future.

**Future Potential.** What does the customer company's future look like? Is it a growing company? Is it in a stagnant industry? It certainly is in your best interest to cultivate customers who have bright futures. They will, after all, be buying more in the years ahead.

Beyond those presented here, there may be other facts of a business nature that you should have. This depends on the selling environment in which you are operating. It is up to you to determine precisely what information you need to sell more effectively.

## Facts of a Personal Nature

In addition to information of a business nature, it is important to gather information of a personal nature about each of your customers.

**Name.** Know how to pronounce and spell the buyer's name correctly. Know the buyer's first name and initials and what the buyer likes to be called. Listen carefully to the buyer's pronunciation during introductions; it is the only correct pronunciation. If you are unsure of the proper pronunciation, ask the buyer's secretary.

**Address and Telephone Number.** In some cases it may be necessary to contact a business customer at home. If a customer provides you with a home address and telephone number, record it carefully so that you don't have to ask again. Many buyers do not like to be contacted outside the office. Therefore, only do so when absolutely necessary and only with the buyer's permission.

**Family.** Know whether the buyer is married and has children. If you have any information about the buyer's family, such as a daughter who is a particularly good tennis player and a son away at college, inquire about them. Most people take great pride in the accomplishments of their children.

**Important Dates.** Make note of birthdays, anniversaries, and other dates that are special to the buyer. Appropriate remembrances can build goodwill.

**Education.** Knowledge of the buyer's educational background may provide a good discussion opener. Knowing that a buyer went to State U and that State U won a big game recently gives you a discussion opener and a means of building a friendly relationship.

**Memberships, Hobbies, and Recreational Interests.** Is the customer a member of any lodge, club, church, charitable, or civic group? Is the customer active in a political party? Does the customer have any hobbies or recreational interests? If so, appropriate and timely remarks can be made about these activities. An awareness of your customer's interests gives you a topic for discussion and a common bond through which you can develop a long-term friendship.

**Sales Call Preferences.**   Does the buyer prefer sales calls in the morning or afternoon? Early in the week or late in the week? Does the buyer enjoy talking business over lunch or only in the office? Does the buyer enjoy a little friendly conversation or prefer getting right to business? Knowing the answers to these questions will help you plan your sales calls for more rewarding results.

**Likes and Dislikes.**   Know your customer's likes and dislikes so that you don't criticize things your customer is fond of or raise issues that may be offensive or irritating. Does the buyer object to smoking in his/her office? Try closing a sale after making a joke about a particular politician and then finding out that your customer is a strong supporter of that politician.

The discussion to this point has dealt with information about buyers for business firms. What if you are calling on customers who are buying for themselves? For example, you may be selling insurance, securities, or real estate. Much of the personal information just discussed would still be appropriate information to have. In addition, you may want to have information on the age of the prospect, occupation, income, family size, age of children, medical history, current assets, pension plans, home ownership status, smoking and drinking habits, and similar information. Again, what is appropriate information depends on what you are selling and what information will help you to complete the sale.

# SECURING CUSTOMER INFORMATION

Information about customers is learned over time and from many different sources. Most information is obtained simply by keeping your eyes and ears open.

## Observe, Listen, Ask Questions

Keep your eyes open during your sales calls. Pictures in your customer's office may indicate whether the person has a family. Decorations, books, and magazines may suggest something of the customer's interests and hobbies. Pins or buttons worn on a coat may show club memberships or political affiliation. Lack of an ash tray may indicate that the buyer isn't a smoker and may not appreciate smoking in the office.

Listen to everything that your customer has to say. Your customer will reveal much information about personal interests, likes, and dislikes during conversations.

The best means of obtaining information is to ask questions. If you want to know whether the buyer has final purchase authority, what certain company policies are, or if the buyer has any hobbies, ask. If you are selling insurance and need specific information to set up the right type of policy for the prospect, ask the questions you need answered to serve the needs of the customer.

## Your Company

Your company may have information on your customer. This may have been gathered through past transactions with the customer or by a previous salesperson who called on the customer. Your sales manager, branch manager, or supervisor may have information about the customer. Some companies supply their salespeople with manuals describing various types of customers and accounts. Specific suggestions may be provided on how to deal with various types of customers.

## Other Salespeople

You may come in contact with salespeople representing noncompeting companies. It is to the mutual advantage of noncompeting salespeople to exchange nonconfidential information about customers. In fact, you may be able to work with other salespeople to exchange leads on potential customers. In any place where salespeople gather, stay alert for information that might be valuable to you.

### Additional Sources

Depending on the information you want, there are many possible sources. Information about customers who are buying for personal use may be available from the customer's friends, relatives, neighbors, and other companies that have done business with the individual. You might also contact the local credit agency and the bank your customer uses for additional information.

**Illustration 3-2   An alert salesperson might take advantage of any situation where people gather.**

Information about a buyer's company is available from many sources. You can use trade associations, credit agencies, banks, trade directories, trade magazines, newspapers, and other periodicals. Official and legal records are often very helpful. Further sources of information include other supplier firms, chambers of commerce, local building and business exchanges, the Better Business Bureau, bonding firms, current and former employees of the company, the National Association of Manufacturers, and various local manufacturers' associations.

# MAINTAINING CUSTOMER INFORMATION

Your system of maintaining customer information may be elaborate or very simple. Personal computers can be used to store customer information. Information stored in this way can be accessed and updated easily. Most salespeople use a diary or a small notebook with a page or more devoted to each customer. Some use 3 × 5 index cards arranged alphabetically for easy reference. Whatever system is used, the files should contain all information gathered about the customer, the customer's company, and previous contacts with the customer.

**Illustration 3-3   Personal computers can be used to store and maintain customer information.**

A new customer file should be created each time you identify a new prospect. Information should be added to a customer's file as gathered. If you discover new information about a customer during a sales call, record the information in your files immediately after leaving the customer's office or home. Don't wait to record the information; you may forget. Figure 3–1 shows an example of how a 3 × 5 card file might be organized.

Your customer files should be organized in a manner that provides information that is of use to you. The card shown in Figure 3-1 is organized to contain mostly personal information. You may want to organize your files primarily for business-related information, or to keep a historical record of the transactions with the customer. Once established, you should refer to your files to refresh your memory on pertinent information just before your sales call.

*Tip  Donna Herrod, a new salesperson for the Perry Graphics Co., was having difficulty developing rapport with her customers. She asked Sarah Gage, a senior salesperson for the company who seemed to be on very good terms with all her customers, how she did it. "It's simple," said Sarah. "I make notes on my customers' likes and dislikes, hobbies, interests, information on their families, important dates, and anything else that might be useful. I also note whether the customer likes to talk a bit before getting down to business. Thus, I've learned to treat all customers the way they like."*

## CUSTOMER TYPES

You will encounter different types of customers. When you first meet a new prospect, you must quickly size up the prospect and determine the best approach to take. This is difficult, but you will improve with experience. Your sales success will depend on your ability to correctly classify the prospective customers you meet. Perhaps the most practical approach to identify customer types is (1) by stage of buying action, and (2) by personality or disposition. Most customers can be classified along both dimensions.

### By Stage of Buying Action

Potential customers may be classified by how close they are to buying. You can determine this by watching the customer's actions, asking pertinent questions, and listening to what the customer has to say. Customers may be placed in one of three buying action categories.

**Interested Observer.**  This prospect does not intend to buy at the present time but is interested in your product or service. Your job in this situation is to stimulate the customer's interest,

**Figure 3–1**

## SAMPLE CUSTOMER INFORMATION FILE

### MASTER CARD

Date _____

Name _____  Spouse: _____

Address _____

City & State _____ Zip _____ Phone: _____

Age _____ Birthdays: Husband ____ Wife ____

1  Childrens' names & ages  2 _____ 3 ____

4 _____ 5 _____ Pets ____

Business _____ Phone: _____

Business address _____ Zip ____

Position title _____ How long? _____

Know from or through _____

Estimated worth & income _____

Colleges _____ Church _____

Call preferences _____

---

Political party _____

Sports _____

Hobbies _____

Special interests _____

Clubs _____

Organizations _____

Special honors _____

Mutual friends, relations _____

Remarks _____

**(Always prepare follow-up card and dates-to-remember cards for birthdays & anniversaries)**

present facts about your product or service to help the prospect make a buying decision, and develop a good relationship so that future sales result.

**Undecided Customer.** This prospect has identified a need and wants to satisfy that need but is not sure what product or service to buy. Your job is to listen so that you, too, understand the need and can recommend the product or service that will best satisfy the customer.

**Decided Customer.** This customer has decided on a purchase and knows exactly what is wanted. Your job is to hear the customer out and try to provide the appropriate product or service under mutually acceptable terms.

It should be relatively easy for an alert salesperson to identify these customer types in personal buying situations. In a matter of minutes, a retail salesperson should be able to classify a person entering the store as an observer, undecided, or decided customer. These categories apply just as well to business buying situations. For example, some business buyers have no intention of buying now but are simply seeking information for future buying situations. Other business buyers may be in the market at the present time but want to compare product features, prices, terms-of-sale, trade-ins, and delivery schedules before buying. Still other buyers, in the decided category, know what they want and simply have to finalize the purchase.

**Illustration 3-4 The experienced salesperson can determine readily the type of buyer a customer is.**

## By Personality

The second customer classification is by personality, disposition, or temperament. These terms refer to the general mood or nature of the buyer. Certainly moods change. The normally talkative customer may be quiet on a particular day, or you may find the normally trusting customer skeptical at times. Over time, however, most customers will exhibit a personality consistent enough for you to classify them into one of the following types.

| Customer Personality Type | Sales Strategy |
| --- | --- |
| 1. Talkative | Don't let this customer take you into a wide range of topics that are unrelated to your sales call. Take every opportunity to steer the conversation back to the topic you came to discuss. |
| 2. Silent | This situation is very difficult because the customer says little. Don't be impatient. Ask questions that cannot be answered by a simple "yes" or "no." Be more personable than usual until the customer opens up. |
| 3. Procrastinating | This customer listens but puts off buying. Forcefully handle all objections raised. Summarize the benefits the customer will lose if action isn't taken. If prices are likely to increase, point this out. |
| 4. Disagreeable | Resist the temptation to argue or fight back. Remain calm; listen to the customer; be cheerful and optimistic. |
| 5. Timid | Provide guidance, assurance, and support. Help the customer overcome buying fears. Reassure the customer and take it slow and easy. |
| 6. Ego-Involved | This customer exhibits a superior attitude. Listen attentively and flatter the customer's ego. Where appropriate, ask the customer for advice. |

| | |
|---|---|
| 7. Decisive | This customer is confident and knows what is wanted. Omit a lengthy sales presentation. Stick to the facts; omit details. |
| 8. Shrewd | This customer plays the angles and often pits one salesperson against another to get the best deal. Use subtle flattery; express respect for the customer's judgment and bargaining abilities. |
| 9. Skeptical | This customer tends to be distrustful. Do not argue or become impatient. Be conservative; admit to shortcomings; and use logic and proven facts. |
| 10. Grouchy | This customer is always in a bad mood. Be especially cheerful. Do not let the customer's mood dampen yours. Try to understand what is bothering the customer. |
| 11. Methodical | This customer moves slowly and appears to weigh every statement you make. Adjust your tempo to that of the customer. Slow down and expand on details. |
| 12. Dependent | This customer needs help in making a buying decision. Ask questions so that you understand the customer's need. Be patient; present supporting facts; and show the customer how your product or service will be in his or her best interest. |
| 13. Chiseler | This customer will never accept your quoted price. Stress quality and emphasize service to show that your product is worth the price. |

A number of customer categories have been identified above. However, the largest customer category has not yet been mentioned. This is the *pleasant customer*. You will find that most of your customers fall into this group. They are pleasant, open-minded, and willing to give you full attention. So if you are properly prepared for your sales presentation, you will have a good opportunity to close a sale.

## WHY CUSTOMERS BUY

Most behavior, buying behavior or otherwise, is motivated. When you are thirsty, you get a drink; when you are hungry, you get something to eat. Also, when a person buys something, the purchase action is the result of some form of motivation. People do not spend their money, or their company's money, without a reason. You must, therefore, understand what motivates customers to buy if you are to become a successful salesperson.

It is important to recognize that, just as there are many different types of customers, there are many different buying motives. The same product may be purchased for many reasons. Customers buying a new car may purchase on the basis of price, economy of operation, resale value, safety, appearance, or prestige. A salesperson stressing economy to a status-conscious prospect who wants to impress friends with the new car will probably lose the sale. Even products as simple as toothpaste appeal to many different buying motives. One brand claims low price, another good taste, while another stresses cavity prevention. Still others offer fresher breath, brighter teeth, and even sex appeal.

The best way to gain insight into buying motives is to examine the customer's past behavior. The habits people develop usually change little over time. Consider how difficult it is for a compulsive eater to diet or for a smoker to quit. The same is true of buying motives. The customer who has always been price conscious is likely to respond to price appeals in the future. Hence, the importance, as described earlier, of maintaining a detailed transaction file on each of your customers.

In addition to a customer's history, there are a number of forces that influence a customer's buying behavior. These forces operate individually and in combination when a customer is making a purchase decision, as shown in Figure 3-2.

Economic forces certainly are basic to purchase decisions. What a customer buys, the quality of what is purchased, and the quantity purchased depend on ability and willingness to pay. The demographic characteristics of the buyer are also important. These include a wide range of factors such as the buyer's age, education, occupation, religion, family status, nationality, and

**Figure 3–2**

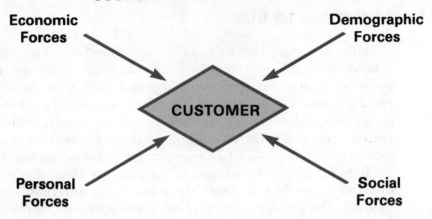

## SOURCES OF BUYING INFLUENCE

Economic Forces

Demographic Forces

CUSTOMER

Personal Forces

Social Forces

sex. Social forces include the influence of friends, neighbors, business associates, and organizations to which the buyer belongs. Finally, personal forces include the buyer's personality, ambitions, hobbies, and needs. Hence, the importance of maintaining a personal file on your customers.

Beyond an awareness of past purchase behavior and the economic, demographic, social, and personal forces influencing buying behavior, you should also be aware of basic buying motives. An awareness of these motives will help you to develop the appropriate appeal for each customer. Buying motives may be classified as either rational or emotional.

### Rational Buying Motives

Rational buying motives refer to purchases that are made on the basis of a logical, objective review of available facts. The buyer reviews information available on the product or service with the intention of purchasing that offering providing the best value for the money spent. Rational buying motives are most generally associated with business buying situations. Examples of rational buying motives include: (1) dependability, (2) durability, (3) low price, (4) economy in use, (5) installation and service, (6) performance, (7) speed, and (8) long life. The best way to prepare for a customer who is influenced by rational motives is to be familiar with all facts about your product or service as well as the features of competitive offerings.

**Illustration 3-5** All buying is influenced by rational and emotional buying motives.

### Emotional Buying Motives

Emotional buying motives represent purchase decisions made to satisfy personal feelings. It is impossible to identify all emotional motives; feelings are complex and all buyers possess a broad range of emotions. However, some examples of emotional buying motives include: (1) pleasure, (2) comfort, (3) relaxation, (4) pride, (5) status, (6) power, (7) belongingness, (8) sex, (9) fear, (10) security, and (11) distinction.

Although buying motives can be classified as either rational or emotional, it should not be assumed that purchases are based on only one or the other. Most purchase decisions are likely based on some combination of rational and emotional motives. The business buyer purchasing an executive jet for business travel, for example, may have made the purchase primarily on the basis of the rational facts presented, but appeals to an emotional motive such as status may have also influenced the decision.

# FROM INFORMATION TO ACTION

The previous material has provided the basic information you should have about each of your customers. Based on what you know about your customers, you must now develop the appropriate sales appeal to use. Just as there are many different customer types and buying motives, there are many possible sales appeals. Some examples will be presented here; more detail is provided in Chapters 7 through 12 of this book, which describe the various parts of the sales presentation.

| Appeal | Where to Use |
|---|---|
| 1. Prestige | This appeal may be used with ego-involved customers who wish to impress others. These customers are attracted to prestigious brand names and to expensive merchandise. They will buy if told that other important people are purchasing. |
| 2. Follow-the-Leader | This approach will often be successful with timid and dependent customers or customers who have a need to belong. These customers want the security of "going with the crowd." |
| 3. Comfort | Appeal to comfort with customers who have a desire for physical and mental well-being. |
| 4. Guilt | Guilt is a strong emotional appeal that is best used when the product or service will aid the buyer's loved ones. This appeal is often used when selling life insurance, encyclopedias, or products for young children. |
| 5. Price | The price issue is best used in business settings where the buyer is interested in cost savings or money gains. It can also be used successfully for major consumer products such as homes, automobiles, and major appliances. It is always useful for the price-conscious consumer. |

| 6. Status | Status is important to many customers. A wide range of offerings from club memberships, clothing, cars, opera subscriptions, to homes in exclusive neighborhoods, can be sold on the basis of status. |
|---|---|
| 7. Service | Many customers are interested in service after the sale. This is true of business buyers as well as consumers of automobiles and appliances. |

This is just a partial list of sales appeals; you should be able to think of many more. Appeals may be directed to a buyer's loyalty, desire for beauty or romance, sense of justice, desire to be different, desire for power or recognition, and many others. Your job is to determine the right appeal for each selling situation. You may want to try out several different appeals during your sales presentation. Once you have identified the appeal that seems to be of most interest to your customer, focus on it for the remainder of your presentation.

*Tip Tim Doyle had done some preliminary checking before calling on a prospect for duplicating equipment. Tim felt that he had the right machine to sell to this economy-minded customer. The prospect, however, showed little interest. Sensing this, Tim asked, "Mr. McCartney, have you already found a less expensive copier?" "What I have in mind," replied Mr. McCartney, "is something that makes higher quality copies; copies that look like originals. You see, these copies will be going to our customers." Discovering this, Tim produced samples from his company's more expensive duplicating equipment. At the same time, Tim switched from an economy appeal to a prestige appeal.*

## A FINAL WORD

When you turn the key in your car's ignition, you expect the car to start. When you turn on a water faucet, you expect water to run. However, when you call on a customer, you never know exactly what will happen. Customers are complex individuals. Although they may possess certain things in common, each is different.

Your customers are valuable friends whom you should never take for granted. Just as you are subjected to pressures that may result in your being happy one day and angry the next, so are your customers. There is no way you can predict how your customers will respond to your call on a given day at a given time. However, having the appropriate customer information and being knowledgeable about your product(s) will pave the way for your sales success.

## QUESTIONS

1. What is meant by segmenting a market? How might a salesperson for a pharmaceutical company use an awareness of market segmentation?

2. What is the difference between geographic, demographic and psychographic segmentation? Give one example of how each might be used.

3. How might the lack of adequate customer information lose a sale? Give one example.

4. Your records indicate that the customer you are about to call on is the silent type. What might you do to prepare for this sales call?

5. You are about to make your first sales call on a buyer for a particular business firm. What should you do before the call? What should you do during this call?

6. Why is it necessary for you to have a file on each of your customers? What information would you maintain in your files?

7. How might your customer files be used to identify buying motives?

8. "It's good to work as many appeals as possible into your sales presentation." Do you agree with this statement? Explain.

9. For what types of products and customers might prestige appeals work?

10. You are about to make a call on a person you have classified as a shrewd customer. How would you prepare for this call, and what type of appeal would you use?

# SALES CHALLENGES

1. Identify three well-known people. They might be entertainers, political figures, athletes, or top business executives. Based on what is known about them publicly, classify each into a particular customer type category. Identify the sales approach that you would use for each, then explain in detail how you arrived at your conclusions.

2. Because Tuesday mornings are usually slow in the Fashionwear Department Store, you are the only one working in the men's department. On this particular morning you are trying to wait on two customers at the same time, while a third customer has been browsing around waiting for service. A fourth customer walks in, selects a size 44 long sport coat off a rack, and hands it to you with the comment, "I'll take this coat. Could you ring it up right away?" How would you classify this customer? Explain how you would handle this situation. Would you ring up the sale and make the other customers wait? Would you ask the fourth customer to wait? What other alternatives are possible?

3. Pat Culley has just walked out of Amy Laser's office shaking her head. She thought she had a sale. As Pat was working out details on the purchase of some very expensive equipment, she casually mentioned the current high interest rates and the lack of government action to bring the rates down. Suddenly Pat found herself in an argument over politics. Within ten minutes the call was over and she was leaving without a sale. What went wrong? Why did this situation develop? What has Pat learned for future reference?

# CASES

### 3-1  A New Home for the Trudells

Margaret and Ken Trudell have been married for seven years. Margaret is an editor for a publishing company and Ken is an accountant for a large manufacturer. They both have cars and they are currently living in a very tastefully decorated two-bedroom apartment on the fifteenth floor of a luxury building. Each has been saving a portion of their income every month, and they now feel they are ready to make a down payment on a nice home.

The location of the home is very important. There are only a few areas around the city that Margaret and Ken will consider. These are the newer, more fashionable areas where many of their friends live.

There are a number of features that Margaret and Ken are looking for in their home. The home must have at least three bedrooms, a family room with a fireplace, an enclosed back porch, a large basement that can be remodeled into a recreation room in the future, a two-car garage, at least two full bathrooms, a large back yard that could accommodate an in-ground pool, and a separate dining room. Other features that Margaret and Ken would like, but which aren't as important, are a wet bar in the family room, a large foyer, and a laundry room next to the kitchen.

Margaret and Ken realize that the home they are looking for will be quite expensive. However, since many of their friends have homes with these features, and Margaret and Ken plan to do a lot of entertaining, they want a home that will be equal to the homes of their friends. Furthermore, with a large down payment, Margaret and Ken feel that (based on their combined incomes) the monthly payments will be within a range they can afford. They realize they will need additional furniture and appliances but are confident that they can budget for these items if they are careful.

Margaret and Ken have been watching the real estate market and think that now is the right time to buy. They have called you as a salesperson for Real Estate One and have made an appointment to see you.

1. Identify the various buying motives exhibited by Margaret and Ken. Would you consider the Trudells rational or emotional buyers?
2. As a salesperson, how would you go about discovering the important facts about Margaret and Ken that were presented in this case?
3. What sales appeal(s) would you use when showing homes to Margaret and Ken?

## 3-2 The Glidden Glaze Company

Bruce Fynes sells glaze that is used to coat ceramic floor and wall tiles. Bruce is calling on Rhonda Holden, a new purchasing agent for the Terrazzo Tile Company. Bruce has called on Terrazzo Tile in the past, but he has not been successful in completing a sale. This is also Bruce's first meeting with Ms. Holden. Bruce has been kept waiting 20 minutes beyond the appointment time that was made by telephone. Finally, Ms. Holden's secretary shows Bruce into Ms. Holden's office.

**Bruce:** How do you do, Ms. Holden? I'm Bruce Fynes with the Glidden Glaze Company. I'd like to talk with you about some of our products. (Ms. Holden does not return Bruce's smile but simply nods toward a chair in front of her.)

**Holden:** Have a seat. I should tell you right off that I have a six-week supply of glaze on hand, and I'm very satisfied with my current supplier.

**Bruce:** (Taking a seat) Thank you, Ms. Holden. As you know, Glidden is one of the largest suppliers of glaze coatings in the country. Our service and prices can match those of anyone in the industry.

**Holden:** What makes your service so good?

**Bruce:** Because of our strategically located inventories across the country, we guarantee 24-hour delivery. If we don't have the proper glaze in our warehouse, we will air freight it to you direct from our plant. We're the only company in the industry offering that service. Also, our glaze provides a tougher finish. What volume do you order in, Ms. Holden?

**Holden:** It varies.

**Bruce:** Most companies order in two-month volumes. How much glaze do you use in the course of a year?

**Holden:** How much glaze we use is privileged information between us and our suppliers.

**Bruce:** I understand. I just wanted to get an indication of your volume so that I could quote a price to you.

**Holden:** I'm sure your price would not be lower than we're paying now.

**Bruce:** It's true that prices are highly competitive. However, when you combine Glidden's price with a superior product and service, you are getting a very attractive package.

**Holden:** I'm sure you think so, but so do all of your competitors.

**Bruce:** You know, Ms. Holden, many companies are buying from more than one supply source. That ensures a continuation of supply even if something happens to one of the sources. Glidden would certainly like to be one of your sources.

**Holden:** I'm not concerned about what other companies are doing. By concentrating my purchases with one supplier, I get a larger discount.

**Bruce:** Have you considered alternating your orders? You can order from one supplier one time and the other supplier the next. That way, you get the same discount, and still hedge against disruptions in supply.

**Holden:** Well, let me think about it. Leave your product catalog and price list.

1. In which customer category would you put Rhonda Holden?
2. How do you think Bruce handled this customer?
3. What would you have done differently? What type of appeal might work with a customer like Rhonda Holden?

# 4

# YOUR INDUSTRY, COMPANY, AND PRODUCTS

Would you take your car to a mechanic who lacks adequate auto repair knowledge? Would you have your income tax returns prepared by an accountant who is unfamiliar with current tax laws? Would you trust the health-care needs of your family to a doctor with insufficient medical knowledge? In the same fashion, why would a customer buy from a salesperson who lacks the knowledge to satisfy the customer's needs? Like all other skilled professionals, you must have a thorough knowledge and understanding of the essentials of your job if you are to perform to the satisfaction of your customers.

Figure 4–1 expands upon the diagram shown in Chapter 2, page 32 and identifies the five areas in which thorough sales knowledge is needed. These five areas are: your industry, your company, your products, your customers, and territory and self-management. Customer knowledge, because of its importance, is covered in Chapters 3, 5, and 6. Territory and self-management is covered in Chapter 14. This chapter will focus on industry, company, and product knowledge.

## SALES KNOWLEDGE IS IMPORTANT

Your customers demand facts. If you are to provide the information your customers need, answer their questions, and handle objections, you must possess pertinent information about your company, your company's offerings, and your competitors' offerings.

Having the right information gives you credibility with your customers and helps you to service their needs. Just as you would feel more assured when dealing with knowledgeable professionals, so do your customers. Furthermore, the better your knowledge, the better you will be able to devise ways of satisfying your customers' needs through your company's offerings.

Figure 4–1

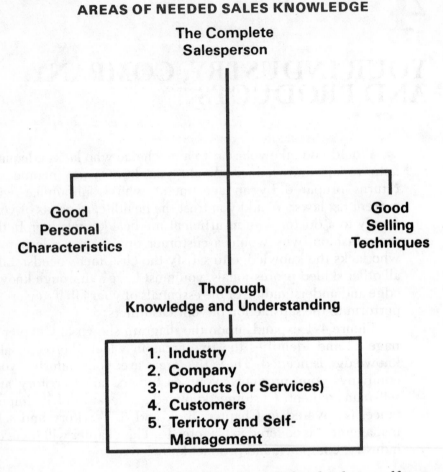

**AREAS OF NEEDED SALES KNOWLEDGE**

**The Complete
Salesperson**

**Good
Personal
Characteristics**

**Good
Selling
Techniques**

**Thorough
Knowledge and Understanding**

1. **Industry**
2. **Company**
3. **Products (or Services)**
4. **Customers**
5. **Territory and Self-
Management**

Finally, your thorough sales knowledge leads to self-confidence and personal development. Possessing the facts you need gives you confidence as you approach each sales call. You have faith in your knowledge and your ability to handle any questions or problems that may arise. This confidence helps you to be the best salesperson you are capable of being and paves the way for promotions as openings occur in your company.

## YOUR INDUSTRY

To provide the proper background for your selling efforts, you must have insight into your industry with particular reference to your competition and your territory. From a broad

**Illustration 4-1** Attaining knowledge of current developments in many industries is important.

*Intel Corporation, photo by Chuck O'Rear*

viewpoint, you should understand how your industry fits into the overall economy. Economic changes affect customer requirements. This, in turn, may necessitate changes in selling techniques. For example, information about expected inflationary pressures in your industry may be used to convince customers to buy now.

You should also understand the relationship between your industry and related industries. If you are a distributor to auto supply companies, how will changes in auto production affect the needs of your customers? Knowledge of current developments, understanding of how current news events will affect your industry, and awareness of what industry trade associations are doing will help you to anticipate sales opportunities.

From a narrower perspective, salespeople must have detailed knowledge about their present customers. You must know the buying policies, patterns, and preferences of your customers. You should possess some knowledge of the products and services of your customers. In some cases, salespeople need to be knowledgeable about their customers' customers. This may be especially true if you are selling to wholesalers, distributors, or are acting in a missionary capacity where you are expected to assist your customers with their sales problems.

## Your Competition

When you are in the market to buy a video game, a television, an item of clothing, or almost anything else, you examine several brands or styles before making your purchase. As such, you should assume that your customers will be examining various offerings as well before they make a purchase. Your customers, especially business buyers, require certain products and services. Therefore, the decision they are making is not whether to buy but what, from among a variety of choices available to them, they should buy.

Business buyers will rarely make a purchase decision without comparing competitive offerings. In many sales situations, a customer will ask questions about competitors' products and services. One of your responsibilities is to make sure that buyers have the correct information. For example, a buyer may feel that your price is too high, not realizing that your price includes many options for which your competitors charge extra. Your knowledge of the competition will clarify this situation.

The information you should have about your competitors includes such things as design, features, options, price, quality, sizes or models, packaging, overall performance standards, delivery, and after-sale servicing. As an example, a sales representative for a textbook publisher must know what books other publishers have for the same courses, their strengths and weaknesses, and the material they cover. Other factors such as the caliber of students at which the books are directed, the availability and quality of supplementary materials, user opinions, and prices must also be known. Acquiring competitive information may seem time-consuming and difficult, making it easy for you to excuse yourself from this task on the grounds that you don't work for the other companies. However, you end up working for them every time you lose a sale because you didn't have appropriate competitive information.

Keep in mind that competition is not limited to those firms selling the same products as yours. Your competitors include all firms whose offerings fulfill the same customer needs. If you sell television advertising time, your competitors are not only other

TV stations but radio stations, newspapers, magazines, bill-boards, transit space, direct mail, and any other form of com-munication that advertisers might use.

Information about the offerings of other companies can be obtained from competitors' advertising messages, trade associa-tions, company laboratories, publications such as *Consumer Reports*, sales meetings, conventions, trade shows, and from other salespeople. You may be able to obtain price lists and catalogs from your competitors. Much information can be gained by asking questions. Ask users of competitive products why they buy them and what they like about them. Comparative shopping might be used. Visit an outlet that sells competitive products and listen to a salesperson's presentation. You may want to buy a competitive product to get first-hand information about features and operations of the product. Keep a notebook on your competitors' offerings adding new information as you acquire it. Make special note of all areas where your products compare most favorably against the competition.

*Tip    Juan Mendels sells a line of plumbing products to wholesalers, plumbing and building contractors, and retail outlets for Atled Industries. Over the years, Juan has acquired a great deal of competitive information by being very alert. With this information, Juan has developed his own cross-referenced notebook. Each section of the note-book contains detailed information about competitive products, features, and prices with comparable informa-tion about the products that Juan sells. When buyers comment on competitive offerings or ask questions, Juan can check his notebook to verify the information, note inaccuracies in the buyer's information, or comment on the features of competitors' products. Juan can point out the particular advantages his firm's products have over each competitive offering. It is no accident that Juan has consistently been one of the most successful salespeople at Atled.*

## Your Territory

Sales territories differ in many ways. The nature of the market in your territory may be substantially different from that faced by other salespeople for your company in other territories. It is important that you understand the uniqueness of your own territory.

A sales territory may be dominated by a specific industry such as the auto industry in Detroit. Factors affecting the auto industry may have more impact on this territory than on other territories. Some territories may be urban in nature; some rural. Some territories may have a smaller number of large customers, while other territories may be populated by a large number of small customers. Some territories may have a disproportionately large number of people of a specific religion or ethnic origin. You must understand the unique attributes of your territory if you are to successfully cultivate its sales potential.

## YOUR COMPANY

Just as you need thorough information about your industry, so must you have a detailed understanding of your company. When competitor's offerings are nearly identical, company information may be more important to the buyer than product information. The customer may prefer buying from the company with the best reputation for service and delivery.

### Size and Standing in Industry

If your company is very large, particularly if it is a leader in its industry, this can serve as a very useful sales tool. Companies are large for a reason. The reason is that they have many customers, and a firm that has many customers is doing something right. Customers are patronizing them for a reason, and that reason is the products and services offered. Many customers feel more confident when buying from large companies. Use this to advantage in your sales presentation.

### Company History

Company histories often make interesting reading. More important, learning about the history of your firm and its founders provides a better understanding of current company policies and philosophies. In addition, knowledge of the history and growth of your firm makes you feel more a part of the organization and often provides interesting anecdotes that may be used during a sales presentation. Assume that you are a salesperson for Apple Computer and a prospective customer asked you how the company got its name. It would be more interesting to be able to say that one of the company's founders,

Steve Jobs, eats only fruit and named the company after one of his favorite foods than to say, "I don't know."

## Organization

Most companies prepare organizational charts that identify lines of authority and responsibility. You should be familiar with the internal organization of your company. Successfully filling an order and servicing a customer's needs are often the joint responsibility of a number of different departments such as accounting, traffic, production, credit, and purchasing. If a customer problem or complaint arises, you should know who to contact to resolve the problem or expedite a shipment.

**Illustration 4–2  It is important to become familiar with the internal workings of your company.**

## Personnel

Who are the top managers of your company and what is the background of each? What have they done for your company? Are they well known and important figures in the industry? Are they well known for their service to the community? If so, the names of these people can be used effectively in your sales presentation. The reputation of your company's management and their willingness to stand behind your products is important. Your customers would be reluctant to deal with you if they had little faith in your management.

## Policies

Most business firms have rules or policies that guide their actions. These policies ensure uniform action and indicate what the firm can and cannot (or will and will not) do. You must know and understand these policies so that you don't make promises to customers that your firm cannot satisfy. Here are some of the more important policy areas with which you should become familiar.

**Credit Policies.** Extending credit to customers, allowing them to receive goods now for a promise to pay later, is a very important customer service. You must know your firm's credit policies, particularly with regard to credit worthiness, conditions under which credit will be granted, and credit limits. Customers will ask about credit policies.

Although credit policies are normally established by the company's credit department, salespeople play an important role in administering credit policies. The salesperson is in an excellent position to obtain credit information on customers. Figure 4–2 is an example of a typical form that salespeople are asked to complete when a new customer requests credit.

**Price Policies.** Salespeople generally do not have a say in establishing their company's list prices. However, salespeople do have considerable authority in granting discounts off the list price. As such, salespeople must be thoroughly familiar with their company's pricing policies to know what discounts can be offered and under what circumstances.

What sort of discounts does your firm offer that would be of interest and use to your customer? There are cash discounts for prompt payment, trade discounts for the performance of certain services, seasonal discounts for buying out-of-season, quantity discounts for buying in large volume, and advertising allowances granted when your customers promote your products in their advertising. You must be aware of these policies and how they are applied. Also, know your firm's policy on trade-ins, which is another form of discount off the list price.

**Service Policies.** What services are available to your customers? Under what conditions are the services offered? Good service is important to sales success. Service may be the difference in making a sale when competitive products and prices are similar. Don't promise services, however, that your firm can't deliver. This is a sure way to lose customers. Be familiar with

**Figure 4–2**

## TYPICAL CREDIT INFORMATION FORM

Date _____

Account Name _____

Address _____

_____

Officers or Owners _____

_____

### BALANCE SHEET

| Assets | | Liabilities & Capital | |
|---|---|---|---|
| Cash | | Accounts Payable | |
| Accounts Receivable | | Notes Payable | |
| Inventory | | Other (Loans, etc.) | |
| Other | _____ | | |
| Total Current | _____ | Total Current | _____ |
| Plant & Equipment | | Long-Term Debt | |
| Other | | Total Liabilities | |
| | _____ | Net Worth | _____ |
| Total Assets | _____ | Total Liabilities & Capital | _____ |

### OPERATING STATEMENT

For Period _____ Through _____

| | | | |
|---|---|---|---|
| Salary | | | |
| Rent | | Sales | |
| Taxes | | Cost of Goods Sold | |
| Other | _____ | Gross Profit | _____ |
| Total Expenses | _____ | Less Expenses | _____ |
| | | Net Profit | _____ |

Signed _____

your company's delivery, installation, repair, and maintenance policies. Understand the policies concerning returned goods, as well as services such as prepackaging, prepricing, merchandising aids, and advertising assistance. Know when these services can be offered and under what conditions.

### Socially Responsible Activities

Is your firm engaged in programs that are beneficial to the community? These might include environmental programs, programs to aid charitable organizations, or providing jobs for the handicapped, just to name a few. Be aware of these activities of your company. Other things being equal, a customer would prefer to patronize a firm that supports worthwhile causes.

Just as you would record and keep industry information, so should you keep a detailed record of company information for easy reference. Keep this information up to date. You will acquire additional information through sales meetings, company newsletters, annual reports, and correspondence and mailings from your company. More information will be obtained by visiting company manufacturing and distribution facilities, talks from company officials, news reports, and trade journals.

## YOUR PRODUCTS

A thorough knowledge of your products or services is essential for sales success. The most successful salespeople are those who can communicate the value of their offerings to potential customers. To communicate effectively, you must thoroughly understand the products or services you are selling. Product knowledge is so important that some companies seek out people who have highly developed product knowledge. Textbook publishing companies hire former teachers, pharmaceutical companies hire druggists, computer manufacturers hire systems engineers and programmers, while industrial distributors hire mechanical engineers.

Customers depend on salespeople for information. The amount of information needed varies by type of customer and complexity of product. A salesperson for IBM would require more product knowledge than a salesperson for Avon. However, the Avon representative still requires adequate product knowledge to answer questions and handle objections. Not being able

**Illustration 4–3** Visiting your company's manufacturing facilities is one way to obtain information.

to provide the information a customer has requested may end your chance to make a sale; providing the wrong information could lose a customer forever.

*Tip    Ching-yu Jen has been a successful salesperson for Allen Adhesives for a number of years. When asked about her consistently high sales by a new salesperson for the company, Ching-yu related the following story. "A number of years ago I lost a very large account. I thought that I knew everything about the products I was selling. In truth, I didn't really have adequate product knowledge. I recommended the wrong epoxy to a manufacturer for a certain application. The result really messed up their production process. Soon after, they gave all of their business to another salesperson who knew what she was talking about. From that day on, I started learning everything there was to know about our products and their applications. I'll stack my product knowledge against that of any salesperson in the industry. My sales are high because buyers have confidence in me."*

### Know the Research and Development History of Your Product

Most companies spend a great deal of time, effort, and money in the development of their products. The product may be tested, modified, and retested many times before it is made available for sale. The testing and modifications result in many product improvements. Once offered for sale, the product may be further improved as additional information is gathered. The product may be tested under many highly demanding situations. You should be familiar with the research efforts behind your products. This information assures your customers that your products are well suited to their needs and have benefited by improvements brought about through testing.

## Know How Your Products Are Produced

Your customers desire assurances that your products will perform as promised. Information on how the products are produced and the raw materials used can provide this assurance.

**Materials Used.** You should know exactly what materials your products are made of and what characteristics they possess. Just as the ingredients used by a chef determine the flavor of the finished meal, the materials used in the production of a product determine its qualities. The materials used in the construction of your products can often be translated into important selling features. Because your product is made of aluminum instead of steel, for example, it has the benefits of being lighter, rustproof, and 100 percent recyclable; features that may be very important to your customers.

Under certain circumstances, buyers may be interested in the manufacturing process for your products. For example, clothing buyers may be interested in the weaving and dying processes used. They may want to know how particular yarns are interwoven for effect. The buyer may be interested in knowing that your product is made by a continuous manufacturing process, thus ensuring a uniform pattern. Many companies encourage customers to visit their plants to observe their manufacturing procedures.

Customers may be interested in the quality control procedures used by your company. Product quality may be monitored by visual inspection, electronic sensors, optic scanning, x-rays, or other means. These procedures ensure that defective parts are not sent out. Where consistent quality is of vital concern to your customers, knowing the quality control procedures used for your products can provide the assurances necessary to complete a sale.

**Illustration 4-4** Encouraging customers to visit your company's facility may be beneficial.

## Know the Performance Characteristics of Your Product

When someone buys a product, what they're really buying is the performance of that product. You don't buy a drill because you want to own a drill. You buy a drill because you want or need the holes that the drill will make. As such, customers are interested in product-performance information.

There are many types of performance questions that a customer might ask. Will the lubricant work at high temperatures? Will the metal buckle under stress? How much maintenance does the product require under normal use? What is the machine's output per hour? How much fuel is required? What is the amperage required to operate the equipment? What is the top operating speed? What is the life expectancy of the product?

What is the 'R' value of the storm windows and doors? The list of possible questions depends on the interests of the customer and the characteristics of the product.

Successful performance examples can be useful selling tools. You may want to compile case histories of successful applications of your products. Case histories are accounts of experiences users have had with your products. A customer may be more confident in buying your product knowing that it has a successful performance history by other users.

### Know How Your Product Is Promoted

In many selling situations, customers are interested in how well your products are promoted in the market place. This is especially true when selling to wholesalers and retailers. Retailers are more willing to stock products that are heavily advertised since the advertising presells the products for them. Products like Coca-Cola, Tide, Crest, Pampers, and many others are given premium shelf space because the advertising support they receive creates considerable buyer interest in them. Know how your company supports your products. This information can be used as part of your sales presentation.

Does your company provide dealer aids? These are brochures, displays, and point-of-purchase materials that are set up in the retail store to help sell the displayed merchandise. Retailers may be more willing to stock products, or stock larger volumes of products, for which dealer aids are available. Not only should you make sure that you bring available aids to the attention of your customers, but you should also be available to assemble the aids, clean and replace damaged displays, and show retailers how to use the sales aids most effectively.

### Know the After-Sale Support of Your Company

Another important concern for many buyers is what your firm will do for them after they have purchased your product. Many products require complex or difficult installation. Does your company provide this installation? If not, what type of installation assistance or advice is provided? How can you be of assistance to the buyer to ensure that installation is performed properly so that the product performs as promised?

If your product requires servicing over time, your customers must be informed of service contracts or servicing assistance that is available. Does your product come with a performance guarantee? This can be a strong selling point. Make sure, however, that you point out any limitations that may exist on the guarantee to prevent misunderstandings.

Know what your company policy is regarding repairs, replacement parts, and returns. Your customers will want this information. Know who to contact in your service or parts department when a customer has a problem. When customer assistance is needed, you cannot pass the buck; customers expect you to have the answers.

### Know the Advantages of Your Product

In addition to knowing as much as you can about your products, be particularly aware of the advantages your products have over the competition's products. These advantages will serve as your main selling points. Look for differentiating features that are unique to your company's offerings. Are your products more durable? More versatile? Faster? More energy efficient? Carry a better or longer warranty? Your knowledge of your products and of the competition should help you to develop a long list of advantages to use in your sales presentation.

## SOURCES OF SALES INFORMATION

There are many sources available to obtain the industry, company, and product information that you should have. Although it is impossible to identify all available sources, the most commonly used will be presented. The wise salesperson will stay in constant contact with these, as well as other information sources.

### Sources Within Your Firm

Your company is an important and readily available source of information. Be sure you take advantage of this resource.

**Sales Training Programs.**   Most companies conduct sales training programs for new sales recruits. These programs may run from several days to several months in situations where very technical knowledge is required. Company executives, sales managers, experienced salespeople, and outside experts may be involved in various aspects of the training. Films, cassettes, lectures, role playing, round-table discussions, literature, and visits to company facilities are among the training methods used.

The typical content of sales training programs, based on a survey of 152 companies, is shown in Table 4–1. As can be seen, training programs cover the most important areas of knowledge described in this chapter.

**Table 4–1**

| Topics Covered In Sales Training Programs | |
|---|---|
| TOPIC | PERCENT OF TRAINING TIME |
| Product Information | 42% |
| Market-Industry Information | 17 |
| Company Information | 13 |
| Selling Techniques | 24 |
| Other Topics | 4 |
| | 100% |

Source: *David S. Hopkins,* Training the Sales Force: A Progress Report *(New York: The Conference Board, 1984), p. 1.*

In addition to training programs for new recruits, most companies conduct ongoing training programs for their experienced salespeople. These programs serve to introduce information on new products, changes in company policies, new promotional programs, new selling techniques, or any other information that the company believes would be of importance to the sales force. Information may also be conveyed at routine sales meetings.

**Company Literature.** Most companies supply printed bulletins, brochures, sales manuals, catalogs, merchandise manuals, annual reports and other literature to their salespeople. Much valuable information is available through these sources. It is often wise to carry this information in a briefcase during sales calls so that it can be referred to when customers ask technical questions.

**Sales Supervisors and Other Salespeople.** Your sales manager and experienced salespeople with your company represent a good source of information. These people have been in the field, possibly much longer than you, and have accumulated valuable information. When you are with these individuals, be a good listener; ask questions and take advantage of their insight and understanding.

**Your Products, Manufacturing Facilities, and Research Labs.** Study your products so that you understand their features. Use your products as your customers would so that you understand their operation or function. Read the labeling on the products. Labels contain much valuable information. Visit your company's manufacturing facilities. Ask questions of the people producing your products. If your company has research facilities, visit them as well. The people in your research labs subject your products to continual testing and, as such, possess valuable insight into your products that you may not have.

### Sources Outside Your Firm

In addition to the many sources of information within your firm, there are even more outside sources.

**Customers.** Your customers can be a valuable source of information. As users, they have opinions about your products—things that they like and might not like about them. Since these people are generally called upon by your competitors, they are often a good source of competitive information. They may also be familiar with things going on in your industry of which you are not aware. Be sure to listen carefully during your sales calls and ask questions.

**Business Publications.** There are a wide range of business publications that can be very valuable information sources. Periodicals such as *Business Week* and *Fortune* provide broad information about the economy and various major industries. Publications such as *Business Marketing* and *Sales & Marketing Management* concentrate on sales information. In addition, there are many highly specialized periodicals devoted to specific industries. If you were selling plumbing products, for example, you might want to be familiar with *Hardware Age, Hardware Merchandising, Hardware News, Hardware Retailing, Hardware World, Do-It-Yourselfer, The National Home Center News,* and *Plumbing Digest.* Become familiar with the publications in your industry.

Public libraries are a valuable source of printed information. Reference guides such as *The Reader's Guide to Periodical Literature* and *The Business Periodicals Index* list information sources on a wide variety of subjects. Many libraries now have computerized information search facilities. If you are not familiar with these, ask the librarian for assistance.

**Trade Shows.** Trade shows are events where many companies in an industry display their products and generate customer interest. These shows provide a good opportunity for alert salespeople to obtain valuable competitive information. Inspect the offerings of your competitors, watch any demonstrations they may conduct, and pick up their product literature. Also, talk to customers who are visiting the show.

**Testing Bureaus.** There are many independent laboratories that test products and provide performance information. Consumers Union and Underwriters' Laboratories are examples. Consumers Union publishes *Consumer Reports*, which provides test results, classifies products as "acceptable" and "not acceptable," and indicates "best buys" in various product categories. A salesperson whose product has received a best buy rating in *Consumer Reports* can certainly use this to advantage during the sales presentation.

> *Tip*    *Richard Allen, a salesperson for the Duo-Fast Company for 15 years, was called into the office of his sales manager, Anne Lesperance. "Rich," Anne began, "you've been with us for a long time. Sales of most of the people on our staff show a leveling pattern after eight to ten years. Your sales, however, have continued to show significant increases every year. What's your secret?"*
>
> *"It's no secret at all," replied Rich. "My philosophy is that a professional salesperson is like any other professional. You must keep learning. You expect a doctor to be more of an expert after ten years in practice than right after finishing medical school. In selling, products, product uses, competition, and customers change; the professional salesperson keeps up with these changes. I read trade journals, attend trade shows on my own time, pay attention at sales meetings, read all the literature that the company puts out, spend time in the library, and, most of all, listen to what my customers have to say. The more I know about my customers, the industry, our company, our products, and the competition, the better prepared I am to sell."*

## CONVERT KNOWLEDGE INTO CUSTOMER BENEFITS

This chapter has concentrated on the kind of knowledge required for successful selling. Customers, however, are not just interested in facts; they are interested in benefits. Your job is to convert your knowledge into customer benefits. A person buying a new pair of shoes isn't interested in product features such as welt, filler, lining, insole, or stitching. The customer is interested in how these product features bring about benefits such as comfort, long wear, and good appearance. The salesperson stressing customer benefits is more likely to complete a sale than the salesperson stressing product features.

It is your responsibility to convert product features into customer benefits. This is not a difficult job, but it does require some effort. The starting point is to identify all the features of the products you are selling, no matter how unimportant the feature may seem. Once you have listed all the product features, identify ways your customers can benefit from each feature. One easy way of translating features into benefits is to read each feature on your list and then ask yourself the question, "So what?" The answer to this question will often be a benefit that the feature brings about. Table 4–2 lists some sample product features and corresponding customer benefits.

**Table 4–2**

## Product Features and Customer Benefits

| Product Feature | —— "so what" —— | Customer Benefit |
|---|---|---|
| Hammer forged screwdriver | | Bit won't slip from screw slot in use |
| Balanced shovel handle and blade | | Less back strain in use |
| Hammer handles that are sanded, polished, and shaped | | Comfortable, sure grip, and splinter-proof |
| Polycotton fabric | | Looks fresh in use and easy to care for |
| Permanently lubricated, shielded bearings | | Less maintenance required |
| High 'R' value | | Provides better insulation |
| Low amperage rating | | Requires less energy |

In each of the examples presented in Table 4–2, would a customer buy because of the product feature or the resulting benefit? Keep in mind that in addition to product features, you can convert company features into customer benefits. This is often overlooked. A company with many geographically dispersed inventory locations offers the benefit of fast delivery; a company with a highly trained service department offers efficient, worry-free repairs; while a company with a wide selection of products means a customer can benefit by doing all of their buying from one source.

> **Tip** *Lara Marie sells real estate. She is currently showing a home to a family just moving into the city. "This is a fine house," Lara tells the couple, "but I'll have to know more about your family before we can tell whether you will be happy here." Lara proceeds to ask for such information as the number and age of the children, where the husband will be working, where the wife will be working, the religious affiliation of the family, and the family's hobbies. Receiving this information, Lara checks her notebook. From her notes, Lara is able to point out to the family how many children of a similar age there are in the neighborhood, where the nearest schools are, the distances and shortest routes to the places of work, the location of the nearest church, and the upcoming activities at the community center that the family members can join. From this, the couple can clearly picture what it will be like living in the home. Lara sells many homes because she sells the benefits the homes offer to her customers.*

## KNOWLEDGE IN SELLING SERVICES

Most of what has been said about products applies to selling services as well. Those who sell services should thoroughly understand and explain the benefits of their particular services. Thus, the telephone company stresses the convenience of having several phones in the home. Telephone salespeople stress the beauty of their products by presenting streamlined instruments in many appealing colors. Other telephone services are sold by demonstrating various uses, such as answering and recording equipment, automobile telephones, low service rates during special time periods, conference calls, WATS lines, and many others. The service salesperson can develop tantalizing appeals to potential customers simply by explaining how the service will make the customer's life easier, more successful, or more enjoyable.

## CAN A SALESPERSON HAVE TOO MUCH SALES KNOWLEDGE?

The question might be raised as to whether you can know too much about what you are selling. The best answer to this was supplied by one sales veteran who stated, "No, it is not possible to know too much about what you are selling, but it is possible to talk too much about it." Each customer is not interested in everything you know about what you are selling. Find out what the customer is interested in and concentrate on those issues. Use your product knowledge wisely. Do not overburden the customer with facts. Concentrate on customer benefits—not product features.

## QUESTIONS

1. "Salespeople who don't know their competition often end up working for them." What is meant by this statement?
2. Identify what you believe to be the five most important types of information to have about your company. Why have you selected each of these?
3. A professional salesperson is often viewed as the manager of his or her territory. Do you agree with this statement? Why or why not?
4. Why is it important to understand the organizational structure of your company and to know the people in the various positions?
5. "To be an efficient problem solver, you must have adequate product knowledge." Do you agree or disagree with this statement? Explain.
6. Would a customer be interested in how your products are made? Why or why not?
7. How might your products be supported in the market? Why might your customers be interested in this information?
8. Product guarantees are a frequent source of disputes. Why do these disputes arise? How can they be prevented?

9. What is the difference between product features and benefits? Which is more important in your sales presentation?
10. Is product knowledge important in retail selling? Explain your answer.

## SALES CHALLENGES

1. It is important for salespeople to know something about their industry. Select an industry that you are interested in. Visit a library with which you are familiar. Examine some of the general business periodicals such as *Fortune* and *Business Week*. Find some specialized periodicals dealing with the industry you have selected. Use the periodical guides described in this chapter. From all of these sources, put together a report describing the industry that includes overall industry sales, sales of the major firms in the industry, and current industry trends.

2. Salespeople should know many facts about the products they sell. Facts differ in importance, however, depending on the nature of the products that are being sold. Visit a local department store. Select an expensive consumer product (priced above $150). Examine this product and identify as many product features as you can. Convert each product feature into a customer benefit that can be used as a selling point in a sales presentation for the product. Prepare a short report identifying as many customer benefits as you can.

3. Among other things, Duane Wilbur sells disposable paper seat covers to be used at athletic events to protect fans' clothing from dirty seats. Duane has just contacted Moe Lewis, the general manager of Exposition Stadium.

Duane: Good morning, Mr. Lewis. I'm Duane Wilbur of Continental Paper. I have a product just suited to your needs. It's a disposable seat cover to be sold to fans at your ball games. We can sell the covers to you for $.20 each, and you can sell them for $.50. If you sell just 5,000 at each game, that's a profit of $1,500 for you. Pretty good, eh?

Moe: That sounds OK, but what am I going to do with the 15,000 canvas rental covers that I have now?

Duane: Rental covers? You have rental covers?

**Moe:** If you can figure out what to do with the rental covers, give me a call.

**Duane:** OK. Thanks for your time.

Why didn't Duane make the sale? What should he do before his next sales call?

## CASES

### 4-1  Ondecker Bathware Supplies

Al Pilecki of Ondecker Bathware Supplies is calling on Ruth Meyer, a buyer with Tecumseh Hardware and Tire. Ondecker is a manufacturer of a wide range of plumbing products while Tecumseh Hardware and Tire is a regional chain of retail home center outlets. Over the years, Ondecker has not been very successful in getting their products into the Tecumseh stores. However, Ondecker has recently introduced a new hand shower that Al Pilecki is certain will be of interest to Ruth Meyer.

Al has been in Ruth's office for about 15 minutes. Pleasantries have been exchanged and Al has described some of the main features of the Ondecker hand shower, including the adjustable spray, the all-brass wall bracket connection, the four decorator colors the plastic model comes in, the chrome finish available on the more expensive model, and the five-year guarantee. Al has also gone over the price list with Ruth. At this point, the following conversation takes place:

**Al:** I think I've covered the main features. Do you have any questions?

**Ruth:** Just a few. Is your spray cover needle or aerated?

**Al:** I'm not sure. Let me check my product manual . . . I don't seem to see anything. Yes, here it is. It has an aerated spray.

**Ruth:** Is your wall bracket fixed or swivel?

**Al:** I'll have to check the manual on that. (He searches for several minutes.) I can't find any reference to swivel in the manual, so I'd have to assume its fixed.

**Ruth:** Does your hand shower have a water saver feature like some of the other new models on the market?

**Al:** I'm sure it must, our product has most of the latest features.

**Ruth:** What mounting accessories come in your shower package?

**Al:** Gee, that's a good question. I'll have to check with the office and get back to you. Can I answer any other questions?

**Ruth:** No. I don't think you can.

1. Why do you think Ruth didn't ask any more questions?
2. Was Al prepared for his sales call? Explain.
3. Do you think that Al is going to make a sale to Tecumseh Hardware and Tire? Why or why not?
4. What advice would you give Al before he makes his next sales call?

## 4-2   Marcotte Auto Supplies

Marcotte Auto Supplies was founded in 1938 by Santos and Theresa Marcotte to manufacture parts for auto repair. The company began with only five products but currently manufactures and distributes more than 250 separate items that are commonly needed by automotive repair outlets. The company began with 11 employees. For the first several years of operation, Santos Marcotte did all of the selling. Today, the company employs more than 500 people and has a sales force of 18.

Although the company produces over 250 parts, this is a relatively small number compared with all of the parts used in auto repair work. For many years, Marcotte produced only engine parts but in recent years has begun offering selected drive train and brake parts. Marcotte does not manufacture any component parts (parts such as batteries, tires, and headlights). These parts are heavily advertised and well known by brand name.

The replacement parts market is highly competitive. There are many independent manufacturers such as Marcotte, and the automobile manufacturers themselves have become very active in the replacement parts market. The auto manufacturers direct large amounts of advertising to repair outlets encouraging them to stock original equipment parts. They have also started advertising directly to consumers to encourage them to ask for brand name parts. In addition, many of the other independent producers are starting to advertise.

There are nearly 3,000 independent jobbers who carry a complete line of auto replacement parts. A jobber is an independent middleman who purchases parts from a number of different supply sources and resells the parts to auto repair outlets. Industry estimates indicate that there are more than 125,000 auto repair outlets across the country. This does not include automobile dealerships that would normally only carry parts from the respective auto manufacturer.

Marcotte Auto Supplies has never used media advertising. The only promotional material used has been direct mail pieces. These have been sent to jobbers and repair outlets. Car owners are generally not familiar with the Marcotte name. However, the company does not view this as a drawback. When experiencing car problems, the average car owner wants the car fixed and generally doesn't care about the name of the replacement parts used. In fact, the typical car owner seldom sees the parts that have been replaced.

The Marcotte sales force calls on both jobbers and on auto repair outlets. Sales are made, however, only to the jobbers who are encouraged to carry the Marcotte line. The repair outlets are contacted to get feedback on the Marcotte line, to identify any problems they might have had with the Marcotte line, and to encourage them to patronize jobbers that handle the Marcotte line. The salespeople do not sell directly to auto repair outlets.

1. Is the company providing adequate support to the sales force? If not, what else should Marcotte be doing?
2. What are some of the major issues that the Marcotte sales force should emphasize during their sales calls?
3. Would different points be of interest to jobbers than to repair outlets? Explain.

# PART
# TWO

## UNDERSTANDING
## YOUR
## CUSTOMERS

The first part of this book provided an overview of selling and the background preparation needed for success in a sales career. As part of this overview, Chapter 3 identified customer types, buying motives, and sources of customer information.

Part 2 of the book expands the discussion about your customers. As your customers are your most valuable asset, you must thoroughly understand what motivates them to buy if you are to develop the right sales appeals. Chapter 5 examines internal motivations. This includes emotions; need satisfaction; wants; perception; the learning process; values, attitudes, and beliefs; personality; and self-image. Chapter 6 examines external factors that influence customer behavior. Among the many external influences discussed are society, culture, social class, group pressures, and family.

# 5

# CUSTOMER BEHAVIOR—
# INTERNAL MOTIVATIONS

Customers are the most valuable possession of every salesperson. As such, salespeople should strive to know and understand their customers better. They should attempt to view life through the eyes of their customers.

Each customer is different. Many salespeople take little or no notice of these differences; they operate with a single approach and presentation that they use almost without change for all customers. Standardized approaches, like a shotgun approach, will convert a certain number of potential buyers into customers. Repeated to new groups of buyers or to a sufficient number of individuals, a standardized approach will ensure continued, moderate success, which may be satisfactory to the salespeople and their employers.

Energetic, progressive salespeople, however, should not be satisfied with using one standard approach with customers. Each presentation should be adjusted to the individual. The sooner a salesperson learns to tailor a sales approach specifically to each potential customer, the faster sales will increase.

Successful salespeople are constantly studying, learning about, and evaluating customers. When they approach new prospects, they try to learn as much about them as possible.

## AID TO EFFECTIVE SELLING:
## KNOWLEDGE OF BEHAVIORAL SCIENCES

Personal observation and analysis provide the starting points to customer understanding. In addition, you can apply behavioral science principles. This application of principles can be done even before you contact customers, thus developing a firm background that enables you to develop personal observation and analysis skills.

**Illustration 5-1 The astute salesperson caters to the unique characteristics of the potential customer.**

*Vince Streano ©1985; STREANO/ HAVENS*

The behavioral sciences deal with the study of human actions. The three behavioral sciences that are most important to the salesperson are psychology, sociology, and anthropology. Psychology deals with individual behavior; sociology with group behavior; and anthropology with the study of total cultures and their histories. Each of these sciences has much bearing on why and how an individual buys.

Useful information drawn from the behavioral sciences will be introduced in this and the following chapter. The salesperson who can adopt and apply at least some of this information will be able to increase sales by learning how better to satisfy customer needs. For discussion purposes, all of the conditions, influences, characteristics, sensations, and feelings that affect individual behavior may be grouped under two headings: (1) internal and (2) external or environmental.

Although many internal factors affect behavior—perception, learning, attitudes, beliefs, personality, and self-image—the salesperson will generally be most concerned with motivation, or the actions resulting from felt needs and wants. The remainder of this chapter is concerned with those internal factors that influence behavior. The next chapter will cover external factors and the interpretation of their effect upon the buyer.

# EMOTIONS

Each of us is a highly complex being with a complicated physical makeup, a tremendously flexible mental makeup, and a variety of individual characteristics that cause actions and reactions to occur in particular ways. Most people exhibit remarkable consistency in thinking and acting that is partially independent of the situation they are facing. Many of these actions are quite noticeable, but others are inconspicuous. The salesperson seeks to be aware of both the evident and the obscure actions in acquiring new customers or keeping repeat customers.

Whether an individual's actions in a given situation are influenced by internal factors or external factors, emotions play a significant part in the ultimate decision to buy or not to buy. Emotion has been defined as a "stirred up condition of the organism."[1] As you read this chapter and the following one, you will see that emotions play a major part in every aspect of behavior.

## Intensity of Emotions

The intensity of an emotion may be governed by the perceived importance of the problem or subject causing the emotion. Some people are easily aroused if they feel they have been wronged financially, given a raw deal on the job, or have been deceived in some way. These same individuals, however, may not be influenced by social injustice or the suffering of others. Another type of person, less influenced by worldly possessions, may be easily angered by suffering and injustice. There are many degrees of emotion, varying from the exuberant joy of a child to the mild happiness of a senior citizen. The same stimulus may arouse distinctly different degrees of emotion across different people.

## Identifying Emotions

Emotions arise from a variety of causes and are demonstrated in numerous ways. They vary in intensity and outward appearance depending on many factors. The alert salesperson can look for numerous clues to identify a customer's emotions.

---

[1]Gordon W. Allport, *Pattern and Growth in Personality* (New York: Holt, Rinehart and Winston, 1961), p. 198.

**Emotions—The Face.**   When making a sales presentation, you will generally focus on the face of the customer. The face controls the source of information through the voice and through facial expressions that reinforce the voice. "Emotions are shown primarily in the face . . . the face is the key for understanding people's emotional expression, . . ."[2] These statements are substantiated by Ekman and Friesen based on a large number of studies about facial expressions as described in their book, *Unmasking the Face.* Their findings may be very helpful to one pursuing the study of customers.

Certain emotions are more easily identified than others. A close examination of a customer's facial expressions should alert you to the emotions of surprise, fear, disgust, anger, happiness, and sadness. These emotions can be identified as follows:

**Illustration 5–2   Facial expressions are indicators of a customer's varying emotions.**

### Surprise
— The brows are raised, so that they are curved and high.
— The skin below the brow is stretched.
— Horizontal wrinkles go across the forehead.
— The eyelids are opened; the upper lid is raised and the lower lid is drawn down; the white of the eye—the sclera—shows above the iris, and often below as well.
— The jaw drops open so that the lips and teeth are parted, but there is no tension or stretching of the mouth.

---

[2]Paul Ekman and Wallace V. Friesen, *Unmasking the Face* (Englewood Cliffs, NJ: Prentice-Hall, Inc., 1975), p. 7. We recommend that the creative salesperson purchase this book (hardcover or paperback) for intensive study.

**Fear**
— The brows are raised and drawn together.
— The wrinkles in the forehead are in the center, not across the entire forehead.
— The upper eyelid is raised, exposing sclera, while the lower eyelid is tensed and drawn up.
— The mouth is open and the lips are either tensed slightly and drawn back or stretched and drawn back.

**Disgust**
— The upper lip is raised.
— The lower lip is raised and pushed up to the upper lip; or is lowered and slightly protruding.
— The nose is wrinkled.
— The cheeks are raised.
— Lines show below the lower eyelid, and the lid is pushed up but not tense.
— The brow is lowered, lowering the upper eyelid.

**Anger**
— The brows are lowered and drawn together.
— Vertical lines appear between the brows.
— The lower lid is tensed and may or may not be raised.
— The upper lid is tense and may or may not be lowered by the action of the brow.
— The eyes exhibit a hard stare and may have a bulging appearance.
— The lips are in either of two basic positions: pressed firmly together, with the corners straight or down; or open, tensed in a squarish shape as if shouting.
— The nostrils may be dilated, but this is not essential to the facial expression in anger and may also occur in sadness.
— There is ambiguity unless anger is registered in all three facial areas.

**Happiness**
— The corners of the lips are drawn back and up.
— The mouth may or may not be parted, with teeth exposed or not.
— A wrinkle (the naso-labial fold) runs down from the nose to the outer edge beyond the lip corners.
— The cheeks are raised.
— The lower eyelid shows wrinkles below it, and may be raised but not tense.

— Crow's-feet wrinkles go outward from the outer corners of the eyes.

**Sadness**
— The inner corners of the eyebrows are drawn up.
— The skin below the eyebrow is triangulated, with the inner corner up.
— The upper eyelid inner corner is raised.
— The corners of the lips are down or the lip is trembling.[3]

Individuals communicate with gestures as well as with facial expressions. Just as the eyes can indicate approval, so can gestures. However, great variations in interpretation exist in different countries. "There are, in fact, dozens of gestures that take on totally different meanings as you move from one country to another."[4] For example, the way in which we would gesture with our hand to indicate to someone to come toward us is a way of waving goodbye in some parts of the world. Even in the same country, gestures take on many different meanings.

**Emotions—The Body.** A sensitive salesperson can learn much from body communication, especially if well acquainted with the customer. There are certain movements that can be interpreted easily; others are more subtle and may not be applied generally.

Certain body postures are more appealing than others. Some seem to attract, some repel, others are neutral. If a person leans forward during a conversation, it conveys interest to the speaker; sitting passively back may portray little interest. There are a number of different stances that can be assumed when approaching someone. The position of arms during conversation may indicate the degree of interest. Orienting the head and body to the speaker and leaning forward and smiling show warmer association; drumming fingers shows impatience.

Hand gestures can be excellent indications of inward feelings but may also deceive. Do not use only one indicator to analyze your customer but sum up the use of hands, facial expressions, eye changes, body movements, and voice. Some individuals are more outwardly expressive than others.

---

[3]Ekman and Friesen, pp. 45, 63, 76, 95, 97, 112, and 126. With permission.

[4]Paul Ekman, Wallace V. Friesen, and John Bear, "The International Language of Gestures," *Psychology Today*, Vol. 18, No. 5, (May 1984), p. 69.

Some salespeople become experts at judging the feelings of customers, others remain unsure of themselves. It is easy to misread others if you are unfamiliar with their backgrounds. "Body postures and movements may have vastly different meanings to people in different cultures. For this reason it is probably not feasible to speak of an *overall* ability and accuracy in interpreting body language."[5]

Body movements and facial expressions may be simulated to deceive the watcher. They may be used to get rid of an unwelcome person, or to encourage an early end to a sales presentation. In other words, a salesperson may not know if what is observed is true or merely assumed to get rid of an unwanted person. This is the point of separation between the ordinary and the accomplished salesperson.

**Tip**  *Nora Reese sells life insurance. In her sales presentation, Nora uses a trial-and-error approach. That is, Nora emphasizes many different sales appeals in her presentation. As Nora goes through different appeals such as protection, fear, investment, prestige, and safety, she watches the prospect's face and body movements closely for clues. In this way, Nora can determine which appeals seem to interest the prospect and which do not arouse any interest. Once determined, Nora concentrates on those appeals that have ignited positive facial and body responses from the prospect.*

**Emotions—The Voice.**   Your tone of voice or pattern of speech can strongly affect customers. Although a prospect begins to form an impression of the salesperson from physical appearance, eyes, distance, behavior, and body language, the prospect may reserve the final appraisal until hearing the voice in conversation or in a sales presentation.

Individuals speak in patterns that aid the hearer in determining emotions and traits. How much one talks, how often one interrupts, how one responds to statements and questions, all these may contribute to the listener's appraisal. Rapid speech or speech disturbances such as stuttering, omitting words, using incomplete sentences, and making slips of the tongue often indicate anxiety.

---

[5]Chris L. Kleinke, *First Impressions; The Psychology of Encountering Others* (Englewood Cliffs, NJ: Prentice-Hall, Inc., 1975), p. 60.

A speaker expressing confidence may speak more loudly, be more enthusiastic, show dominance and be more self-assured than a speaker who is doubtful. People who do the most talking, within limits, often are believed to be stronger. Less vocal people, if judged by voice alone, attract less attention. Persuasive speakers talk faster, with more force, and greater volume than those who are neutral.

### Emotions in Perspective

Most salespeople have learned about emotions through their own experiences, but many have not considered the implications of using emotions effectively to aid in selling. The salesperson who can capitalize on the use of emotions has advanced far in selling skill. Many salespeople do not understand how to make their product emotionally attractive, nor do they sense degrees of attraction or aversion. Even under pressure, where the buyer has little choice, lessening aversion may make the sale easier.

The salesperson should remember that emotional changes may increase tension and hinder communication, or they may facilitate communication. If the sales presentation is charged with fear, distrust, and reluctance, communication is difficult; if anger and loathing are added, communication is probably nonexistent. But if there is a feeling of receptiveness, calmness, interest, and anticipation, communication can be highly successful. The attention-holding power of a presentation is enhanced if it is delivered in a way that agrees with the emotional reaction of the listener.

## UNDERSTANDING MOTIVATION

If emotional, biological, and social drives are the keys to motivation, then motivation is the force that unlocks human behavior. Motivation is responsible for all behavior, buying behavior or otherwise. Emotions are a vital aspect in motivation. Motivation is the impetus for people to act and to achieve goals, and all motivation arises from needs or wants that people experience. People are seeking to satisfy physical, mental, and emotional desires. They are constantly trying to reach a goal, that goal being greater satisfaction.

## Needs and Wants

There are differences of opinion as to the distinction between "needs" and "wants." An individual may *need* dental work but may *want* to spend the money on something not as necessary, perhaps a vacation to the Bahamas. Other wants, such as an attractive appearance or comfort, may not be important to one individual but may be very important to others. You can see, then, that it is difficult to define people's needs and wants except in a general way.

Generally, a need is an essential requirement for the well-being of an individual; a want is a strong desire for something. Therefore, although a need may be a want, wants also extend to things that may seem unessential or unnecessary.

**Illustration 5-3   The purchase of a new car is in response to both needs and wants.**

## Effort Is Required to Satisfy Needs and Wants

People must exert effort to satisfy needs and wants, and this is where motivation enters the picture. One definition states that ". . . a motive is an inner state that energizes, activates, or moves (hence 'motivation'), and that directs or channels behavior toward goals."[6]

Certain goals require greater effort to achieve than others, and some people must work harder than others to attain goals. If minimum effort is required to satisfy a need or want, people will

---

[6]Bernard Berelson and Gary A. Steiner, *Human Behavior: An Inventory of Scientific Findings* (New York: Harcourt, Brace & World, Inc., 1964), p. 240.

probably attach little value to it. Most people, for example, attach little value to air. It has always been free, and as long as it was available for the taking, few consciously valued it. (Of course, air pollution has caused radical changes in people's thinking.) On the other hand, if great effort is involved in satisfying a need or want, people will probably attach great value to it. Most of us attach considerable value to owning a comfortable home or a new car because there is effort involved in obtaining these goals.

## Needs and Wants Change

People are never satisfied—they are always wanting. Once they satisfy one need, they focus on another. Needs that have already been fulfilled today may increase tomorrow or may change as people change. Thus, the family satisfied with owning two cars this year may want to buy a boat next year. The family who camps in a tent one summer may want a tent-trailer the second year; a trailer the third year; and a luxurious camper, a home-on-wheels, the fourth year. There are "breaking points," however, to the ever-changing, ever-increasing nature of needs and wants. A family with a moderate income may enjoy owning and using a boat and motor. They may start out with a rowboat and a five-horsepower outboard motor. In successive steps over several years, they may eventually own a sizeable boat with an inboard-outboard motor. But this family, if it remains in the moderate income bracket, is not likely to desire a yacht. They will realize that such a boat is beyond their means, and likely will not be frustrated by the realization.

A series of needs and wants are common to most people, while other needs and wants vary from individual to individual. The needs of some could not by any stretch of the imagination become the needs of others.

There are certain basic needs, appropriately called physiological and safety needs, that are more or less common to all of us and that take primary demand on our time and earnings. These physiological needs include food, clothing, exercise, and shelter. Safety needs include protection against deprivation and exposure to injury and threat. After meeting physiological needs —or, in some cases, concurrent with them—people endeavor to reduce or eliminate deprivation and threat. Social needs are apparent when people exchange friendship and love with others.

Ego needs vary greatly. Some people are content to be obscure. Others have crushing desires for recognition, prestige, and power; they will spend large sums of money to meet these needs. Some will even willingly sacrifice basic needs, such as health and physical care to satisfy a drive, such as ambition. Self-fulfillment needs focus on self-development and concern with reaching one's full potential.[7]

## A Fulfillment Pattern

Each person has a mental list of needs; as soon as the basic ones are fairly well satisfied, desires transfer to the next category. Thus, there are always a few needs at different levels being fulfilled and a few still unfulfilled. Although people are unique and have different fulfillment patterns, some generalization about fulfillment patterns can be made: (1) As one need is satisfied, it is replaced by another. (2) Needs are organized in a series of levels. (3) Only after lower level needs have been at least partially satisfied will higher level needs be focused upon. (4) Because of the limited opportunity to fulfill higher level needs, people concern themselves with satisfying lower level needs. This is caused by unequal distribution of income, level of education, location, and other factors.

Five categories of needs have been identified—physiological needs, safety needs, social needs, ego needs, and self-fulfillment needs. These five categories of needs form a fulfillment pattern for an individual. Each individual has a different fulfillment pattern, and the pattern may change over time.

A fulfillment pattern might be visualized as a series of steps. In Figure 5–1, you can see that the pattern is organized in a series, in a hierarchy of importance. Lower-level needs must be reasonably satisfied before an individual can move up to higher-level needs. The hierarchy of importance pertains to the fact that only when lower-level needs have been satisfied adequately do higher-level needs begin to become important. This scale is basically the same for all people. The degree of fulfillment refers to the attainment of a certain level of satisfaction for each category of needs. Therefore, the degree of fulfillment will vary from individual to individual. The individual proceeds to a higher level of needs after a lower level is reasonably satisfied.

---

[7]Douglas McGregor, *Leadership and Motivation* (Cambridge, Mass.: The M.I.T. Press, 1966), pp. 8–11.

**Figure 5–1**

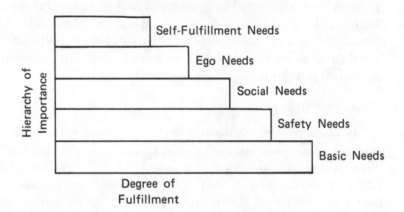

NEEDS HIERARCHY

Figure 5–2 shows different fulfillment patterns for people with low incomes, people with moderate incomes, and people with high incomes.

From these illustrations, we can see that people with low incomes will not be able to reach as high a degree of fulfillment in any category as people with high incomes. Basically, the amount of money required to buy a certain quantity of food is the same regardless of the level of income; however, the cost of the food has a greater impact on the lower-level income recipients because it requires a greater percentage of their income. People with moderate incomes will also not be able to fulfill needs to the same degree as people with high incomes, but will reach a higher degree of fulfillment than low-income people.

### Why Fulfillment Patterns Are Important

Salespeople selling to different groups of customers must be aware of the variation in fulfillment patterns. At the poverty level, "needs" and "wants" may be synonymous. The satisfaction of basic needs consumes the majority of this person's income. At the other extreme of the income scale, "needs" and "wants" may diverge greatly. A person in the upper income bracket will give little thought to physiological and safety needs since the majority of these needs are easily satisfied, but will concentrate on satisfying higher-level needs and wants. A person in the middle income bracket, while conscious of satisfying physiological needs, is likely to spend time and money fulfilling safety, social, ego, and self-fulfillment needs.

**Figure 5-2**

# NEEDS BY INCOME LEVEL

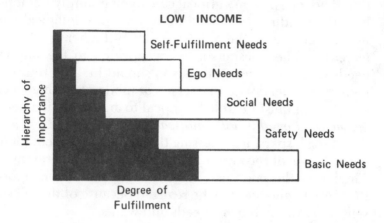

LOW INCOME

Hierarchy of Importance

Self-Fulfillment Needs

Ego Needs

Social Needs

Safety Needs

Basic Needs

Degree of Fulfillment

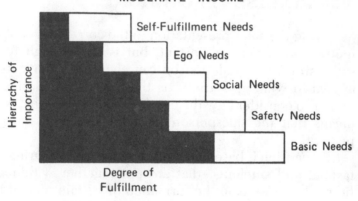

MODERATE INCOME

Hierarchy of Importance

Self-Fulfillment Needs

Ego Needs

Social Needs

Safety Needs

Basic Needs

Degree of Fulfillment

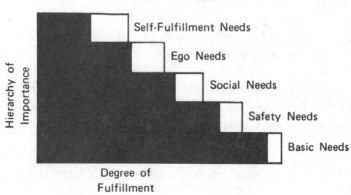

HIGH INCOME

Hierarchy of Importance

Self-Fulfillment Needs

Ego Needs

Social Needs

Safety Needs

Basic Needs

Degree of Fulfillment

The salesperson selling to customers at the lower income level is faced with a need-demand that is physical and imperative. The salesperson's appeal can involve simply demonstrating how the product will meet the buyer's physiological needs. As income increases, the ability to satisfy higher level needs also increases. The salesperson who appealed to the physiological needs of the low-income person should be able to appeal to a higher level need with the person of moderate or high income. A salesperson must be able to appeal to an unsatisfied need since, "A *satisfied need is not a motivator of behavior!*"[8]

The salesperson possessing the skill to tie presentations to the correct level of buyer motivation will find selling relatively easy. The better the salesperson understands the buyer's motivation, the more likely sales will be realized because of the salesperson's sensitivity to the buyer's needs and wants.

## UNDERSTANDING PERCEPTION

Tying the sales presentation to the correct level of a buyer's motivation is very important, but is not enough to ensure a successful sale. A salesperson can choose certain statements to appeal to what appears to be the buyer's motivation, but one must also consider how the buyer will interpret what is said. This means that the salesperson must be aware of the prospect's perception.

Perception is based on sensations—seeing, hearing, touching, tasting, and smelling—that are put together within a person's brain. This results in the formation of certain mental images or relationships.[9] *Perception* is an individual's interpretation of external factors within his or her background of experience. Because people are different, they select, group, and interpret sensory impressions in a variety of ways. Thus, different people may have different perceptions of the same facts. A child's perception of "deep water" might be quite different than that of a sailor.

When presenting certain information, you may be surprised at the reactions of various people. The reception might vary from enthusiastic approval to outright rejection because of dif-

[8]*Ibid.*, p. 9.

[9]Paul Thomas Young, *Motivation and Emotion: A Survey of the Determinants of Human and Animal Activity* (New York: John Wiley & Sons, Inc., 1961), p. 298.

fering viewpoints. As a salesperson, you must not assume that you are right and the other person is wrong, or that the other person is not aware of the qualities of your product. If it appears that the prospect is viewing your offering incorrectly, it is your job to change this viewpoint by changing the prospect's frame of reference.

Perception is not static. In many instances, it is shifting in almost imperceptible stages to reflect changes in the stimulating sources, just as a light meter on a camera adjusts to changing light conditions. The difference, however, is that the light meter, by changing, maintains a fairly constant image to be photographed, while changing perception alters our way of looking at things. It is not uncommon for a person's perception of an object to remain unchanged even when stimuli are changing. This is accomplished by balancing some facts to counteract changes in others, just as the taste of a meal can be controlled by varying the quantity of the ingredients. In selling, this is accomplished by fitting the sales presentation to the prospect, and the challenge is to understand the prospect well enough to tailor a suitable presentation. It is not enough for salespeople to know that different perceptions of the same object may exist for each customer; they must also know which one most closely fits the immediate prospect or customer.

## UNDERSTANDING THE LEARNING PROCESS

The learning process is important to salespeople because behavior is the result of learning. To modify an individual's behavior in some way, salespeople must depend on the customers' ability to learn what they wish them to learn. We generally learn through experience and reflect this learning in our behavior. This behavior may be overt and physical, such as the ability to operate a machine, or indirect and intangible, such as being able to understand new words, or form new mental images.

### Learning

The intensity of a situation and the dramatic support at a particular time can influence learning. For example, if a group were being taught the use of life jackets to prevent drowning, the learning effect would be much weaker in a classroom than on a dock by the water's edge where a person was recovering from a near drowning. Passengers in a plane would pay greater attention to an explanation of safety devices if a recent plane crash were the focus of current news. If salespeople can arouse a high degree of eagerness and willingness to learn, the learning situation improves.

> **Tip** *One of the important features of a small office machine sold by the Yokom Office Equipment Company is its ease of assembly. However, the salespeople for the Yokom Company weren't getting this point across. The normal procedure was for the salesperson to take the product apart in the buyer's office and put it back together.*
>
> *To enhance the learning process, Hazel Nez uses a more creative approach. When Hazel enters the customer's office, she dumps a box of disassembled parts on the customer's desk. This arouses the customer's attention. As Hazel begins her sales presentation, she starts putting parts together. Within ten minutes, Hazel has assembled the machine she is talking about and finished her presentation. The buyer's curiosity makes him hear every word of the presentation and he watches the assembly process intently.*

In a customer learning situation, it is better for the salesperson to begin with simple elements and proceed to the complex. Interesting illustrations should be used whenever possible to maintain attention. Salespeople should also know that some people learn readily while others learn slowly and only after repeated reinforcement. One might liken this situation to driving a nail to fasten two pieces of wood. Some wood yields readily, and the nail is easily driven in. Other wood resists penetration and requires many more hammer blows to get a secure fastening.

## Forgetting

Remembering and forgetting are intrinsic parts of the learning process. Obviously, salespeople would like to prevent prospects from forgetting sales points they have made. Forgetting is natural, but salespeople can help to prevent it. First, salespeople should know that forgetting is slowed down if the learning occasion was spectacular or the rewards for learning were exceptional. It is likely that you will always remember buying your first car. Although salespeople cannot always match the drama or emotion of such a situation, they can try to make presentations as interesting and dramatic as possible.

A prospect will probably learn little and remember less from a sales presentation if the prospect was disinterested, skeptical, or hostile. As such, the salesperson must find a method of converting the disinterested or hostile prospect into an attentive listener. Response and interest may be lacking because the listener does not understand the presentation or is unable to follow it.

Another point to remember is that the rate of forgetting is rapid immediately after learning. Thus, if the information is highly important, the salesperson should groove it deeper into the prospect's mind through immediate reinforcement. If at all possible, the salesperson should arrange for a quick return appointment to reinforce the learning. To aid remembering, the salesperson should contact the customer frequently enough to maintain cordial relations, but not so often as to become annoying. Neglecting a customer is dangerous; the salesperson who forgets a customer through lack of attention is soon forgotten by the customer. Also, the speed of forgetting increases when competing salespeople give attention to the customer.

## Behavior

Repetition of a particular act reinforces learning and may develop the behavior into a habit. A habit is a connection between stimuli and response that, through experience, becomes automatic. A person does something over and over until the response can be made without conscious thinking. For example, the typical automobile driver, when traveling as a passenger, will instinctively press on the floor when danger is approaching as if in control of the brakes. Once salespeople have determined that their product is the right one for a customer, they seek to build habit-based behavior in that customer. They want that customer to buy initially and then continue to buy the product over time.

The more automatic a particular response becomes, the easier it is for a salesperson to continue selling to a particular customer. Sometimes, however, habit-based buying relationships can work to the detriment of a particular salesperson. A salesperson trying to break a purchasing agent's habit of buying from a competitor may find great difficulty in changing this buying pattern. Often, however, the supplying salesperson becomes complacent and careless in giving the buyer proper attention. Since every year there are changes in buyers, salespeople, producers, and other circumstances, a salesperson soon finds possibilities to challenge almost any established seller-buyer relationship. Skill and perseverance should result in getting a toehold in some such relationships each year. By the same token, skill and perseverance can help maintain such relationships year after year.

*Tip   Although other salespeople for Unro Electronics have a difficult time maintaining long-lasting relationships with customers, this doesn't seem to be a problem at all for Lauren Washington. Lauren follows two simple rules to keep her customers happy and to get them into habit-based buying relationships with her. First, right after a major sale is closed, Lauren gets back in touch with the customer. If it is a new customer, Lauren calls the next day to thank the customer again for the order. In addition, Lauren reaffirms the terms of the sale and the delivery date with the customer. If the sale was made to a regular customer, Lauren sends a letter to the customer thanking the individual for the continuing confidence shown in Lauren and her firm. Second, after the order is delivered, Lauren contacts the customer to see that everything arrived in workable order. If everything is acceptable, the customer appreciates Lauren's attentiveness. If the customer has a complaint, Lauren is there to handle it.*

## UNDERSTANDING ATTITUDES AND BELIEFS

Combined with a salesperson's need to understand a prospect's motivation, perception, and learning process is the need to understand the prospect's attitudes and beliefs.

### Nature of Attitudes

An attitude is an individual's view or feelings about another person, object, idea or anything else in the individual's environment. "Attitudes have generally been regarded as either mental readiness or implicit predispositions that exert some general and consistent influence on a fairly large class of evaluative responses. Attitudes are thus internal, private events whose existence we infer from our own introspection or from some form of behavioral evidence, by word or deed. A verbalized attitude is called an *opinion*."[10]

We develop attitudes over time as we learn through our experiences. An attitude is not a physical object; it must be inferred from one's actions. For example, people are often characterized as having a positive or negative attitude as a result of their statements or actions. We express our attitudes in words, actions, or deeds. We may have attitudes of disdain, disrespect, intolerance, generosity, attention, or consideration.

## Changing Attitudes

Attitudes develop through experience or observation of external factors. The individual expresses an opinion based on environmental influences. Many attitudes are strongly fixed in the individual. Others are less well entrenched. As such, the salesperson attempting to change customer attitudes will find wide variation in difficulty in doing so.[11]

Attitudes are formed through a variety of means. You may influence an individual's attitude by offering a reward. Attitudes may be shaped by observing the behavior of others. The mass media may shape attitudes. Television is a powerful influencing medium. Our home and school provide many standards of behavior that shape our attitudes. Religion has developed attitudes for millions of people over thousands of years. One must also include the power of the written word over long periods of time as a potent attitude influence.

One approach to achieving attitude change is an effective communication that stresses attention, comprehension, acceptance, and retention. The salesperson cannot communicate until the prospect gives attention. Explanations are of minimum value unless they are understood. Just because a prospect hears the salesperson this does not imply acceptance. Considerable persuasion, perhaps amplified by illustrations and testimonials, may be required for even partial acceptance and agreement. Finally,

---

[10]Philip G. Zimbardo, Ebbe B. Ebbesen and Christina Maslack, *Influencing Attitudes and Changing Behavior* (2nd ed., Reading, Mass.: Addison-Wesley Publishing Company, 1970), p. 20.

[11]For wider discussion in this area see Ronald L. Applbaum and Karl W. E. Anatol, *Strategies for Persuasive Communication* (Columbus: Charles E. Merrill Publishing Company, 1974).

if the buying decision is delayed or depends on several individual buyers, it is important that the message be remembered. Each step, separated here, must blend into a continuous message to be effective.

Another approach to attitude change is through group influence. If peoples' beliefs and inclinations vary from those of their reference groups—social, business, religious, and family—the salesperson may use pressures of group conformity to bring about attitude change.

**Tip** *Mark Burso is a salesperson for Volane Sporting Goods. Mark is attempting to sell a supply of baseball bats to Jean Moto for the little league baseball team Jean coaches. Jean likes the price of the WHALLOP brand bats but is hesitant to buy because she is unfamiliar with the brand name. Realizing that he must do something to develop a positive attitude toward his brand, Mark mentions that Casey Martin, the coach of the local high school team, always buys the WHALLOP brand. Jean, conceding that if they're good enough for the high school team, they're good enough for the little leaguers, buys the WHALLOP bats.*

## Nature of Beliefs

Beliefs are more deep-seated and more basic than attitudes. We may have a strong belief in the free enterprise system and, therefore, a negative attitude toward anything that threatens it. Many of our religious beliefs, coming from strong authority and long exposure to a definite religious climate, are very deep-rooted. Beliefs are not uniform, however. We may characterize some as strong and others as weak. This range of beliefs can promote or hinder a sale.

Some beliefs are basic, primitive in origin, and almost unshakable. These beliefs give salespeople a tremendous help if they are favorable to the salesperson's offer. Salespeople must train themselves to become aware of customer beliefs and capitalize on them, while at the same time disassociating themselves with beliefs regarded as unfavorable by the buyer. If your sales presentation gets involved in an area where primitive and deep-seated beliefs are present, be wary lest you upset the prospect by attempting to discredit such beliefs. If the prospect's objections appear to be based on weak beliefs, they can be overcome or reversed.

# PERSONALITY AND SELF-IMAGE

In its own way, all of the elements that have been discussed —motivation, perception, learning, attitudes, and beliefs—determine an individual's personality and self-image.

## The Nature of Personality

Everyone has a certain way of behaving and responding that is unique. This is our personality. This is what identifies you as the person you are. Personality refers to those individual factors or characteristics that reflect a behavior pattern.

A more in-depth explanation suggests that "personality is the unique, or individual, pattern of a person's life. It is the fundamental organization of an individual's characteristic adjustment to his environment. Total adjustment includes the individual's characteristic attitudes toward others, his interests and ambitions, his plan of life, and his attitude toward life in general."[12]

A third way of looking at personality is to identify traits that fit the individual. These traits are internal forces manifesting themselves in observable behavior. Particular and distinctive traits reveal an aspect of personality. A trait is a consistent form of behavior or reaction to particular stimuli.

Thousands of different traits have been identified at various times. To reduce this number to manageable proportions, Cattell and Eber combined and adjusted the available information and came up with 16 primary personality dimensions which appear in Table 5-1.[13] These 16 groupings do not cover all personality traits; a number of other authors have done similar work and arrived at different groupings. The serious salesperson should study several of the books related to personality to become acquainted with the rich and growing literature in this area. This will help to develop a greater awareness of customer behavior.

If salespeople have knowledge of a buyer's personality, they can approach the buyer with a measure of assurance—providing,

---

[12]George Kaluger and Charles M. Unkovic, *Psychology and Sociology, An Integrated Approach to Understanding Human Behavior* (St. Louis: The C. V. Mosby Company, 1969), p. 146.

[13]*Ibid.*, p. 150.

of course, they have spent time investigating other information such as income, position in society, age, type of work, and other relevant factors. A professional buyer with a strong personality may attempt to browbeat salespeople or intimidate them. The same buyer may also behave calmly, but be so exacting and ask so many questions that an ill-prepared salesperson finally gives up and leaves without an order. The professional buyer's job is to best serve the interests of the company.

**Illustration 5–4** The potential customer's age and income are relevant in all sales situations.

**Table 5-1**

## The Sixteen Primary Personality Dimensions of Cattell and Eber

| | | |
|---|---|---|
| Reserved, detached, critical, cool | vs. | Outgoing, warmhearted, easy-going, participating |
| Less intelligent, concrete-thinking | vs. | More intelligent, abstract-thinking, bright |
| Affected by feelings, emotionally less stable, easily upset | vs. | Emotionally stable, faces reality, calm, mature |
| Humble, mild, obedient, conforming | vs. | Assertive, independent, aggressive, stubborn |
| Sober, prudent, serious, taciturn | vs. | Happy-go-lucky, heedless, gay, enthusiastic |
| Expedient, disregarding rules, feeling few obligations | vs. | Conscientious, persevering, staid, rule-bound |
| Shy, restrained, diffident, timid | vs. | Venturesome, socially bold, uninhibited, spontaneous |
| Tough-minded, self-reliant, realistic, no-nonsense | vs. | Tender-minded, dependent, over-protective, sensitive |
| Trusting, adaptable, free of jealousy, easy to get on with | vs. | Suspicious, opinionated, hard to fool |
| Practical, careful, conventional, regulated by external realities | vs. | Imaginative, wrapped up in inner urgencies, careless of practical matters |
| Forthright, natural, artless, unpretentious | vs. | Shrewd, calculating, worldly, penetrating |
| Self-assured, confident, serene | vs. | Apprehensive, worrying, depressed, troubled |
| Conservative, respecting established ideas, tolerant of traditional difficulties | vs. | Experimenting, liberal, analytical, free-thinking |

**Table 5-1** (continued)

| Group-dependent, a "joiner" and good follower | vs. | Self-sufficient, prefers own decisions, resourceful |
|---|---|---|
| Undisciplined self-conduct, careless of protocol, untidy, follows own urges | vs. | Controlled, socially precise, self-disciplined, compulsive |
| Relaxed, tranquil, torpid, unfrustrated | vs. | Tense, driven, over-wrought, fretful |

Source: *Adapted from Cattell, R.B., and Eber, H.: 16 personality factor handbook, Champaign, Ill., 1962, Institute of Personality and Ability Testing.*

You should regard knowledge of personality as just one more tool in your selling kit. Such knowledge brings many advantages when used in combination with other selling tools.

## The Nature of the Self-Image

Everyone has conscious experiences. Some of these, such as feelings of right and wrong, sensations of pleasure and pain, and other self-experiences are personal in nature. Over time these inward self-experiences crystallize and become a base for social conduct. This leads to degrees of self-awareness that guide interactions with others. Because of the multiplicity of environmental factors, one cannot develop a self-image in isolation. "The self cannot be understood in isolation but only in relation to other persons; the very language of the self—the language of intentions, desires, motives and the like—can only be an intersubjective language."[14]

Self-evaluation may be greatly influenced by social contacts, and one's self-assessment may vary depending on the strengths of associates. One may feel important in one social group and inadequate in another.

---

[14]Theodore Mischel, "Conceptual Issues in the Psychology of the Self: An Introduction," *The Self: Psychological and Philosophical Issues*, edited by Theodore Mischel (Totowa, NJ: Rowman and Littlefield, 1977), p. 25.

For example, as a student you probably feel more comfortable exchanging ideas with your friends in the cafeteria than serving as a representative on a committee composed of administrators, faculty, and students.

Each person develops a concept of self—the image this individual gives to others, and an image this person desires inwardly and may believe others recognize. This image includes not only outward appearance but also inward characteristics. These inward factors—such as generosity, pleasant disposition, integrity, and many others—go a long way to shape behavior, and affect reactions to sales presentations.

Each individual develops a personal identity that distinguishes that person from every other person. Development as a child is influenced by parents. As the individual grows, a series of idols or images of outstanding people develop. Imitations of these people may follow by adapting some of the things they do, say, or wear. An individual discouraged and criticized early in life may pick up a negative self-image that creates timidity. Some people do not prepare the self to meet adult problems; some people hide inferiority complexes behind a brave exterior. Watchful salespeople can find various approaches to handle people with different self-images if they are willing to learn more about people, try to understand them, and try to gain empathy by fitting presentations to prospects' self-images. This approach develops increased buyer confidence.

## RECENT STUDIES OF PSYCHOLOGICAL MAN

The decades of the 60s and 70s and now into the 80s have been notable for the great contributions by psychologists to the problems of man in this rapidly changing environment.

Studies have shown that when people in primitive tribes, maintaining low blood pressure over many years, were exposed to the cities of today, their blood pressures tended to increase as it does with many of us. Using laboratory experiments, researchers have discovered that animals react in ways similar to people. "When mice that have not previously lived together are placed in a colony . . . have constant confrontations with one another while seeking food, this exposure to chronic stress causes them to develop progressively higher blood pressure; they die early deaths from heart attacks, kidney trouble, or strokes."[15] Such research has led to "a variety of human behavioral treatments—psychotherapy, assertiveness training, meditation, and relaxation training."[16]

It appears that highly successful salespeople would fit in what is called the *leadership motive syndrome*. Such people want power, are high in self-control, and have little or no inhibition. Many probably worked their way to the top of an organization through aggressiveness and persuasiveness. "Young managers who displayed [assertiveness] when they entered AT&T were more likely to have been promoted to higher levels of management in the company after 16 years."[17]

Although this type of individual is probably on the way to success, the physical results may be higher blood pressure, and symptoms of stress that increase the possibilities for illness, as has been revealed in various studies. Meditation research should be useful for such individuals. "Early research, summarized in Herbert Benson's *The Relaxation Response*, suggested that meditation reduces anxiety . . . and it quiets the symptoms of the fight-or-flight response from activation of the sympathetic nervous system."[18]

The growth of the electronics revolution is affecting the lives of people and may in many areas change the approaches a salesperson uses in contacting customers. The sales job may include finding new solutions for current problems that revolve about the human conditions of the individual. That does not say that one should abandon efforts to understand the basic human phenomena but rather should develop greater appreciation and understanding of each individual. Recognize that although people have many similar likes, dislikes, needs, and aspirations, so can different prospects choose unlike solutions to meet similar needs. If these solutions are inimical to the salesperson's normal presentation, if there is one, it is necessary for the salesperson to reach an understanding and accord with the prospect to achieve a successful sales conclusion.

---

[15]Jerome Bruner, Richard S. Lazarus, and others, "Understanding Psychological Man," *Psychology Today*, Vol. 16, No. 5 (May, 1982), p. 52.

[16]*Ibid.*, p. 52.

[17]*Ibid.*, p. 55.

[18]*Ibid.*, p. 56.

# QUESTIONS

1. Why do customers warm up to some salespeople more than to others?
2. How can emotions be used in the sales presentation? Define emotion.
3. How do facial, body, and voice mannerisms suggest emotion? How can emotions be identified?
4. Is motivation essential to a salesperson? What is motivation? How is it acquired?
5. Not all people feel a need for or want the same things. How do you account for this?
6. In what way are perception and product presentation tied together? What is perception?
7. Is it important to you as a salesperson to know how a customer learns? Why?
8. Is there a relationship between motivation and learning? Between motivation and forgetting? What is the relationship?
9. Would you say a salesperson could hinder forgetting? How?
10. How can habit-based behavior hinder or help make sales?

# SALES CHALLENGES

1. There are many sales situations in which customers are likely to mistrust the salesperson. For example, most of us seem to be skeptical of what any salesperson tells us about a used car. Many prospects seem to be skeptical of the sales presentations of door-to-door salespeople. What are other sales situations in which prospects are likely to be doubtful or uncertain of the salesperson? What can the salesperson do in such situations to gain the confidence of the prospect?

2. Gus Gustafson works in the men's department of the Bartoma Department Store. Gus has just sold two $479 imported suits. The first suit was sold to Josh Nakosha who owns his own business, lives in one of the most expensive areas of the city, and earns over $90,000 a year. The second was sold to Jon DeMay, a recent college graduate who works for an accounting firm and earns about $23,000 per year. What common buying motives were probably at work for two

relatively unlike customers? What differences in sales presentations do you think Gus made to the two customers?

3. Examine your buying motives for three recent important purchases. What buying motives were at work? What needs and wants did these purchases satisfy? Evaluate these purchases with respect to your self-image. In any case where a salesperson was involved, what motives did the salesperson appeal to? Did the salesperson correctly identify motives that were important to you? If so, how did the salesperson correctly recognize them? If not, why was the sale made anyway?

# CASES

## 5-1 Addy Electric

Sean O'Grady is a salesperson for Addy Electric, one of the leading companies in the electrical equipment industry. Addy manufactures a wide line of electric motors, generating equipment, control devices, and related machinery. Sean is calling on Joan Caswell, general manager of Harlton Manufacturing.

**Sean:** Ms. Caswell, I'm Sean O'Grady of Addy Electric. I'd like to talk with you about some of our equipment.

**Ms. Caswell:** (Putting down a copy of *Business Week*) Have a seat, Sean. I was just reading about the budget deficit. Pretty bad, isn't it? What do you think of the policies of the current administration?

**Sean:** I'm sure that the deficit will be corrected. And when it is, the economy will spurt. Business firms like yours had better be ready. Is Harlton Manufacturing planning any expansion, Ms. Caswell?

**Ms. Caswell:** We might build a new plant in Peoria in a year or two. Did you see this article in today's *Wall Street Journal?* The government is thinking about free medical care and increasing business taxes to pay for it! What do you think of that?

**Sean:** I always hate to see taxes increased but medical expenses are getting beyond the means of many people. Ms. Caswell, I've been studying your generating equipment. Do you realize how old the equipment is and how much more you're paying to operate your equipment than is necessary?

**Ms. Caswell:** Yes, the equipment is pretty old. What do you think will happen in the next election?

**Sean:** It's hard to say. I'm sure whoever is elected will do a good job. Ms. Caswell, I've drawn up some plans based on my examination of this plant. I can show you how the savings in operating costs by installing one of our new generators will pay for the generator in less than ten years. Would you like to see my figures?

**Ms. Caswell:** Yes. I would like to see what you have. Let's go over your figures.

1. What kind of communication problems did Sean run into?
2. Did Sean handle the political questions properly? Should Sean have stated his political views?
3. Did Sean do a good job of getting Ms. Caswell on to the topic of Sean's presentation? What might you have done differently?

### 5-2 Campau and Mullay, Inc.

Marie Gonzalas has just been hired as a sales representative for Campau and Mullay, Inc. Marie's territory includes the heavy industrial area of southeastern Michigan and southern Ontario. Marie will be handling a line of drills, taps, and reamers. She will be selling to a wide range of industrial customers, including the large automotive customers in Detroit and Windsor.

The previous salesperson, Frank Rosenburg, had compiled detailed notes about each of his customers. Frank turned these notes over to his sales manager upon retirement, and the sales manager, in turn, turned the notes over to Marie.

Marie was very happy to receive these notes. Listed under each customer's name was information such as birthdays, anniversaries, family and personal achievements, likes and dislikes, organization memberships, hobbies, educational background, and other pertinent facts.

Marie obtained the following information about two customers she would be calling on during the upcoming week. Christopher Palm enjoys hockey, and Nelda Zeldonrust is fond of Benny Goodman recordings. Although Marie doesn't know much about hockey, she decided that she could sit through a hockey game if it would make her customer happy. In addition, Marie decided that she would try to find a Benny Goodman recording that Nelda didn't have.

Marie wanted to be a successful salesperson but began to wonder about the lengths to which she should go to please her customers. Marie wondered whether she was willing to cater to the whims of all of her customers and to what degree.

1. Can a salesperson spend too much time trying to please a customer?
2. Is one's personal integrity to be considered in the interest of satisfying customer interests?
3. Is there a place for individualized gifts rather than the usual luncheons or dinners to promote sales?
4. Recording details about customers takes time and effort; is it really necessary?

# 6

# CUSTOMER BEHAVIOR—
# EXTERNAL INFLUENCES

In most buying situations, an individual's internal characteristics become so bound up with external influences that it becomes difficult to disassociate them and treat each independently. It is imperative, therefore, that salespeople be aware of, and able to sort out these outside influences and understand the impact each has on sales. External influences involve all environmental variables that may have a bearing on an individual's buying behavior.

## INFLUENCE OF CULTURE AND SOCIETY

An individual is frequently torn between personal desires and what society says is proper. How far and in what direction will a person go to express individuality without sacrificing society's demand for conformity? One who goes just far enough is often admired and rewarded with approval; on the other hand, one who goes too far may be ostracized from a group or from the entire society.

### Culture and Society Defined

The terms "culture" and "society" are often used interchangeably, but there is a distinction between the two. A society is a grouping of people with common traditions, institutions, and interests; a culture is the collective beliefs, traits, and traditions of a grouping of people. Each society has its own culture. The people of the United States, for example, constitute a society; as a society, we have our own culture. This culture includes all the common values and standards that we observe when we interact with other people within our society.

Each society may have its subgroupings or subcultures. Often these subcultures are founded upon race, religion, national origin, language, age, and social class. In our society, we have many subcultures, each of which has behavior patterns that distinguish it from other subcultures.

## Behavior Norms Imposed by Society

Our actions are governed to a considerable extent by what society considers proper. To enable it and its members to function most efficiently, each society sets up certain standards of behavior. These standards are called norms, and they are imposed on each individual. All behavior norms are developed over time to meet certain needs of a society. Different societies have different norms that are suitable in particular environments. Some of these norms may appear odd, barbaric, or even silly to outsiders, but for those who established the norms, they may be helpful and perhaps even essential for survival.

Society imposes three kinds of norms on its members: folkways, mores, and laws. A folkway is what we often call a custom, such as giving gifts at Christmas. Mores are those norms that govern moral conduct. An example that has been very strong in our society is that parents should provide for the welfare of their children. Some norms are written down and thus become laws. Breaking folkways or mores usually brings some type of punishment, such as disapproval by our associates or expulsion from a group. Breaking laws brings a definite type of punishment, such as a fine or imprisonment.

Our lives are surrounded and strongly governed by behavior norms. These norms are powerful factors in determining what we buy. Some people openly flaunt behavior norms, but the majority of us conform to the norms imposed by society. Since norms are persuasive and powerful, the salesperson cannot ignore their influence on buying patterns. Although most buyers will not admit to it, or even be consciously aware of it, the norms of society control their many desires. A salesperson cannot succeed by violating behavior norms or ignoring folkways, mores, and laws pertinent to the buyer.

## Social Stratification

Our society is stratified into a number of levels or social classes. Although social stratification is most often determined by income, factors such as education, ethnic origin, property ownership, occupation, and many other elements are also used to stratify the population. Each social class—like the total society—has its own norms of behavior and its own patterns of buying. It may be difficult to say which norms exert the most influence on the individual. However, since social classes are closer to the individual than is the total society, the norms of social classes are the more powerful in many cases. Social class norms are generally the same as those of society, but they can be more specific and more personalized. Most people feel the desire to conform to the norms of their social class. Many individuals feel the desire to conform to the norms of the social class above them in order to elevate themselves to this class.

Salespeople often misjudge buyers because they do not understand that each buyer's thinking process is dictated in part by social class norms. A family in one social class living in one part of town may be satisfied with the old car and furniture. Once their income increases, however, and they move to a more affluent neighborhood, their outward expenditures change to fit their new social class and environment. Sometimes people dabble in attempts to fit into a different social class, only to learn that they are unable to cope with the norms of that class, and so retreat to their original behavior patterns.

## INFLUENCE OF GROUPS ON BUYING BEHAVIOR

Within each society and social class are reference groups. There are many kinds of reference groups and they differ for each one of us. The family is a powerful reference group for most people. Other reference groups are ethnic groups; informal groups, such as associates on the individual's job or in the neighborhood; and formal groups, such as membership in organizations like the Rotary Club. We associate closely with such groups, desire the approval of group members, and are strongly motivated to conform to the behavior norms of such groups.

*Tip  Sonia Ramos used a very special group, the customers of her customer, to keep from losing a sale. Sonia sells specialty advertising products. One of Sonia's customers, Mr. Diaz, informed her that he did not intend to continue his program of sending his customers pocket appointment calendars. Sonia suggested that before the use of the appointment calendars is discontinued, the customer conduct a little postcard survey. To the custo-*

*mer's surprise, the overwhelming majority of postcards returned indicated that the receivers of the appointment calendars used them all year and definitely wanted to continue receiving them. When discovering this, Mr. Diaz not only renewed his order but expanded his mailing list for the appointment calendars.*

## Family

The family exerts a dominant influence on behavior, whether the influence is confined to the immediate family—husband, wife, and children—or whether it includes other relatives. Some individuals are excessively dominated by relatives, others are minimally dominated. In some nations and races, relatives have a greater influence than in others.

**Illustration 6-1** Marriage and family change the buying habits of young adults.

The position of the individual in the life cycle determines how great an influence the family group has on that member's spending. Each part of the life cycle sets up different buying patterns triggered by needs and financial resources. In childhood, a child's buying may be heavily controlled by the adult members of the family. This diminishes as the child grows older and begins earning money. As children mature, they become independent of parents and make their own buying decisions with money they earn. Marriage changes the buying habits of most young adults and orients their purchases to satisfy needs and some luxuries of the young family. As the family grows, additional responsibilities alter buying patterns. Prior to the arrival of the first baby, the young couple may have been concerned with purchasing clothes, stereo equipment, entertainment, cars, and shelter. The focus of the young couple shifts when a new baby arrives, since they must now purchase baby clothes, diapers, baby furniture, toys, and additional food. For some couples, income may be temporarily or permanently reduced when one parent stays home to care for the infant.

The careful salesperson attempts to sort out those influences relative to the product and aims the presentation at the dominant influence in each selling situation. If a salesperson can characterize the prospect and the buying influences, it is possible to visualize a buyer profile that is susceptible to a particular kind of selling stimulus. Sometimes a salesperson's thinking can be aided by constructing a pattern of information in table form. This serves to differentiate buyers in a manner that helps the salesperson to understand them. A sample of the tables a salesperson might use are provided in Table 6–1.

### Ethnic Groups

An ethnic group is one distinguished from the rest of a society by race, religion, or nationality. Sometimes an ethnic group can actually be an entire subculture. Many of us are part of some ethnic group and are under its influence. For example, Scandinavians have particular food that they enjoy during the Christmas holiday season, but most of these foods are not consumed at other times of the year. This same custom is common to other ethnic groups. Some groups are opposed to certain foods, and some enjoy foods prepared in particular ways. A greeting card suitable for one nationality or ethnic group might not be appropriate for another.

A salesperson should never think of an ethnic group in a derogatory way, but rather as a particular group drawn together by some common bonds or interests. Salespeople should learn the habits, desires, and thinking of the group they are to work with, conduct their selling efforts in ways to please this group, and be compatible with its standards. Not only should sales-

**Table 6-1**

## PROSPECT PROFILES OF A CAR SALESPERSON

| PROSPECT | AGE | OCCUPA-TION | MONTHLY TAKE HOME PAY | SPOUSE WORKING | FAMILY SIZE | TYPE OF HOUSING | PRESENT CAR | CAR DESIRED | TYPE OF FINANCING |
|---|---|---|---|---|---|---|---|---|---|
| SMITH | | | | | | | | | |
| KUNKLE | | | | | | | | | |
| HITTI | | | | | | | | | |
| PERRY | | | | | | | | | |
| ABERNATHY | | | | | | | | | |

## INDUSTRIAL BUYER PROFILES

| BUYER | EXPERI-ENCE | FAMILY | INDIVI-DUAL TRAITS | COMPANY POLICY | ORDER SIZE | COMPANY CREDIT | AUTHOR-ITY | PRICE | COMPE-TITION |
|---|---|---|---|---|---|---|---|---|---|
| HINCHMAN | | | | | | | | | |
| FREDHOLM | | | | | | | | | |
| HESTON | | | | | | | | | |
| ONISKI | | | | | | | | | |
| HYMAN | | | | | | | | | |

people learn the particular likes and dislikes of an ethnic group to which they sell, but they should also try to learn the "why" behind such likes and dislikes. This will help develop firm relationships with customers.

## Reference Groups—Organizations

As social beings, we desire acceptance from other people; and we have a bewildering number of organizations in our society that attempt to fulfill this need. Since each individual in an organization wants to be recognized as a part of the group, an organization can exert pressure on its members to conform to the group's standards. During organization meetings, members are exposed to both visual and verbal communication. Members see other members who have new cars and new clothes; they hear about vacation trips, shopping experiences, and the results of using certain products.

Individuals may imitate respected members of the organization by buying similar things. They may make these purchases even though it means buying something beyond their customary price range. For example, some people may buy large homes in a certain suburb to impress people they admire, even though such purchases are beyond their financial capacity. The attentive salesperson will be aware of the interplay of these organizational forces on customers. The sales presentation can be improved by making the purchase appeal to this need to be accepted by other members in the organization.

**Tip** *Yang Lin has become the top salesperson for Pleasure Pools. Yang is constantly outselling salespeople with far more experience than she. Yang's formula for success is the result of applying something she learned in a sociology class while in school.*

*Yang learned that reference groups often exert a strong influence on what people buy. As a result, every time Pleasure Pools installs a swimming pool in someone's backyard, Yang inquires as to who the closest friends and associates of the new pool owner are. After several weeks, giving the friends of the new pool owner a chance to see the pool, Yang will start making sales calls on these friends. Yang realizes that because a close friend of theirs has recently bought a pool, they are probably thinking about a pool. Yang is thus reaching prospects at the right time.*

The type and number of organizations to which an individual belongs are determined by many factors—age, income, social conscience, family, ability, availability of time, desire for recognition, and ambition. You may find that an individual with membership in many organizations is more susceptible to buying than one who belongs to none or to only a few.

### Reference Groups—Position and Role

Every reference group has its own hierarchy of importance. An individual's rank in that hierarchy may come from birth, exemplary conduct, or outstanding contributions. Each position in the group has its own rights and responsibilities.

To be a nonconformist invites reproach. Being different invites criticism that bothers sensitive people. The fear of being unwanted, left out, laughed at, or ridiculed is more than some can bear. Some people buckle under the strain.

The motivation to conform has many sales advantages. It opens up a large demand for standard products and equipment that can be mass-produced and mass-sold. Production and marketing thrive on sameness. The standard of living is raised for millions of people willing to accept mass production. Individuality may be sacrificed, but comforts increase. Although mass production can provide the majority of our needs, we still prefer some custom-made products. The much smaller group of nonconformists, who still conform in some ways, and the large group of conformists, who still are nonconforming in minor ways, furnish a healthy market for salespeople specializing in customized merchandise, made and sold in a smaller volume but at a much higher price.

## PRODUCT ADOPTION CYCLE

Every product goes through an adoption cycle that lasts from the time of its introduction until the time it is accepted or rejected by the buying public. The place that the product—and the prospect—occupies in this cycle is quite important for the salesperson to understand, as it should influence the sales presentation.

### Stages in the Adoption Cycle

The product adoption cycle includes five stages: (1) awareness that the product exists, (2) interest in the product, (3) evaluation in relation to other products, (4) trial usage, and (5) total adoption or rejection. Knowledge of where a product is in the adoption cycle will aid the salesperson in determining the right presentation and the most receptive group of buyers.

## Opinion Leaders and Followers

There is a hierarchy of adopters of a new product or of a well-known product in a new area. Those people who adopt a new product almost as soon as it appears are called innovators. Such people are usually well-educated, well-read, and quite mobile. They are often opinion leaders, and their actions may influence other people to buy the products they buy.

A salesperson should watch opinion leaders for clues in selling, particularly if some of the products are new to the firm. Leaders, whether in a community or in industry, lend authority and respectability to a product or activity and influence many others to follow. For example, if the leading banker, president of the Chamber of Commerce, or a prominent individual signs to buy a product or advocate a cause, others of lesser stature will more readily follow.

*Tip* *Brad Schechter sells various household and kitchen supplies through the party system. This is a sales technique in which friends are invited to someone's home for refreshments, conversation, and the opportunity to view and place orders for the merchandise Brad sells. Brad is consistently one of the sales leaders for his company.*

*Brad's success is attributable to the sound planning of where the parties will be held. Brad identifies people who are very active in a wide range of community activities. Once they are identified, Brad attempts to get these community leaders to host his sales parties. Brad believes that by having an influential person from the community host the party, those attending will be more likely to purchase. Brad's sales success would seem to indicate that his system is working.*

As a product is accepted in the market, it filters from the innovators to other adopter groups. The innovators are followed, in order, by the early adopters, early majority, late majority and laggards.[1] The later adopter groups are generally more con-

---

[1]Everett M. Rogers and Floyd F. Schoemaker, *Diffusion of Innovations* (New York: The Free Press of Glencoe, 1962), p. 114.

servative than the earlier groups. The later groups hold off trying a product until they have some indication of market acceptance for the product.

People tend to fit fairly consistently into the same stage of the adoption cycle. It is dangerous, however, to assume that a certain type of person will always occupy the same place in the cycle. For example, an individual who was slow to adopt a VCR might be one of the first to try a new gun or fishing pole.

A product presentation to an innovator would be different from the same product presentation to a laggard several years later. There are advantages as well as disadvantages accruing to the buyer early in the cycle and also to the one who buys late in the cycle. One advantage for the slow buyer of new products is accrual of the benefits of product improvements. An advantage for the innovator is the immediate enjoyment of using a new and perhaps revolutionary product. In stressing advantages, it is important to dwell on those pertinent to the particular buyer.

## COMMUNICATION AND THE ART OF PERSUASION

Communication and persuasion are included in our study of external characteristics because they are the means by which certain outward forces—in our case, the salesperson—can change the attitudes and the perspective of the individual.

### Communication Process—Elements

In any communication process, there must be a sender or source, a message, a channel or medium of communication, and a receiver. In selling, the sender is the salesperson; the message is the sales presentation; the channel generally is the voice; and the receiver is the customer. To be transmitted, each message must be put into a form mutually understandable by both source and receiver. This process is called *encoding*. Writing, speaking, and illustrating are all methods of encoding or giving form to the message.

After a receiver has picked up a message, it must be interpreted and comprehended within the brain so that it can be understood. This process is called *decoding*. Few messages are decoded exactly as the sender intended. This is because everyone's perceptions differ and the same words will mean different things to different people. The salesperson can help to ensure that the message will be decoded as intended by learning about the customer's environment and by encoding the message accordingly.

## Persuasion—Its Nature

*Persuasion* is communication designed to change behavior. The types of communication that will result in effective persuasion vary among individuals because individuals vary in such characteristics as intelligence, motivation, and emotional factors. For example, people who rank low in intelligence and education can be persuaded to buy with a one-sided, perhaps emotional, approach. Better-educated people respond more readily to presentations that are factual, supported by reputable evidence, and that appeal to reason.[2]

## Persuasion—Its Elements

The elements of persuasion need to be considered in some detail before applying them to customers.

**Source.** Source credibility refers to the confidence the receiver has in the message source. Two major factors affecting source credibility are trustworthiness and expertness. A source is considered to be trustworthy when the receiver perceives the source to be believable. If the source is perceived to be skilled, experienced, and informed, the receiver will feel that the source is an expert on the message topic. Many other qualities exist and may be extremely important in particular situations, but *trustworthiness* and *expertness* might be considered universal.

High credibility sources are more effective than low credibility sources. Salespeople may enhance their credibility by the use of words, pauses, inflections, and force. Speech hindrances such as hesitating, stuttering, excessive word repetition, and tongue-slip corrections are irritating and can hinder persuasion. However, in a certain television commercial for fertilizer, a farmer who hesitated and spoke haltingly was used to impress user credibility on the listeners.[3]

---

[2]Irving L. Janis, "Personality as a Factor in Susceptibility to Communications," *The Science of Human Communication* (New York: Basic Books, Inc., 1963), pp. 57–58.

[3]"Some Farmers Hoe an Unfamiliar Row: As Stars of TV Ads," *The Wall Street Journal*, Vol. CXCII, No. 106 (November 30, 1978), p. 1.

Salespeople often try to identify with their customers by using similar language, showing similar attitudes, and fitting into each customer's image. A conversational style reinforces trustworthiness and can be quite effective in certain situations and with some individuals. A salesperson may be a member of the same organization as the customer. Showing salesperson-customer similarities can build friendship or bridge a gap. A status position or role often influences others since many people attribute greater strengths to one in a higher position. Often a person of prestige—doctor, professor, clergy, or high ranking business manager—is very influential. If your product is endorsed by one or more such people, many prospects will be impressed.

**Illustration 6-2 The endorsement of a product by a famous person helps to sell a product.**

*Courtesy of American Express Travel Related Services Company, Inc. Copyright: 1985*

**Message.** The message will be discussed under three parts: (1) form, (2) content, and (3) presentation. Much of this information is covered in detail in later chapters. The approach here is in more general terms.

The form of the message often depends on its specific purposes. Sometimes a formal introduction helps to prepare the setting for the body of the message. Sometimes it's desirable to state conclusions; other times it is preferable to let listeners draw their own conclusions. ". . . when using highly complex messages, addressing less intelligent receivers, or when receivers are initially unfavorable, it may be wise to state the conclusions explicitly. When dealing with an intelligent audience, particularly with simple problems, it would be best to have implicit conclusions."[4]

An ordered message is superior to one that is disordered. If the listener is very interested, the most important points should be stressed toward the end of the presentation. If the listener is indifferent, place your important points early in the message to create greater attention. If, in your opening section, you can introduce factors or ideas with which the listener agrees, there will be more response to your entire message. If you are the first one of several to make a presentation to a buying group, bring in your strong arguments forcefully and early. The listeners are fresh and will remember. Although later presentations may become tiring and be followed with less intensity or even ignored, many salespeople have mentioned that, if possible, they try to be last with their presentation. The assumption in this situation is that the last presentation, if it can capture the listeners' interest, will be best remembered.

The content of the message may vary from highly factual data to strong emotional appeals. A highly credible speaker gains ready acceptance of factual data; a speaker with low credibility is wise to have factual data supported by documented case histories. Presentation of one side of the argument may be quite effective before a less intelligent audience. A highly intelligent audience will be more impressed if the salesperson presents two sides.

The content of some messages is geared to getting an immediate response. For example, insurance presentations revolving around protection of loved ones may ignite immediate interest. As such, it is important to close the sale of the policy at this point in time. If the salesperson requires a day or more to prepare the policy, the prospect may have a change of heart.

A strong message inadequately presented could easily fail while a weaker message eloquently presented would close the sale. An effective delivery includes a strong message spoken distinctly with emphasis on salient points supported by proper explanations to an interested audience insulated from outside noise and distractions.

---

[4]Ronald L. Applbaum and Karl W. E. Anatol, *Strategies for Persuasive Communication* (Columbus: Charles E. Merrill Publishing Company, 1974), p. 92.

**Illustration 6–3   An effective delivery includes a strong message supported by appropriate sales aids to an interested customer.**

**Channel.**   There are a number of possible channels of communication used to present a message. In this discussion we confine ourselves to the sales presentation where the channel is the spoken word. When you are communicating face-to-face with a customer or prospect, it is your message the customer hears. As you talk, you provide the prospect with opportunities to make comments, ask questions, and raise objections. You see the immediate reactions to various propositions. As you talk, you perceive the interest or lack of interest in what you say and adjust your message as you continue in order to touch responsive chords. If the customer does not understand, you can amplify and clarify to the individual's satisfaction. Words and expressions may have different meanings to others and as you watch your listener you strive to make your meanings compatible with that of the listener.

**Receiver.**   The receiver is the person to whom you are trying to sell. Receivers' personality variables greatly influence their attitudes to sales presentations. Individuals with high self-esteem may have greater stability and evaluate critically each element of the salesperson's message. Low self-esteem customers have less confidence in themselves and can be persuaded with less difficulty. Insecure people are hesitant to accept your statements. To overcome this situation, identify yourself with the listener by finding the cause of the insecurity.

Authoritative customers have great regard for high-level people or those they consider powerful. They are willing to buy if you can show them that their action is aligning them with the behavior of such people. Closed-minded individuals are difficult to change unless such change coincides with their behavior or that of someone they admire. Open-minded individuals are willing to evaluate, compare, and weigh your message more on its merits. Egotistical listeners must be addressed with expressions showing you recognize their importance and are striving to enhance their positions.

## Applying Persuasion Techniques

The customer must be guided to give attention to your message. A salesperson not only wants the prospect to listen to the message but to give primary attention to it. Some salespeople forget that the prospect is bombarded constantly by communications from many sources, including many competing sales messages. As such, you must expertly position your message within this barrage of attractions and guide the listener to pay attention to it. This is best done by encoding the message in line with what you know about the prospect's motivation and perceptions.

**Tip**  *Haru Moon sells data processing equipment for Info Systems, Inc. A major industrial customer contacted Haru to explain their data processing needs and to invite Haru to make a sales presentation. Haru discovered that three of her competitors had also been invited to make presentations. Haru quickly went into action to see that her presentation would be the most forceful and best remembered.*

*Haru's efforts began by asking the potential customer if she could spend a day at their headquarters to examine their present system and equipment. From her observations, Haru identified an opportunity to reduce the prospect's data processing costs by more than 20 percent. In addition, to counter the presentations of her competitors, Haru (1) prepared a presentation that pointed out at least*

*one advantage her product had over each of the competi-*
*tive products, (2) arranged for a demonstration with the*
*'right' people, (3) arranged a lunch meeting with the key*
*buyer to take place right after the presentation of her*
*major competitor, (4) prepared an impressive list of users*
*of her equipment, and (5) brought the controller of the*
*customer firm to a trade show to see Info Systems' prod-*
*ucts in action. Haru's success was the product of thorough*
*planning.*

It is almost impossible for a salesperson to get the sales message through to a customer if that customer is preoccupied with a weighty problem. In such instances, it is better for the salesperson to request to be excused and arrange for another interview at a better time. When a salesperson wants an industrial buyer to make an important decision, an invitation to go out for lunch or dinner can avoid interruptions common in the office. If a major purchase is involved, and if convenient, the salesperson might also invite the buyer to the salesperson's home office where there is a minimum of confusion and interruption.

When two competing salespeople must make individual presentations to a buying committee, there may be a slight advantage in being second. If, however, the first salesperson is capable of getting some kind of commitment from any member of the buying committee, the second salesperson will have difficulty changing the views of those who have expressed themselves strongly for the first salesperson's products.

It is easier to sell a person if need-arousal precedes product selling points. Presenting a strong sales appeal first, followed by mentioning somewhat less favorable characteristics, is better than the reverse order. For example, it is better to sell a person on your product first and then follow up with precautionary suggestions in using it than to emphasize dangerous elements first and then try to make a sale.[5]

**Develop Your Customer's Faith in You.** Efforts at persuasion are most effective when people have faith in the source of the message. If people have faith in others, they will tend to follow their suggestions. For example, people follow the instructions of their physician with regard to health problems because

---

[5]Winston L. Brembeck and William S. Howell, *Persuasion: A Means of Social Control* (New York: Prentice-Hall, Inc., 1952), pp. 406-407.

they have confidence in suggestions from such a source. Similar situations are common for ministers, lawyers, salespeople, or anyone looked up to by the message receiver. Thus, it is important for you as a salesperson to build your customers' faith in you and in what you say. Otherwise, it is doubtful whether your attempts at persuasion will ever be successful.

**Adapt the Message to the Prospect's Expectations.**  Another means of ensuring that your persuasive efforts will be successful is to encode your message in line with the prospect's expectations. One buys a particular product because it promises to give specific results. For example, the person who buys a correspondence course expects or at least hopes it will help in acquiring a particular job. The person buying cosmetics expects them to enhance their appearance.

People who wish to be persuaded are easily swayed. For example, the parent anxious for a child to succeed in music is easily persuaded to buy the deluxe rather than the standard accordion; a fishing enthusiast will buy almost any bait if persuaded by an expert that it will catch fish. If a salesperson paints a word picture of satisfactory use and then helps a customer achieve this expectation, repeat sales will be very easy. Keep in mind, however, that painting pictures of success not usually attainable will bring about frustration, disappointment, and unhappiness.

Even industrial salespeople must be aware of emotional buying motives in addition to practical product appreciation. It has been found that many firms have bought equipment because other firms had it; even though they were ill-prepared to use the equipment. Business people may be reluctant to admit that they spend money on fads like the average consumer, but studies reveal instances of poor judgment and bad timing in business purchases that have been motivated by emotional behavior patterns rather than by sound judgment.

## APPLYING WHAT YOU KNOW ABOUT THE BEHAVIORAL SCIENCES

The material in this chapter and the preceding one provides a basis for inviting further study to help salespeople understand their customers. Trying to understand people is a complex, fascinating, and never-ending experience. You will gain increasing awareness of buyer motivation through reading pertinent literature and analyzing people, and you will be able to develop better sales presentations that stress the fulfillment of customer desires.

The salesperson who feels bewildered by the mass of information covered in this chapter and the preceding one can advance successfully by sorting out that which is familiar and can be handled and then applying it skillfully. Progressive salespeople will earnestly study this material because increased success hinges on greater perception of customer beliefs, feelings, and inclinations. As you become more familiar with the behavioral sciences and absorb more information, you can convert it to use and widen your understanding of buyers, thereby increasing your sales effectiveness.

## QUESTIONS

1. How is individual purchasing behavior influenced by culture and society?
2. In what way does buying behavior conform to social class norms?
3. In what manner do some people deviate from social class norms?
4. What kind of influence over purchasing behavior does the family exert?
5. How does the product adoption cycle affect the points stressed in a sales presentation, the original selection of promising contacts, and the salesperson's approach?
6. In the product adoption cycle, are buyers always in the same category? Explain.
7. Is there a difference between encoding and decoding? If there is, explain the difference.
8. How can salespeople enhance their credibility? What is meant by source credibility?
9. If you wanted to send a message to influence a possible customer, how would you build in persuasive language?
10. In what way(s) does customer expectation influence their buying?

## SALES CHALLENGES

1. Develop customer profiles assuming you are a sales representative for a (1) computer manufacturer, (2) radio station, and (3) real estate firm. What pertinent customer information will be needed in each situation? How will this information be used? How will the customer profiles differ in each of the three situations?

2. To the extent you can, form several groups with individuals of entirely different backgrounds. Each group should contain people of different nationalities, educational backgrounds, income levels, ages, religions, and occupations. Discuss various topics, openly disagree when there are differences of opinion, point out strong attitudes and beliefs, voice likes and dislikes. Encourage everyone to participate. After the session, ask yourself these questions: What have I learned? Can I learn anything from angry discussion? Did my experience increase my tolerance toward others? Have I been wrong in my views toward others? Will I now be more sensitive to the needs and feelings of others?

3. Make contact with three or more salespeople. Find out from each any pending or completed sales that would be considered large. Question them about external influences that affected the sale and how they reacted to these influences. Apply the material presented in this chapter to help you understand the sales situation better. Discuss the uses and limitations of the material in this chapter with these salespeople. Is there anything you can point out from this chapter that would have helped or could now help them?

## CASES

### 6-1   Educational Products, Inc.

Ted and Melinda Gretzky are a young, hard working couple. They own a modest home, a three-year-old car, and have a small savings account. Ted works on the assembly line for one of the major automobile companies. Melinda works part-time at a local retail florist shop. Ted and Melinda did not have the benefit of a very good education. Ted, in fact, is a high school dropout. Everything Ted and Melinda have, they have had to work very hard to get. As such, Ted and Melinda are very concerned that their two children receive a better education than they had.

Early on a Wednesday evening, as Ted and Melinda are watching television, there is a knock at the door. Bart Flohr, a sales representative for Educational Products, Inc., is at the door.

**Bart:** Good evening. I am Bart Flohr with Educational Products, Inc. I have a rather unique offer that you will be interested in, but it only runs through the rest of this month; that is only six more days. Would you like to hear about it here or inside where the light is better?

**Ted:** I suppose so. Won't you come inside?

**Bart:** Thank you. *(Bart enters home)*

**Ted:** This is my wife, Melinda.

**Bart:** How do you do, Melinda. My name is Bart Flohr from Educational Products, Inc.

**Melinda:** Won't you have a seat?

**Bart:** Thank you. *(As Bart takes a seat he notices a picture on one of the end tables.)* Are these your children? Very nice looking family.

**Melinda:** Thank you.

**Bart:** We are running a special offer this month on one of the finest products my company makes. You may have heard of our encyclopedias. They are among the best available. Let me show you one of our sample volumes. The binding is genuine leather with gold-leaf engraving. The 30 volumes look very impressive in any bookcase.

**Ted:** They do seem to look very nice, but they must be expensive.

**Bart:** We offer an easy payment plan. And look at all of these features. The books are organized in alphabetical order so that you can easily find information on any topic you want.

**Melinda:** *(Realizing that the encyclopedias could be of use to their children in school to help them with their work.)* Can you tell me something about the information in the books?

**Bart:** The books are filled with beautiful full-color illustrations. Look at these pictures. See how deep and clear the colors are.

**Melinda:** Yes, but what I really want to know . . .

**Bart:** *(Interrupting)* And, as I said earlier, we are offering a special this month. If you buy now, we will give you at no additional charge this World Atlas. As you can see, the Atlas matches the encyclopedia set and all maps are in beautiful color.

**Melinda:** We have two children, and . . .

**Bart:** *(Interrupting again)* I know what you mean. Children are always getting into everything and you wouldn't want this beautiful set damaged. To guard against damage, we have available a bookcase with glass doors that can be locked. The price of the bookcase can be included in your easy payment plan.

**Ted:** Do you have an encyclopedia that comes with a less expensive binding?

**Bart:** Yes, but it doesn't look nearly as nice. Besides, you don't get the free Atlas with that set.

**Melinda:** Does the less expensive set contain the same information as this set?

**Bart:** Yes, but it doesn't look nearly as nice. Let me explain our easy payment plan to you. Did you say that you would be interested in the bookcase?

**Melinda:** Ted and I would like to think this over for a while.

**Bart:** You better act fast. The free Atlas offer ends this month.

**Melinda:** Thank you, but we'd like to think it over.

**Bart:** Can I call back tomorrow?

**Melinda:** No, but you can leave a telephone number in case we're interested.

**Bart:** Thank you. Please give a call if you decide to buy. Remember, the free Atlas offer ends this month.

**Ted and Melinda:** Goodbye.

1. Were Ted and Melinda good prospects? Explain your response.
2. Bart missed a real opportunity to sell because he was not what?
3. Knowing what you do about selling at this point, how would you have approached Ted and Melinda?

### 6-2  Rationalizing a Purchase

Akeo and Tatsu Doi operate a dry cleaning plant employing 20 people in Northberg, a town of 60,000 people. Their income is about $70,000 a year.

The Dois are ardent city boosters, and Mr. Doi is a member of the Chamber of Commerce. They are both members of a luncheon club and several other organizations. They attend church regularly and are active in the church.

The Dois, in their early forties, live in a home purchased 15 years ago for $37,000 that now has a market value of $84,000, drive a new car purchased last year for $14,000, and also have a second car, now five years old. They have no debts other than current expense items.

Northberg is a pleasant city located on a lake that is five miles long and one mile wide. It is one of three connecting lakes that together make up a waterway 12 miles long. A navigable river six miles long connects the middle lake to one of the Great Lakes.

Many citizens in Northberg own boats, and quite a few, including the Dois, belong to the Viking Boat Club. The Dois have owned a boat for 15 years and keep it at a local marina. They have had several boats during this period and presently own the Clam, a boat they purchased three years ago for $20,000. They paid the balance they owed on this boat two years ago. The Clam has a 40-horsepower outboard motor. It is still a sound, durable boat useful for water skiing, fishing, and pleasure riding. It has a canvas top that may be raised or lowered.

The Doi family walks into your marina on a Monday evening at about seven o'clock. Mr. Doi tells you they had just checked on their boat, at another marina half a mile away, and were just driving around a bit. Mr. Doi informs you that he spent last Saturday at a boat show in Barstow, a city at 200,000, about 50 miles away. You notice by looking at the Doi children that a couple of them will be starting college in a few years.

You casually begin talking with the Dois, showing them the new boats. In a short time you see Mr. Doi's interest in a new Claremont that came in last week. This boat is larger than the boat the Dois now have. Powered by a 125-horsepower inboard-outboard motor, it has a small cabin, including modest living facilities for cooking or an occasional overnight stay for those who would want to go out to the big lake. It is a beautiful boat, exhibiting luxury without being overpowering. It has many practical features that make it ideal for fishing as well as pleasure boating. There is room for nine people, but the boat could not sleep that many. The price is $90,000; you could allow the Dois $15,000 on their present boat.

As the entire family gathers around this boat, you detect a strong sales possibility, but it means stepping them up from a $20,000 to a $90,000 investment.

1. What customer behavior factors brought out in this and the previous chapter might affect this sale?
2. What rationalizations will Mr. and Mrs. Doi probably use if they buy this boat?
3. What might their friends and neighbors say, among themselves, about this purchase?
4. Prepare a dialogue covering part of a sales presentation in which something in your behavioral science learning plays a part. Indicate in the beginning the specific point you are covering. Indicate any assumptions you are making.

# PART THREE

## SELLING TECHNIQUES AND PROCEDURES

The previous six chapters have provided background information necessary to understand and appreciate the selling process. Part 3 will now focus on the specific stages of the selling process. The sales job is broken down into six parts and each is discussed in detail. Chapter 7 examines the start of the selling process—how to find and qualify customers. Chapter 8 describes the beginning of the sales presentation—how to gather background information and arrange for an appointment. The making of the sales presentation is the topic of Chapter 9. Techniques for developing effective presentations are presented. The focus of Chapter 10 is on developing creative and appealing product demonstrations. In every sales presentation, some customer resistance is encountered. As such, various approaches for handling customer objections are presented in Chapter 11. Finally, Chapter 12 covers the important topic of closing the sale and getting an order from your customer.

# 7

# FINDING AND QUALIFYING CUSTOMERS

It would seem quite obvious that to make a sale, a salesperson must have customers. But where do potential customers come from? Do they simply walk in the door and ask to buy something from you? Yes, in some cases they do! This is especially true for the retail salesperson who sells to customers who have come to the store. However, if the typical salesperson selling life insurance, photocopying machines, computers, encyclopedias, and many other products and services did nothing more than wait for customers to come in the door, few sales would be made. In most cases, the salesperson must go out and find customers.

Finding and qualifying customers is the first step in the selling process and begins the discussion of the third branch of the diagram shown in Figure 7–1. This diagram was first introduced in Chapter 2 with the discussion of selling success that centered around the first branch, *Good Personal Characteristics.* Chapters 3 through 6 reviewed all aspects of the middle branch, *Thorough Knowledge and Understanding.* This chapter and the next five will discuss the third branch, *Good Selling Techniques.*

## STAGES OF THE SELLING PROCESS

The process leading to the closing of a sale can be thought of as a series of steps, as shown in Figure 7–2. The material presented in the first six chapters, possessing *Good Personal Characteristics* and acquiring *Thorough Knowledge and Understanding,* brings you to the point where you are ready to take the first step. In this chapter you will find what is necessary to take that first step. The next five chapters will cover what is necessary to take the remaining steps.

**Illustration 7-1   Most salespeople must seek out prospective customers where they work.**

# IMPORTANCE OF PROSPECTING FOR CUSTOMERS

The process of looking for customers is known as prospecting. This is certainly an appropriate term to use since prospecting originally meant the search for valuable minerals such as gold. Finding customers is as important to a salesperson as finding valuable minerals was to a prospector in years past.

Many experienced salespeople feel that prospecting is the most important aspect of their job. After all, it doesn't matter how good your sales presentation is unless you have a potential customer to listen to you. Furthermore, it's important to find

**Figure 7-1**

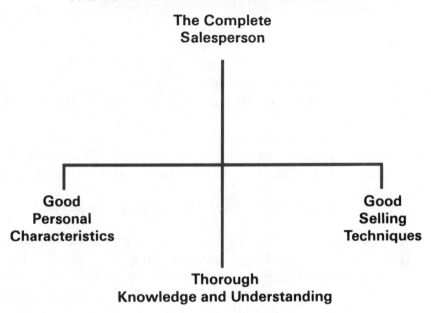

THE FORMULA FOR SALES SUCCESS

The Complete
Salesperson

Good
Personal
Characteristics

Good
Selling
Techniques

Thorough
Knowledge and Understanding

**Figure 7-2**

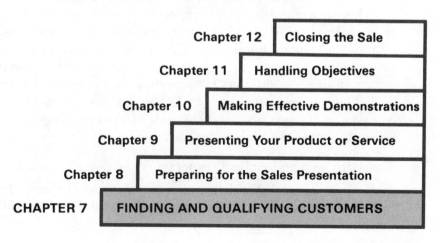

THE STAIRWAY TO SALES SUCCESS

Chapter 12 | Closing the Sale

Chapter 11 | Handling Objectives

Chapter 10 | Making Effective Demonstrations

Chapter 9 | Presenting Your Product or Service

Chapter 8 | Preparing for the Sales Presentation

CHAPTER 7 | FINDING AND QUALIFYING CUSTOMERS

new customers continually because, for a number of reasons, all salespeople will lose some of their old customers over time. Customers may be lost for any of the following reasons:

1. A customer may go out of business
2. A customer's business may be acquired by a larger firm that buys from a different source
3. The buyer you've been selling to is transferred, retires, or resigns
4. A customer moves out of your territory
5. A customer may be lost through death, illness, or accident
6. A customer may have only a one-time need for your product or service
7. A customer may be lost to a competing salesperson

Salespeople who are not continually prospecting for new customers will find their sales declining over time. Joe Girard, discussed in Chapter 1, used to refer to this process as the "Ferris wheel" of selling. Imagine a Ferris wheel at an amusement park with a line of people waiting to get on. The operator will stop the wheel periodically to let some riders off and other riders on. In this way, the Ferris wheel is always fully occupied. In the same fashion, a salesperson must continually prospect for new customers to replace old customers that may be lost for any of the reasons cited earlier.

## METHODS OF PROSPECTING

There are many ways of prospecting for new customers. The right method to use depends on the product or service you are selling. Canvassing homes on a door-to-door basis may be appropriate for a salesperson selling encyclopedias but not for one selling business computers. Prospecting methods can be categorized into three groups: (1) leads obtained through your company; (2) leads obtained through external sources; and (3) leads obtained through personal sources.

### Your Company as a Source for Prospects

Your company is the easiest source to use for prospects. Take full advantage of the assistance available within your organization.

**Current Customers.** In addition to your customers (to be discussed later), other divisions of your company, selling different products, may be selling to people who are not your customers. Obtain customer lists from these divisions as well as any pertinent information that is available. These lists may contain the names of good prospects that you have overlooked.

**Credit Department.** Your company's credit department may be a source of information for past customers who have stopped buying for one reason or another. Also, check for those who were contacted in the past, for whom a credit report was completed, but who never bought from your company. These former and potential accounts may be good prospects today if approached with the right sales presentation.

**Service Department.** Your company's service personnel can be a valuable source for prospects. They are in contact with customers for maintenance or repair work on the products purchased from your company. They are in a good position to identify customers who will need new equipment soon. Encourage your service people to give you information on prospects and reward them when a sale is made through a lead they provided. The delivery people in your company may also be in a position to identify equipment needs of customers. Also, don't overlook the possibility of using service people working for other, noncompeting businesses.

**Tip**  *Peter Stasny has been a successful salesperson for Bouchard Oldsmobile for many years. The other salespeople at the dealership are constantly amazed at the number of prospects who come in asking for Peter. Peter's new customers come about through contacts that he has cultivated over the years with service station mechanics. The mechanics contact Peter whenever they do repair work on a car that is approaching the end of its useful life or when they hear the car owner comment on needing a new car. Peter, in turn, telephones the car owner, promising a good deal if the owner comes to the dealership and asks for him. When a sale is made, Peter shares his commission with the mechanic who provided the lead.*

**Company Advertising.** Most companies receive inquiries in response to their advertising messages. Companies may provide telephone numbers in their TV ads to call for further information; magazine ads may contain mailers to fill in and return; and packages of "free—take one" cards may be posted almost anywhere. As inquiries are received in response to these advertisements, they are turned over to the appropriate salesperson to follow up.

**Trade Shows.** Thousands of trade shows are held every year in almost every industry. There are boat shows, auto shows, camper shows, hardware shows, home improvement shows, computer shows, fashion shows, and furniture shows, to name a few. Companies are normally very careful to take the names and addresses of visitors to their booths during the show. These names are then turned over to company salespeople for follow-up contacts. Be sure to check out these names quickly since other companies represented at the trade show will be contacting many of these prospects.

**Illustration 7-2 Prospective clientele may be found through trade shows and computerized buyer listings.**

**Telephone and Mail Leads.** Many companies send out large mailings with reply cards for further information and/or employ people to generate leads through telephone contacts. Many leads are obtained through these contacts. In addition, all companies receive unsolicited inquiries from potential customers. Make sure that you are receiving your share of these leads from your company.

### External Sources for Prospects

Beyond the leads provided by your company, there are many sources outside your company for finding customers. The best external sources to use will vary depending on the product or service you are selling.

**Other Salespeople.** Salespeople for noncompeting firms may often provide useful leads. While making a call on one of their customers, they may discover that their customer has a need for something you sell. If you have a good relationship with other salespeople, they may pass these leads on to you. Cultivate such relationships; pass on useful information to them when you have a chance.

**Lists and Directories.** Specialized lists of names can be purchased from several sources. The two largest companies that sell names are the R. H. Donnelly Co. in Chicago, and R. L. Polk in Detroit. You can purchase almost any list imaginable. For example, you can purchase the names and addresses of all dance schools in California, all mink producers in the U.S., all high school teachers in Michigan and Illinois, all automotive parts purchasing agents in Canada, or any other specialized listing desired. Local governments will also supply certain listings such as new car registrations, boat registrations, or births. The cost of these lists might range anywhere from $10 to well over $100 per 1,000 names.

In addition to specialized lists, there are many trade directories that list business firms by size, geographic area, and the nature of their business activity (products manufactured). These directories can provide a good starting point for developing a customer list and are available in any major library. The most commonly used directories are *Dun & Bradstreet, Moody's Industrial Manual, Standard and Poor's Corporation Record, Thomas Register of Manufacturers, Fraser's Industrial Manual, Scott's Industrial Directory, The Key Business Directory*, and the *Canadian Trade Index.* Don't overlook such obvious and simple sources as the yellow pages of the local telephone directory. Keep in mind that large libraries contain the telephone directories of all major cities in the country.

**Computerized Buyer Listings.** Several firms now supply specialized computerized buyer listings. If you supply the firm with information on what products you sell, they will provide you with a computerized listing of all businesses known to buy those products. The listing will include the firm's name, its address, the names of top executives, the size, and other relevant company information. One company supplying such a computerized listing is Dun's Marketing Services (New York). The fee for such listings may range from $10 to $50 per 1,000 names.

**Illustration 7-3** Solid prospecting requires a knowledge of many different sources.

**Groups or Organizations.** Does your product appeal to a specialized group such as teenagers, retired people, bankers, advertisers, retailers, lawyers, or artists? If so, it is likely that there is a local club, group, or organization to which they belong. A list or directory of the membership may be available. Many neighborhoods have community centers that put on programs for people interested in a variety of activities such as exercising, ceramics, painting, and crocheting. If you want to reach people with a special interest, you may be able to do so through the community center.

**Centers of Influence.** In every community, there are some people who stand out as leaders. These people may be bankers, business executives, doctors, lawyers, teachers, clergy, or heads of organizations such as the Rotary Club or Chamber of Commerce. These people generally have many contacts throughout the community and are well regarded. A bank executive, for example, knows most people in the community and is aware of most business activity in the community. By building friendships with such people, you may be able to use their recommendations for your product or service. The banker's recommendation, for example, could be very valuable when selling insurance or real estate. Influential people can recommend you and provide you with leads.

### Personal Sources for Prospects

Although your company and specific external sources can be used to find customers, all salespeople must rely on personal initiative and effort to cultivate prospects.

**Cold Canvassing.** This technique relies on the law of averages. It is assumed that if you call on enough homes or businesses, you will find a few interested customers. In door-to-door canvassing, for example, you pick a neighborhood and call on every home. Many products and services such as encyclopedias, vacuum cleaners, cosmetics, home supply products, landscaping, storm windows, furnace repair, and insurance can be sold through cold canvassing. Wholesale salespeople can use this approach by calling on every retailer in a particular area. Industrial salespeople can call on every manufacturing plant in a particular city.

Although not as effective as a personal contact, cold canvassing can be conducted through telephone and mail contacts. A salesperson will choose a particular neighborhood and telephone each home or send a mailer with a reply card or number to each home. An industrial salesperson may also telephone or mail information to all businesses in a particular area.

**Referrals.** Your present customers are often a good source for new customers. After a sale is made, ask your customer if he or she can supply you with the names of some friends who might also be interested in your product or service. This technique is sometimes called the "endless chain" approach because it can be continued from one customer to the next as illustrated in Figure 7–3.

In Figure 7–3, an insurance salesperson, Oki Saga, sold a life insurance policy for $50,000 to Bart Jones, an engineer. Oki asks

Bart to recommend several friends or associates who might need additional insurance coverage. Bart provides three names to Oki. Two of the three express no interest but a policy is sold to the third, Scott Skiles, for $40,000. In turn, Scott is asked to recom-

**Figure 7-3**

## EXAMPLE OF REFERRAL OR ENDLESS CHAIN METHOD

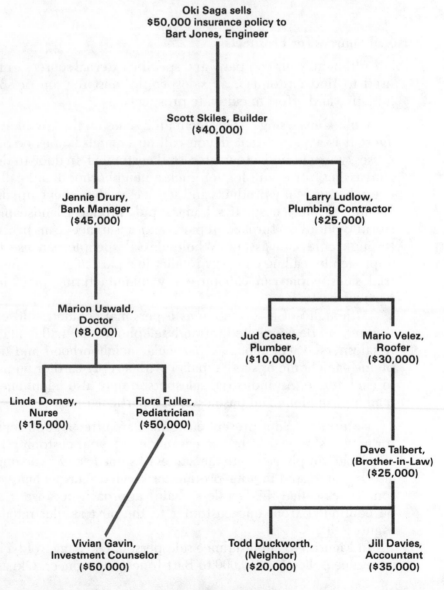

mend several names. Carrying this process through in Figure 7–3, Oki Saga sells $425,000 through the chain of referrals initiated with the sale to Bart Jones.

Referrals can also be used in business selling. Purchasing agents or industrial buyers may be asked if they are aware of other buyers who might need your offering. In some cases, you may be able to get the business customer to write a short letter of introduction for you. This will pave the way for your next contact.

**Bird Dogs.**   Salespeople often develop a network of what might be called bird dogs, spotters, or sales associates. These are people whose services the salesperson uses to find leads. Bird dogs may take many forms. They may be housewives making telephone calls for the salesperson in their spare time, teenagers making door-to-door contacts after school, or people in positions to identify likely prospects such as an employee of a boat dealership who can supply names to a salesperson selling boat insurance. The use of bird dogs saves the salesperson's time and allows the salesperson to concentrate on prospects who have been somewhat pre-screened. Bird dogs can be paid on an hourly basis or on a commission basis when a sale is made.

*Tip*   *Lyla Anderton has been a leading salesperson for Nykonon Furnaces for many years. Lyla sells new furnaces as well as furnace repair and maintenance work. Part of Lyla's success has been due to her creative use of bird dogs through the years. For the last several years, Lyla has been employing high school students who go door-to-door in their neighborhoods after school. The students ask the homeowner if they can attach a small sticker to the homeowner's furnace. The sticker reads:*

> *If experiencing furnace problems or in need of routine maintenance, call Lyla Anderton at 944–4589.*

*Lyla estimates that her stickers are now on more than 10,000 furnaces around town. If a furnace problem occurs in any of these homes, Lyla's number is in the first place the homeowner looks.*

**Friends and Acquaintances.** Good prospects are often close by. Don't overlook people you know as likely customers. Like everyone else, your friends need a wide range of products and services. Many life insurance companies instruct their new salespeople to start out by contacting friends and relatives. This advice could also apply for many other products and services such as automobiles, real estate, securities, vacation travel, home supply products, and magazines, just to name a few.

Try compiling a list of your current friends, relatives, neighbors, schoolmates, members of organizations that you belong to, and people you are in contact with such as milk carriers, mail carriers, doctors, or dentists. How many good prospects are on this list? Cultivate new acquaintances by joining clubs, organizations, civic groups, and bowling leagues. How many people can you meet on the golf course or at little league games? Keep in mind that friends and acquaintances are not only likely customers themselves, but can also be used as the starting point in the referral process discussed earlier.

**Personal Alertness.** All of the techniques discussed in this chapter for finding customers are very useful. There is, however, no substitute for being alert to opportunities that are around you. This technique simply involves keeping your eyes and ears open. Some salespeople are alert to every opportunity; others stumble over promising opportunities and never look back to see what tripped them.

Information picked up in a casual conversation may identify a sales opportunity. The local newspaper is filled with leads. The newspaper contains information on promotions, engagements, weddings, births, deaths, business activities, contracts awarded, building permits issued, new business openings, new product introductions, zoning ordinance changes, as well as many local news stories. A classified ad seeking additional workers may signify a plant expansion. Does this signal a sales opportunity for you?

Many trade publications contain useful information. Religious events and holidays may present sales opportunities. Changes of season and weather may stimulate sales. The alert salesperson will spot and take advantage of these opportunities.

## QUALIFYING PROSPECTS

Once a list of prospects has been developed, the next step is to qualify the prospects. Qualifying the prospect refers to determining whether the prospect is able to buy and is interested in buying. If you are to be successful in selling, it is important not to waste a lot of time with prospects who are not qualified to buy. For example, would a real estate agent want to spend the day showing expensive homes to a couple that has no savings and, hence, would not be able to make a down payment on a home?

Qualifying a prospect involves answering the following questions about the prospect:

1. Does the prospect have a need or desire for your product or service?
2. Does the prospect have the ability to pay?
3. Does the prospect have the authority to buy?
4. Is the prospect eligible to buy?

A positive response to each of these questions indicates that you have a qualified prospect.

## Does the Prospect Have a Need?

If an individual or business has no need or want for your offering, it makes little sense to call on that person or business. A couple living in an apartment would not generally be interested in storm windows; a person who does not have a driver's license would not be interested in a new car; a company that does not perform drilling operations would not need a drill press. In Chapters 3, 5, and 6, various buying motives and needs to which one could appeal were presented. Does your prospect exhibit any of these needs? If so, they are qualified on the basis of need.

## Can the Prospect Pay?

In addition to having a need, a prospect must have the ability to pay. An individual must have sufficient income; a business firm, an acceptable credit rating. How often does a person with a rowboat income waste a salesperson's time by discussing expensive yachts?

## Does the Prospect Have Authority to Buy?

When selling to business firms, it is not always clear where the final buying authority lies. The purchase of machine tools may be the responsibility of production managers, engineers, or purchasing agents in the customer firm. It is important to talk with the right person. In many cases, several people are involved in the purchase decision. If uncertain, ask, "Ms. Hedberg, if your company were to buy, will you be the one making the purchase decision or will others be involved?" In many household buying situations, it may also be important to determine whether the purchase decision will be made by the wife alone, husband alone, or jointly.

### Is the Prospect Eligible to Buy?

In some cases, a prospect may not be eligible to buy. A person in poor health may not be eligible for a life insurance policy. If your company has a policy of selling only to wholesale distributors, a retailer with a need and the ability to pay would still not be eligible. Memberships in some health plans and credit unions are limited to people in certain occupations. Some organizations, such as the Commercial Travellers' Association, limit membership to people in selected professions.

*Tip   Diane Uhouse has been one of the leading salespeople for Richmond Cadillac for the past five years. An important reason for Diane's success relates to her efficient use of time—even when there are no customer prospects in the dealership. Diane has a unique approach to find and qualify customers.*

*Diane selects affluent neighborhoods and drives up and down the streets in her new telephone-equipped Cadillac. When Diane spots a home with an older Cadillac in the driveway, she parks in the driveway right behind the older car. Diane looks up the homeowner's name in an area telephone directory that she carries. Picking up her telephone, Diane calls the house. "Good afternoon, Mrs. Rieger, this is Diane Uhouse from Richmond Cadillac. How would you like to take a test drive in a new Cadillac? I'm sitting in your driveway now." Most people are so surprised and amused that Diane gets very few refusals. Although every test drive does not result in a sale, by combining prospecting and qualifying techniques in one step, Diane has remained a top sales performer for Richmond.*

## SOURCES OF QUALIFICATION INFORMATION

There are many possible sources of information to help a salesperson qualify prospects. Any one, or some combination of the following sources will generally provide all of the information needed.

## Company Records

Most companies keep records of past and present customers. These records include sales and payment information. If the prospect company has been contacted in the past but is not a purchasing customer, the company records may contain a credit report as well as other information gathered during these past contacts.

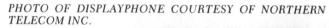

*PHOTO OF DISPLAYPHONE COURTESY OF NORTHERN TELECOM INC.*

**Illustration 7-4   Your company's records furnish information about a customer's qualifications.**

## Published Information

If the prospects are large business buyers, there is generally much information published about them. Trade directories, particularly those published by Dun & Bradstreet, Moody's, and Standard and Poor's, will contain information on the company's history, current size, sales, products, top executives, plant and office locations, and credit rating. Information will also be available through the business press and trade associations. Information can be purchased from many credit rating organizations and 10-K reports, which contain detailed financial and operational information, can be acquired from the U.S. Securities & Exchange Commission.

Many customer organizations publish information about themselves. This includes annual reports, organizational manuals, house organs, product catalogs, and buyers' guides that indicate who has buying authority for different products and services in the organization.

### Referral Source

If the prospect has been referred to you, ask the referral source for information. In the referral example presented in Figure 7–3, Scott Skiles was referred to Oki Saga by Bart Jones as a prospect for an insurance policy. Oki could begin qualifying Scott by asking Bart about Scott's occupation, family status, age, home, and other factors that might indicate the extent of Scott's insurance needs.

### Community Sources

Many of your customers may be known in their communities. The alert salesperson can get information about a person or a business from friends of the individual or from people familiar with the business. Information may also be obtained from local banks, the Chamber of Commerce, the Better Business Bureau, and local government records.

### Ask and Observe

The most direct way to get information is to ask questions and keep your eyes open. If you're not sure whether a business buyer has the authority to buy, ask. If you're not sure whether a prospect qualifies for a particular insurance policy, ask about the prospect's medical history. Observation will give you insight into a prospect's ability to pay. A prospect's home, furnishings, car, and life style will suggest something about what the prospect earns and can afford.

Once you begin gathering information on the prospect, make sure that you record the information so that it isn't lost. Figure 7–4 shows an example of an initial prospect information card. This can be used to record preliminary information as you begin qualifying the prospect. Later, as further information is gathered, you can develop an entire file on the prospect.

**Figure 7-4**

## PROSPECT PRELIMINARY FILE CARD

| P OR S | AGE | OCCUPATION | | NAME | | | | I will See Him On |
|---|---|---|---|---|---|---|---|---|
| **Firm and Address** | | | | | | Phone | | |
| **Residence Address** | | | | Approx. Income | | Phone | | Day |
| Children's Name | Age | Children's Name | Age | Wife's Name | | Age | | |
| | | | | Refer. by/Relat. | | | | |
| Seen Call | Interview | App. | Volume | Annual Premium | | No. Ref. Lds. | | At |
| | | | | | | | | |
| **Other Information** | | | | | | | | Time |
| Just Moved | New Home | First Job | Promoted Or Changed Jobs | Business For Himself | Just Married Or Engaged | | New Baby | Youngsters To School |

# DEVELOP A PROSPECTING PLAN

A major barrier to prospecting is a lack of time. Salespeople often find themselves so busy servicing existing customers, traveling, completing paperwork, and attending sales meetings that little time is left for prospecting. As such, many salespeople take the attitude that they'll get around to doing some prospecting when they have the time. This normally results in doing an inadequate job of prospecting and, over time, not replacing enough lost customers with new customers. To ensure that this does not happen, you must develop a plan. Developing a prospecting plan involves the following four steps:

1. Establish prospecting objectives
2. Allocate time for prospecting
3. Select one or more prospecting techniques
4. Evaluate your prospecting results

### Establish Prospecting Objectives

It is important that you establish clear prospecting goals. It is not enough to say that you want to find some new customers. Identify a measurable goal that you can strive to achieve. For example, an objective can be to find ten new qualified prospects each month.

### Allocate Time for Prospecting

Don't simply say that you will do some prospecting after you have finished your regular sales calls. This normally results in inadequate time being devoted to prospecting. Program your daily activities to devote a certain amount of time, such as one hour every day, to prospecting. Build prospecting into your daily travel plans. Between calls on current customers, call on a potential new customer along your travel route.

### Select Appropriate Prospecting Techniques

Many prospecting techniques were presented earlier in this chapter. Use the techniques that are most appropriate for your offerings and the types of customers that you are trying to reach. Cold canvassing might be appropriate for someone selling a landscaping service, while the use of trade directories might be appropriate for someone selling electrical meters.

### Evaluate Your Results

Over time, evaluate the results of your prospecting activities. Are you achieving your prospecting objectives? If not, there may be something wrong with your prospecting plan. It is possible that you are using the wrong prospecting methods. Some salespeople use prospecting evaluation forms such as the one shown in Figure 7–5. Examining these forms over time can identify which prospecting methods have been most successful. The salesperson can then concentrate exclusively on the successful methods in the future.

## QUESTIONS

1. **What is meant by the "Ferris wheel" of selling? What does this have to do with prospecting?**

**Figure 7-5**

## PROSPECTING EVALUATION FORM

| PROSPECT | REFERRAL | COLD CANVASS | MAIL LEAD | AD INQUIRY | OTHER | SALE |
|---|---|---|---|---|---|---|
| Jack Woods | X | | | | | Yes |
| Linda Carter | X | | | | | No |
| Paul Dermott | | X | | | | Yes |
| Wes Richards | | | X | | | No |
| Laura Dwyer | | | | X | | No |
| Rick Howard | | | | X | | Yes |
| Carrie Bluegrass | | X | | | | No |
| Roy Mulland | | | X | | | No |
| Denise Skirski | X | | | | | Yes |
| Paula Pavan | X | | | | | Yes |
| Cecil Birch | | | | X | | No |
| Doris Gunay | | | | | X | No |

2. Describe any two external sources for prospecting. What type of salesperson would be best suited to each case?
3. Describe the endless chain approach. Do you feel that this is an effective method of prospecting? What are its advantages and disadvantages?
4. Assume that you sell lawn furniture. Who might serve as effective bird dogs or spotters for you?
5. What is the difference between a lead and a qualified prospect?
6 What are the important issues to investigate when qualifying a prospect?
7. What are some of the sources of information that can be used when qualifying prospects?
8. What is the difference between having the ability to pay, the authority to buy, and being eligible to buy?
9. How would you go about establishing a prospecting plan?
10. What prospecting techniques might be most appropriate for someone selling a carpet cleaning service?

## SALES CHALLENGES

1. Assume that you are a sales representative for the National Steel Corporation. You call on manufacturing companies, on

construction firms, and on building contractors. Follow your daily newspaper for one week. Make a list of all items in the newspaper that would be of interest to you in your sales position. Also, go to the closest main library and find one of the trade directories identified in this chapter. From this directory, develop a list of prospects to call on that are within 200 miles of you.

2. You are in the process of interviewing for a sales position with the Mutual of Nebraska Life Insurance Company. As part of the interview procedure, you are asked to develop a list of ten good prospects for life insurance from among your friends and acquaintances. You are also asked to prepare a short report identifying the prospects, listing all information that you have about them, and briefly indicating why you consider each a good prospect.

3. Carlos Palimino has just started a home landscaping and lawn care service. Carlos has gained considerable experience from the five years he worked for another landscaping company. Through this job, Carlos saved enough money to buy a truck and the equipment he needs. Carlos is confident of his abilities and knows that he will be able to retain any customers who give him a chance. The problem is to find customers. In order to break even the first year, Carlos estimates that he needs at least 80 steady customers at an average fee of $45 per month. Recommend ways that would best assure Carlos a list of qualified prospects.

# CASES

## 7-1 Maple Leaf Health Club

Larry Polec has just completed his third year at a major university. He has accepted a summer job with the Maple Leaf Health Club. Larry's job is to sell memberships. The Maple Leaf Health Club offers racquetball and squash courts, indoor and outdoor tennis courts, an exercise room, swimming pool, whirlpool and saunas, locker facilities, small restaurant and lounge, outdoor track, day care facilities, and a pro shop. Membership fees are $165 per year for individuals, $295 for couples, and $450 for family memberships. Larry is hoping to earn enough from the summer job to pay for most of his final year in college. Larry discusses the job with Julie Parascak, the club manager.

**Julie:** Well, I think I've told you as much about the club and its membership as I can. I've given you a supply of membership forms and club brochures. Keep in mind that you'll be paid a straight commission of 15 percent of the memberships you sell. That's $24.75 for singles, $44.25 for couples, and $67.50 for families.

**Larry:** Will I get reimbursed for any expenses I incur?

**Julie:** No. You'll have to cover your expenses out of the commissions that you earn.

**Larry:** How do I find potential members for Maple Leaf?

**Julie:** That's completely up to you. However, it's important that you contact a lot of people. Out of every ten people that you talk to, you'll probably find that eight aren't interested at all in a health club membership, and one is already a member someplace else. That leaves only one out of ten contacts as a possibility.

1. Advise Larry as to the best means for prospecting for club members.
2. On what target markets should Larry concentrate?
3. What might Larry do to prepare himself before going out to prospect?

## 7-2 Home Improvements, Inc.

Edwin Havelock founded Home Improvements, Inc. two years ago. Previously, Edwin had worked in the kitchen department of Naylor Home Centers, a large retail chain, where he picked up considerable experience in kitchen remodeling. Edwin has also taken several night classes where he learned to plan and sketch new kitchen arrangements.

A specialty of Home Improvements, Inc. is remodeling kitchens. During its first year, the company was entirely a sales organization. The actual remodeling work was contracted to outside builders. As business grew, Edwin was able to hire five people to do the remodeling work. One of the five, Tom Mahoney, serves as the supervisor for the group. Tom sees that all jobs are completed as per the contract specifications, puts the finishing touches on jobs that have been held up by materials shortages, and handles any complaints on materials and workmanship.

After two years in business, Edwin Havelock finds that he is operating a relatively successful company. Although the majority of the work has been remodeling kitchens, the company has recently done some attic, basement, and bathroom remodeling. The company has also received some inquiries about room and porch additions as well as building garages.

In considering future growth opportunities, Edwin feels that his company should become a complete home improvement and modernization company. During the past two years, Edwin has been the company's only salesperson. Just last week, Edwin hired a new salesperson, Evelyn McLean. Edwin has also expanded the duties of his secretary, Carey Stratton, who has now become the company's office manager. In this capacity, Carey will be responsible for all paperwork, which includes paying bills, and customer collections. This will free more of Edwin's time for selling.

One of the major problems in selling is finding qualified prospects. Advertisements in the newspapers bring some inquiries. Referrals from satisfied customers contribute some leads. Cold canvassing is also used. Edwin feels, however, that he and Evelyn could be more effective if they had a better system for finding qualified prospects.

1. What do you feel would be the best means of prospecting for Home Improvements, Inc.?
2. Outline a complete prospecting plan for Edwin and his newly hired salesperson, Evelyn McLean.

# 8

# PREPARING FOR THE SALES PRESENTATION

"Good morning, Professor Ganeshan," said Norma Faus, a sales representative for a publishing company, as she entered the professor's office. "May I take ten minutes of your time to talk to you about some of our books? I'd especially like to tell you about two of our new books on advertising and marketing research." "I'm sorry," replied Professor Ganeshan, "but I have a class in five minutes. Furthermore, I don't teach advertising or marketing research and have no use for books on those topics."

This encounter is a typical one for salespeople who do not prepare for their sales calls. The situation would not have occurred if Norma had taken a little time to check Professor Ganeshan's teaching schedule, office hours, and courses. Just as an experienced pilot would never attempt a take-off without first going through a long checklist to be sure that the plane is safe to fly, neither should a salesperson attempt a sales call without preparation.

## THE PREAPPROACH

Once a qualified sales prospect has been identified, many salespeople have a tendency to rush right in to start selling. But before you do, stop for a moment and ask yourself whether you are fully prepared. If you're not, you're liable to make the same mistakes that Norma did.

The advance preparation that a good salesperson undertakes is generally referred to as the preapproach. The term preapproach is used to emphasize the fact that this process covers all activities that you will undertake before approaching or calling on your prospects. The preapproach is complete when you are confident that you are fully prepared for the sales presentation. This chapter takes you through the second step toward sales success, the preapproach, shown in Figure 8-1.

**Figure 8-1**

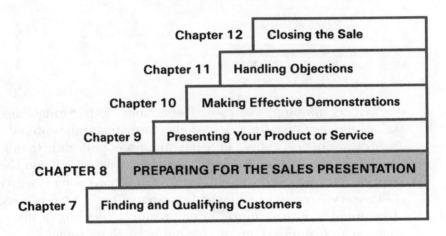

THE STAIRWAY TO SALES SUCCESS

Chapter 12 | Closing the Sale
Chapter 11 | Handling Objections
Chapter 10 | Making Effective Demonstrations
Chapter 9 | Presenting Your Product or Service
CHAPTER 8 | PREPARING FOR THE SALES PRESENTATION
Chapter 7 | Finding and Qualifying Customers

Preparing for the sales presentation involves the following activities:

1. Review of prospect information
2. Review of product or service information
3. Making the appointment
4. Planning the sales presentation
5. Checking appearance, attitude, and equipment

Each of these issues is discussed in the following sections.

## REVIEW OF PROSPECT INFORMATION

With the exception of special situations, such as door-to-door selling, you should possess some information about the prospect you are planning to contact. The facts of a personal and business nature that salespeople should gather about their customers are described in Chapter 3. The information that should be gathered to identify and qualify prospects is discussed in Chapter 7. An example of a prospect preliminary information form is presented in Figure 7–4.

All information collected on a prospect should be reviewed before making a sales call. This will serve as a reminder to you about capitalizing on the customer's interests as well as spotting topics that might best be avoided. For example, Figure 8–2 represents a page from a salesperson's notebook on Alex Essensa, a buyer for a retail organization.

A review of information such as that in Figure 8–2 reminds the salesperson that the customer often enjoys a little small talk at the start of the sales call, suggests topics for the small talk (MSU sports or son's tennis, for example), indicates that an updated catalogue and price list were left during a recent call, and that an order for $3,500 was received during the last call. As further information is gathered this should be added to the customer's file. Make sure that all information is recorded; don't trust your memory.

Depending on the nature of what is being sold, a customer file might contain personal information, industry information, and company information.

## Personal Information

The personal information to maintain in your customer files should include the customer's full name, age, education, occupation, family status, interests, hobbies, memberships, personal peculiarities, and anything else that might be of use during your sales calls. In some selling situations, such as life insurance, only facts of a personal nature should be collected. Personal information sources are identified in Chapters 3 and 7.

## Industry Information

If your customer is a business buyer, you will need industry and company information in addition to personal information. With regard to industry information, you should have some insight into the history of the industry, its current status and economic environment, the major competitors in the industry, the relationship between this industry and other industries, and any current problems facing the industry and its member firms.

Sources of industry information include trade journals, trade advertising, reference books, business directories, trade associations, and government publications. Another good source of industry information is to talk to people in the industry.

**Figure 8-2**

## PAGE FROM SALESPERSON'S CUSTOMER FILES

Essensa, Alexander — *Baumgarten Stores, has been buyer with company for eight years*

Politics: *Republican but somewhat liberal*

Hobbies: *Golf and boating, likes to talk hockey and football but not baseball*

Family: *Married for about 18 years, wife's name is Pat, has three children, oldest son is extremely good junior golfer, has won some tournaments, takes pride in talking about son's achievements*

Interests: *Rotary Club and Junior Achievement*

---

Education: *Graduated in marketing from Michigan State University in 1961, follows MSU sports closely, wife also graduated from MSU*

Reminder: *Enjoys about five minutes of small talk but then likes to get to business*

Recent Contacts:

    *Feb. 22 — Showed some new offerings, no sale*

    *March 28 — Left new catalogue and price list*

    *May 5 — Received fill-in order for $3,500, was told to call again in six weeks*

## Company Information

The company information that you should have on your customer might include the nature of the customer's business, its size, credit rating, company organization and policies, buying practices, purchasing authority, and past relationships with your company. Sources for this type of company information are described in detail in Chapters 3 and 7. All information of a personal, industry, and company nature should be recorded and kept as part of your customer files.

# REVIEW OF PRODUCT OR SERVICE INFORMATION

A review of information on your prospect should provide insight into the prospect's needs. To meet these needs, the salesperson can review appropriate product or service information. Customers depend on salespeople for information. A thorough knowledge of what you are selling, which allows you to communicate the benefits of your offerings to your customers, is essential for sales success.

The product knowledge you should possess includes: (1) how it is produced, (2) the materials used, (3) key performance characteristics, (4) how it is promoted, (5) the after-sale support and services, and (6) the advantages over the competition. For highly technical products, it is often difficult to remember the performance and operating characteristics of all the items you might be selling. Your sales presentation will suffer and your customer will lose confidence in you if you have to look through company literature to find answers to questions your prospect asks. You should have as much information as possible at your fingertips. To ensure this, you must review product and service information before all sales calls.

> **Tip** *Judy Thornbird is a sales trainee for Newport Equipment. As part of her sales training, Judy is accompanying Kate Goodbar on her calls. Kate is an experienced sales representative for the company. Judy and Kate have just left the office of Lewis Stoneman, a purchasing agent for Likert Electric, where a large sale has been completed.*
>
> *"I guess it comes with experience," Judy exclaims, "but I can't get over how well you were able to phrase all of our product features in terms of significant customer benefits for Mr. Stoneman." "Experience helps, of course," replies Kate, "but it's more a case of doing my*

**Illustration 8-1** Review information about your product before a demonstration.

homework last night." "What do you mean?" asks Judy. "Well, last night I reviewed my files on Lewis Stoneman and Likert Electric," explains Kate. "That gave me some idea of what their needs were. Then I reviewed our product literature making note of how our offerings would benefit Likert Electric. I planned my sales presentation around these benefits. Reviewing prospect and product information before calling on my accounts saves everyone's time, shows the prospect that I know what I'm talking about, and helps me to close many sales."

## MAKING THE APPOINTMENT

It is normally much better to make an appointment for a sales presentation than to attempt to call on a prospect without an appointment. Having an appointment will save time and money. Without an appointment you may find yourself spending considerable time sitting in waiting rooms because your prospect is busy or driving across town only to find that the person you want to see isn't in.

When an appointment is made, your prospect knows that you are coming. People are usually more receptive when they are expecting you than when you "pop in" unexpectedly. In addition, when you have made an appointment, the prospect has set aside a block of time for you. This should result in a less hurried presentation and fewer interruptions. Finally, having a formal appointment adds prestige to your sales call.

## Telephoning for Appointments

The most widely used method for making appointments is by telephone. Telephone contacts are generally fast and inexpensive. Many appointments can be arranged quickly by telephoning. The telephone contact to make an appointment should be brief; you are making an appointment, not trying to close a sale. The points to be covered over the phone should include:

1. Introduce yourself and your company
2. Identify the purpose of your call
3. Present a brief message to attract the prospect's interest
4. Ask for and arrange a specific appointment date and time

The key to landing an appointment is to capture the prospect's interest. Here are some examples of telephone introductions that might be used:

### Benefit Introduction

Mr. Elsmore, this is Georgina Cartwright of Cleartone Communications calling from Bloomington, Indiana. Businesspeople such as yourself are saving thousands of dollars on long distance calls through our service. May I explain how your company can start saving immediately on its phone bills? Would next Monday at nine o'clock in the morning or one in the afternoon be better for you?

### Problem-Solving Introduction

Ms. Berlasty, this is Larry Borkowski of Rapid Machine Services calling. Companies manufacturing widgets on continuous process equipment such as yours suffer great losses with machine down-time. Our company offers fast service and repairs to equipment such as yours on a very reasonable

*Photo by Shirley Zeiberg*

**Illustration 8-2  Schedule appointments in a manner appropriate to the sales situation.**

annual fee basis. May I call to explain details of our program on Tuesday at either ten o'clock in the morning or two in the afternoon?

### Congratulations Introduction

Good afternoon, Dr. Eremick. This is Felix Bauer of Universal Life Insurance. I want to congratulate you on the new arrival to your household announced in the paper last week. As your family grows, I'm sure you'll want to review your insurance needs. Would there be a time tomorrow night, say about seven or eight o'clock, that I could meet with you and your husband?

Each of these introductions covers the necessary points for arranging an appointment yet remains brief. There are many other telephone introductions that you can develop that would be suitable to your sales situation.

## Arranging Appointments by Mail

A letter can also be used to arrange an appointment. Like a telephone contact, a letter should identify you and your company, capture the interest of the prospect, and be brief. A lengthy letter is less likely to be read.

A letter request for an appointment may take a number of different formats. The letter may request an appointment time and include a reply card for the prospect to name a suitable time. The letter may indicate that you will call on the prospect at a particular time unless the prospect telephones to indicate that the time isn't appropriate. Another form that the letter may take is to simply state that you will be calling on the prospect in the near future. Finally, the letter may indicate that you will be telephoning in several days to arrange a specific appointment time. In all cases, the letter should be neatly typed on quality stationery. Figure 8–3 illustrates what a typical letter request for an appointment should look like.

## Other Methods for Making Appointments

Although telephone and mail are the most common methods for making appointments, you are only limited by your imagination as to other methods that might be used. Some salespeople use telegrams or cablegrams. These are always attention getters and will normally be read more closely than a typical letter.

Another method that can be used to gain an appointment is through a third party. Salespeople will often ask mutual friends, business associates, acquaintances, or others to telephone or write on their behalf. It's unlikely that a buyer will refuse a request for an appointment when made by a friend.

Finally, appointments can be made through personal contacts. With this method, the salesperson makes an unannounced call on the prospect with the hope of seeing the prospect at that time or making an appointment for a sales presentation at a future date.

**Tip** *Heather Nelligan is a salesperson for Motor City Auto Sales. Heather has devised an interesting way of seeking appointments from prospects that has resulted in increased car sales. In the evenings, Heather walks through the parking lots of shopping centers. On every car more than three years old, she places her card under the wind-*

**Figure 8-3**

## TYPICAL LETTER REQUEST FOR APPOINTMENT

## DRIFAST PAINT COMPANY

9099 Rexdale Road • Clearly, Pennsylvania 13521 • (416)256-2934

September 23, 1986

Mr. Harry Gables
Household Hardware
9336 Winchester
Barley, Ohio 36942

Dear Mr. Gables:

You are losing up to $1.00 on every gallon of paint you are currently selling!

I will be in Barley next week and will be calling at your store on Thursday morning to inform you of our amazing paint offer.

If Thursday morning is not convenient, please call me collect at the above number to arrange a different appointment time.

Sincerely,

*Frances Evans*

(Mrs.) Frances Evans

---

*shield wiper. The card provides Heather's name and telephone number and asks the car owner to make an appointment for a test drive in a new car. Heather also includes an estimate of the older car's trade-in value on her card.*

## Meeting the Receptionist

When you enter a business office without an appointment, you will meet someone in the outer office who will ask, "May I help you?" This person, the receptionist, is very important and can lock or unlock the door to your prospect. When you greet the receptionist, identify who you are and the firm you represent. Hand the receptionist your business card and, if asked, state the nature of your business. Treat the receptionist graciously and with the consideration that this person deserves.

**Illustration 8-3   When meeting the receptionist, identify who you are and the firm you represent.**

Identify by name the person you wish to see. Sometimes, when calling on large firms with many buyers, you may not know the name of the person you should see. In these situations, tell the receptionist what you are selling so that the receptionist can direct you to the correct person. When meeting with the receptionist, act confident. Let the receptionist know that you have something worthwhile to sell and that it would be a mistake if you were unable to complete the office call.

Often when making unannounced calls of this nature, you may not be able to see your prospect immediately. Do not waste a lot of valuable time waiting. Determine from the receptionist how long you will have to wait. If it's going to be a long time, it may be better to arrange a different appointment. If it is a short wait, capitalize on it by planning your sales presentation or reviewing product literature. In some cases, there may be material about the prospect's firm that you can read in the waiting room.

## PLANNING THE SALES PRESENTATION

Once you have reviewed information on your prospect, reviewed material on your product or service, and made an appointment, it is then necessary to develop a basic sales presentation. Do not walk into your prospect's office or home without having planned what you are going to say. As one experienced salesperson put it, "I would no sooner meet a customer without having planned what I want to say than I would plan a trip without looking at a map."

Planning your sales presentation builds your confidence because you know what you are going to say; saves your time as well as your customer's; exhibits the professionalism that you bring to your job; and serves to increase your sales. A thoroughly prepared plan will give direction to your presentation. Furthermore, a prepared presentation is more likely to flow in a logical and consistent fashion.

Planning the sales presentation involves establishing an objective to be accomplished during the sales call, determining the opening statement to be used, identifying the major customer benefits and product or service features to be stressed, anticipating objections that might be raised by the prospect, and identifying a likely closing technique to be used. All of these issues are discussed in the next four chapters. Many salespeople use a sales-call planner to help plan their presentations. An example of such a planner is shown in Figure 8–4.

## CHECKING APPEARANCE, ATTITUDE, AND EQUIPMENT

When you are confident that you have planned your sales presentation adequately and an appointment time has been

**Figure 8-4**

## SAMPLE SALES-CALL PLANNER

PROSPECT NAME: _____

COMPANY NAME: _____

TYPE OF BUSINESS: _____

PREFERRED APPOINTMENT TIMES: _____

_____

RECEPTIONIST'S NAME: _____

CUSTOMER LIKES/DISLIKES: _____

_____

CASUAL CONVERSATION TOPICS: _____

_____

SALES-CALL OBJECTIVE: _____

_____

CUSTOMER'S PRINCIPAL NEEDS: _____

_____

PRESENTATION OUTLINE:
  OPENING REMARKS: _____

_____

  FEATURES/BENEFITS TO STRESS: _____

_____

  DEMONSTRATION: _____

  POSSIBLE OBJECTION: _____

_____

  LIKELY CLOSING TECHNIQUE: _____

_____

OTHER POINTS TO REMEMBER: _____

_____

POST-CALL NOTES:
  REASON BOUGHT/DIDN'T BUY: _____

_____

FOLLOW-UP REQUIRED: _____

NEXT CALL: _____

arranged, your final preparation before the sales call is to check your appearance, attitude, and equipment.

## Appearance

First impressions are very important. As a salesperson, you want to make a good first impression. Keep in mind, the first thing your customer will see is your outward appearance. Your physical appearance, including dress and grooming, has a lot to do with the first impression you make. Keeping yourself physically fit is a constant job. Get sufficient rest and appear to be relaxed. Walk with a firm step, and maintain a pleasant smile and composed appearance.

Appropriateness is the key to the way you should dress. Your clothing should be suitable for the sales situation and the customer upon whom you are calling. If in doubt, dress conservatively. Grooming is also important. No buyer is interested in a salesperson who is careless and sloppy. Furthermore, a good personal appearance will make you feel better about yourself.

## Attitude

Not only should you look sharp, but you should be mentally sharp as well. It is important to approach the sales call with a winning attitude. You should approach the sales presentation with the knowledge that you are going to close this sale. Athletes call this getting up for the game. The better prepared you are for the sales call, the more confidence you will take with you into the prospect's home or office.

Be relaxed, yet alert. Sense the atmosphere and be ready to adapt to the situation. Too often, a salesperson enters a buyer's office with an apologetic air, with a feeling that he/she is intruding on the prospect's time. Do not feel this way. You are selling a worthwhile product or service to a person who can benefit from its use. Furthermore, the person you are calling on has granted you an appointment. This indicates that the prospect is interested in what you have to offer. It is now up to you to show the prospect how the product(s) you are selling will satisfy the prospect's needs.

## Equipment

Many salespeople carry an equipment case, a model for demonstration purposes, samples, or other materials to present to the buyer. Make sure that your equipment is complete and fresh looking. Worn equipment will not make a very good impression on the buyer. As well, it would be rather embarrassing to tell the buyer that you have some samples or product literature to leave only to find that you hadn't packed this material.

It is also important to check that your equipment works before leaving for a sales call. Consider the impression a buyer would have of your product if, during a demonstration, it failed. Be prepared for unexpected occurrences. For example, if your presentation includes the use of a film or slide projector, always carry an extra bulb in case one burns out.

*United Telecom*

**Illustration 8-4  It is important that equipment performs well during the sales presentation.**

## PREAPPROACH TIME AND EFFORT

Successful salespeople recognize the importance of planning their sales presentations. They know that closing the sale is the reward that comes from careful preparation. But just how much advance preparation should be undertaken?

It is claimed that college students should spend two hours in out-of-class preparation for every hour spent in class. If this criterion were applied to the sales situation, a salesperson should spend two hours in preparation for each hour spent with a client.

Given that a salesperson has time available for preparation in the early morning, evening, and between sales calls, the two-to-one ratio may be a reasonable one to follow.

Of course, the actual amount of time and effort devoted to preapproach activity depends on the selling situation. The more complex the selling situation and the larger the dollar volume involved, the more preparation time is needed. Simple selling situations will require much less preparation. This does not mean, however, that *no* advance preparation is needed.

The amount of preapproach activity also depends on whether this is your first call on a prospect or whether it is a customer that you call on regularly. If it is a first call, the preapproach time may be lengthier since you should spend some time gathering information of a personal and business nature on the prospect. For repeat calls, the preapproach time will be shorter; it may only require refreshing your memory by reviewing your customer files.

## FINAL THOUGHTS

It is normal that salespeople experience a little tension as they approach a sales presentation. However, if you have done a good job of qualifying the prospect and planning your presentation, there is nothing to fear. If the prospect is truly qualified, a need exists for what you have to sell. If you are prepared for the sales presentation, you know what you want to say. At this point it is simply a matter of getting in to see the prospect and making your presentation.

You can have a lot of fun in selling by constantly looking for new and creative ways to approach your prospects. People like to have their interest aroused and will respond to your originality.

*Tip* *Ramon Bradour has developed a unique method of arranging appointments that has resulted in his becoming a most welcomed guest by his customers. Ramon is a mystery lover. He is constantly on the lookout in newspapers, magazines, books, and any other sources for very short (a page or two) mysteries. Ramon collects these short mysteries and includes a little whodunit in his appointment letters to his customers. The appointments Ramon arranges are usually about a week after the appointment letter arrives. This gives the customer an opportunity to attempt to solve the mystery. When Ramon arrives for his sales presentation, the customers can then check to see if their solutions are correct. Ramon has found that his customers often anxiously look forward to his arrival.*

## QUESTIONS

1. What is meant by the preapproach? What activities are part of the preapproach?
2. What types of prospect information should be reviewed in advance of the sales presentation?
3. What are some information sources you might use to gather data about your prospect firm's industry?
4. What types of product or service information should you be thoroughly familiar with before attempting a sales call?
5. What are the various techniques that a salesperson might use to arrange appointments? Which of these techniques do you feel is best? Why?
6. Why are sales appointments necessary? Under what conditions might a salesperson not arrange an appointment in advance?
7. In what ways can a prospect's secretary or receptionist help or hinder salespeople?
8. What is meant by a sales-call planner? What information would be contained in a sales-call planner?
9. What does the final preparation before the sales call include?
10. How much time and effort should be devoted to the pre-approach? Are there any "rules-of-thumb" that can be followed?

## SALES CHALLENGES

1. You are a salesperson handling a line of modern, stylish men's sportswear. You have just heard that ownership of a large volume men's shop in a nearby city has changed. In the past, you have not been able to sell your line to the previous owners. Write a letter to the new owners requesting an appointment within the next two weeks to show your line.

2. You have driven 50 miles and have arrived ten minutes early for your appointment with Mr. Costello. This is to be your first meeting with Mr. Costello after several attempts to make an appointment. As you introduce yourself to Mr. Costello's secretary, she informs you that her boss has been unexpectedly detained at a management meeting and will not be available for about 45 minutes.

   You have an appointment with another customer in an hour and a half for which you are not fully prepared. It will take you 30 minutes to drive to your next appointment. There are some magazines, newspapers, company catalogues, and employee bulletins in the waiting room. What should you do?

3. You are calling on Fran Berilko of Terlago Steel Products for the first time. You know very little about Fran Berilko or Terlago Steel. As such, you have arrived 45 minutes early to see what sort of information you can gather before meeting Ms. Berilko. There is a salesperson for a noncompeting company in the waiting room to see Ms. Berilko before you. You want to make the best use of your 45 minutes. How would you approach Ms. Berilko's secretary? What types of questions would you ask of this person? What types of literature might you ask to see? Would you ask anything of the other salesperson?

# CASES

### 8-1 Cooper Business Group

Leona Gorbachev is a representative for the Cooper Business Group. The Cooper Business Group offers a wide variety of business insurance programs. The Cooper Group specializes in offering business insurance to small and medium-sized companies. Although the Cooper Group offers excellent programs at very competitive rates, Leona has often found it very difficult to get appointments. For a variety of reasons, people don't like to discuss insurance. As soon as prospects learn that Leona represents an insurance company, they have a tendency to make excuses as to why they can't meet with her.

Leona, however, knows that her company can develop an insurance program for most small to medium-sized businesses that is better than their current insurance packages. The difficulty is getting the appointment to describe the Cooper programs. Leona has found from past experience that the less information that she divulges when asking for the appointment, the more likely it is that the appointment will be granted. Leona generally likes to set up appointments by telephone. One appointment request used is:

Good morning/afternoon, Mr./Ms. _____ , my name is Leona Gorbachev. I represent the Cooper Business Group. I'm phoning because I would like to meet with you to discuss a service that the Cooper Business Group can provide that will save money for your company. I would like to meet with you personally to tell you more about our service. How is Tuesday morning at 10:30 or Wednesday afternoon at 2:30?

In some cases Leona will secure an appointment based on the above request, but in most cases an objection of one sort or another will be raised. The most common objections are as follows:

"What sort of service are you offering? Tell me more about it."

Why don't you send me some literature describing your service?"

"Cooper? You're with an insurance company aren't you? I don't need insurance."

"I'm very busy. Why don't you tell me briefly about your service now and I'll let you know if it's worthwhile to set up a meeting?"

"Is this about insurance? We don't need any additional insurance."

"Send me a letter describing your service and I'll get back to you."

1.  Put yourself in Leona's position. Provide a response to each of the common objections Leona receives.
2.  What is your opinion of Leona's telephone approach? Can it be improved? Write an alternative telephone appointment request that Leona can use. Keep in mind Leona's objectives and the pointers provided in this chapter.
3.  Write a sample letter that Leona can use should she decide to use mail appointment requests rather than telephone.
4.  This case situation can also serve as a good role-playing exercise. Have someone take the role of Leona and several other people take the parts of prospects raising common objections to Leona's appointment requests.

## 8-2  Sutts Equipment Company

Ron Savitt sells a wide range of equipment and machinery to firms in the metal processing industry. He works out of

Kalamazoo, Michigan and is responsible for the entire southern Michigan market. While reading the *Kalamazoo Daily Chronicle*, an article in the business section catches Ron's attention. The article reads in part:

> Gloria Hollander, president of Hollander Metal Fabricating, Inc., has announced the future opening of two new plant sites. One of the new plants, to employ 50 workers initially, will be located in Kalamazoo.

Ron is excited by the news. He is somewhat familiar with the Hollander company. Its headquarters are in Camden, New Jersey and the company has operations in Ohio, Pennsylvania, and West Virginia.

Ron immediately begins to jot down a few notes for himself. Among the things he wants to do immediately are:

- Check with his boss to see if anyone in the company has had previous contacts with Hollander.
- Check with several business directories to gather as much background information on the Hollander company as possible.
- Request a Dun & Bradstreet report on Hollander.
- Check with suppliers to the Sutts Equipment Company to see if they have had any contacts with the Hollander company.

By early the next week, Ron has pulled together a good deal of preliminary information on the Hollander company. To date, Ron hasn't been able to gather any personal information on Gloria Hollander or any of the executives of Hollander Metal Fabricating. Among the information Ron does have is the following:

Mailing address: Ms. Gloria A. Hollander, President
Hollander Metal Fabricating, Inc.
9780 Esplanade Drive
Camden, New Jersey 07623

Vice-President: J. P. Ducharme

Company founded: 1947

Dun & Bradstreet credit rating: Excellent

Number of plants: Four

Yearly sales: $9,346,292

Ron does not know who is responsible for equipment purchases at Hollander. Some of the strong selling points of the Sutts Company that Ron feels he can stress are:

- In business for more than 40 years
- Recognized in the industry for fast and reliable service
- Always offers a high degree of personal service

1. Has Ron's background preparation been adequate?
2. What additional information does Ron need? How can Ron get this information?
3. How should Ron approach the Hollander company for an appointment?
4. Compose a letter and telephone appointment request for Ron.

# 9

# PRESENTING YOUR PRODUCT OR SERVICE

The previous two chapters described the process of finding and qualifying customers and the preparation that is necessary before calling on a customer. If you have done a good job of prospecting, have gathered relevant background information, and have arranged an appointment, you are now ready for the heart of the selling process, the sales presentation. This chapter describes the next step in the stairway to sales success as shown in Figure 9-1, presenting your product or service to potential buyers.

## TYPES OF SALES PRESENTATIONS

The sales presentation involves a vocal and visual explanation of your product or service offering. Sales presentations may range from highly structured to highly flexible.

### Memorized Presentation

This is also referred to as the "canned" presentation. The memorized presentation is carefully planned and covers all key selling points arranged in a logical presentation order. The salesperson memorizes the presentation and then recites it during each sales call. This form of presentation is used extensively in many routine selling situations such as door-to-door selling.

The memorized presentation is usually developed using the best techniques of a company's most successful salespeople. It is generally better than a presentation developed by just one salesperson. This method ensures that key selling points are covered;

**Figure 9-1**

## THE STAIRWAY TO SALES SUCCESS

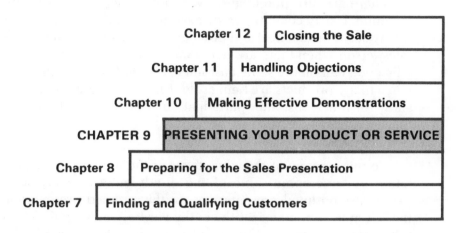

| Chapter 12 | Closing the Sale |
| Chapter 11 | Handling Objections |
| Chapter 10 | Making Effective Demonstrations |
| CHAPTER 9 | PRESENTING YOUR PRODUCT OR SERVICE |
| Chapter 8 | Preparing for the Sales Presentation |
| Chapter 7 | Finding and Qualifying Customers |

*Vince Streano ©1985; STREANO/HAVENS*

**Illustration 9-1** The salesperson should determine the best presentation technique for a given sales situation.

it provides confidence for inexperienced salespeople; and it eliminates repetition of information.

There are also potential drawbacks to the memorized presentation. It may cover topics that are not of interest to the buyer. It may seem mechanical and insincere. It may be difficult for the salesperson when there are many interruptions. It can't be used when you call on the same customers regularly. It is impractical when many products are being sold. Finally, it generally doesn't allow for much customer participation in the presentation.

## Outlined Presentation

To retain many of the advantages of the memorized presentation but overcome some of the disadvantages, many salespeople use outlined presentations. In the outlined presentation, the salesperson memorizes the outline or key selling points. The actual words used are then filled in around the outline or key selling points.

The use of an outlined presentation adds flexibility yet ensures that key selling points are covered in a logical sequence. This allows the salesperson to adapt the presentation somewhat for each customer. However, key points may be overlooked, and it is easier for the salesperson to get sidetracked. Also, the presentation may not be prepared as well as a memorized presentation.

## Need Identification Presentation

This is one of the most challenging and creative forms of presentation. It is highly flexible and is designed to be an "interactive" form of presentation. That is, the salesperson attempts to get the customer actively involved so that the salesperson can adequately identify the customer's needs. Questions such as "What activities do you want computerized?" or "What do you want to accomplish from your investment program?" might be used to open this kind of presentation.

The answers that the customer provides to your opening probes can then serve as the basis for identifying the customer's needs and, hence, the direction that the presentation should take. In fact, an outlined presentation may be used once the customer's needs have been identified. In other cases, a need identification approach might be used for your first meeting with a customer, to be followed by a prepared presentation during your second meeting. This is often the case in industrial selling situations or when highly complex or sophisticated products and services are being sold.

## Need Analysis Presentation

Similar to the need identification presentation, but more detailed, is the need analysis presentation. This is also referred to as the programmed or survey presentation. This approach is generally used when it is necessary to develop detailed insight into a customer's current situation and potential needs before an adequate sales presentation can be developed.

The need analysis presentation is generally used in situations where the sale involves a considerable amount of money and/or a commitment for a considerable amount of time. This approach involves getting the customer's permission to conduct a detailed needs analysis and then developing a presentation around the customer's needs. For example, a computer salesperson may spend many hours studying a business firm's operations and information processing needs. Based on the results of this analysis, the salesperson can then develop a detailed presentation geared to the needs of the particular customer. In some cases, technical experts might be brought in to handle particular parts of the presentation. Although this form of sales presentation may be very time-consuming and costly, it can also be highly personalized and effective.

## Audiovisual Presentation

This integrates audiovisual equipment such as videotape recorders, slide projectors, and overhead projectors into the presentation. The audiovisual equipment is used to illustrate issues the salesperson is talking about and to highlight key selling points. The advantages are in holding the customer's interest, economizing on the use of time, and providing a ready outline for the salesperson to follow.

## Which Is Best?

Each of the presentation methods described will work. You must match the proper type of presentation to the selling situation you are facing. For example, the memorized presentation might be best when little time is available; the outlined presentation might be good for customers you call on regularly; and the need identification presentation is most useful when calling on a

**Illustration 9-2** **Presentations to a large group may require special visual aids.**

*AETNA LIFE & CASUALTY*

customer for the first time. Selecting the appropriate presentation method is part of the preparation process described in the previous chapter.

## GETTING STARTED

You have reviewed background material, prepared your presentation, checked your appearance and equipment, made an appointment, and you hear the receptionist say, "Mrs. Rorseth will see you." It is now time to meet your customer face-to-face. In the next few minutes you want to make a good first impression, capture your customer's attention, and interest your prospect in what you have to sell.

The selling process begins as soon as you meet your prospect. Normally, the first few minutes are devoted to the initial social contact. You will greet the prospect and introduce yourself. Your objective during the social contact is to establish a friendly atmosphere. Your first few words might be a standard opening such as, "Good morning, Mrs. Rorseth. My name is Maria Santos. I represent the Kwick Flash Copying Company."

Do you use a handshake? It depends. Some buyers are always ready for a friendly handshake. Others prefer not to, or prefer shaking hands at the end of the meeting. It might be preferable to wait a moment to see if your prospect offers a hand.

Should you offer a business card? Most salespeople have business cards identifying themselves and their companies. The business card serves as a reminder for your customers in case they want to contact you at some future date. Many salespeople offer their cards at the start of a sales presentation when they are introducing themselves, others prefer waiting until the end of the presentation when they are getting ready to leave.

As you are introducing yourself, size up the situation. Try to formulate a general impression of the customer and the customer's office. Perhaps there is something in the office that will suggest a conversation topic to "break-the-ice." This might be a plaque, picture, sports trophy, or book suggesting a topic of interest to the customer. On the other hand, if the customer appears busy or wants to get down to business immediately, don't waste time with social conversation.

## THE APPROACH

Once initial introductions have been made and pleasantries exchanged, it is time to get down to business. The opening of a sales presentation is generally referred to as the approach. The objective of the approach is to capture the buyer's attention and interest. There are many different approaches that might be used. Here are some examples of common approaches.

| Approach | Example/Description |
|---|---|
| 1. Product | Many interesting or eye-catching products can sell themselves. This approach involves handing the item to the prospect with a comment such as, "Have you ever seen anything like this before?" |
| 2. Compliment | "Congratulations Fran! I read that you were elected president of the National Buyers' Association." This approach would generally be used with a customer that you call on regularly. |
| 3. Benefit | "Mr. Stewart, I'd like to show you how I can help reduce your company's long distance telephone bills by 20 percent." Keep in mind that the benefit offered must be real and must be of interest to your customer. |

| | |
|---|---|
| **4.** Factual | This approach presents factual information that would be of interest to the customer. "Did you know, Mr. Petri, that five of your competitors have reduced their sales force's travel expenses by more than ten percent through our fleet leasing system?" |
| **5.** Curiosity | One successful salesperson opened his presentation by asking, "Ms. Loblaw, how would you like to open a branch office that requires no investment or time on your behalf and will earn $100 a week for you?" After arousing the customer's curiosity, the salesperson explained how his company would install vending machines in the customer's plant area and share the proceeds. |
| **6.** Idea | "I've looked at your machine shop area, Mr. Crimmons, and I have an idea that will reduce your scrap loss." |
| **7.** Showmanship | A salesperson selling advertising space in a major magazine used to walk into prospects' offices and dump bags containing more than $3.5 million in play money on their desks with the statement, "That's how much our readers pay to subscribe to our magazine. Don't you think that if they're paying that much for the magazine, they're going to see what's inside it?" |
| **8.** Question | "Dr. Kentner, you've seen the laboratory results on the testing of this new drug. What do you think of the findings?" The question approach is used to get the prospect involved in the presentation. |
| **9.** Referral | "I was recently speaking with Stan Dueberry at Timmons Products and he suggested that you might be interested in what I have to offer." |
| **10.** Free Service | "Ms. Donaldson, I understand that you have to pick up replacement parts when you need them. How would you like to have the parts delivered to your front door?" |
| **11.** Dramatic | This involves the use of an eye-catching |

action. For example, a salesperson selling unbreakable dinnerware would let the products fall on the floor.

**12. Premium**    You hand your customers a free gift. "Mr. Emerson, I represent the Acme Marker Company. Here are some samples of our markers that you may use to experience for yourself the high quality and long life of our products."

**13. Name**    The use of well-known names may impress a customer. "Ms. Ashe, did you know that our copier is the only one used by NASA?"

**14. Surprise**    Say something the customer wouldn't expect. "Ms. Solomon, I'm here to sell you a word processing system that costs three times as much as any typewriter you've ever purchased!" Emphasizing high price will surprise the customer into attention. At this point, the salesperson can explain how the high initial cost is more than recovered in low operating expenses and fast performance.

**15. News**    Use recent news stories. "What have you read about the fire at Holbrook's Supermarket, Mr. Klein? Although their insurance will cover the fire damage, Holbrook's didn't have business interruption insurance to cover their loss of earnings while the store is closed."

**16. Shock**    This is often used in insurance sales. "Did you know, Mr. and Mrs. Koppel, that the heads of eight out of ten households under the age of 40 do not have enough insurance to allow the family to keep their home if the head of that household should die suddenly?"

**17. Opinion**    "Ms. Caulifretti, what is your opinion of Data Fast Business Computers?" This approach serves to get some initial reaction from the customer as well as getting the customer involved in the presentation.

All of these approaches will work. Your objective is to find an approach that you feel comfortable with and that works for you. The approach you use should, of course, be altered to suit different situations and different customers.

## THE PRESENTATION

If everything has gone well, your approach has captured the *attention* of your prospect. Now that you have their attention, you can move into your presentation. Your presentation should ignite an *interest* in your prospect, create a *desire* for what you have to offer, and ultimately move your prospect to take *action*.

A complete presentation will (1) thoroughly describe what you have to offer, (2) show how your offering will be of benefit to your customer, (3) cover all details essential to completing a transaction, and (4) close the sale.

### Presenting Yourself

Often as important as what you say is how you go about presenting your offering. The following guidelines should be followed.

|  | **Correct Action** |
| --- | --- |
| Eye contact | Look directly at your customer |
| Facial expression | Friendly and relaxed |
| Posture | Sit or stand erect, directly facing your customer |
| Distance | Stay three to four feet from your customer |
| Voice | Speak distinctly, changing pitch for emphasis |
| Gestures | Emphasize important points |

## Ask Questions

Plan for two-way conversation. Get your prospects involved in the presentation. To do this you must ask questions. When they are talking, the prospects reveal facts and ideas. Their needs can be discovered. This helps you to see what interests your prospects.

By getting your customers to talk, you also force them to think. They may identify for themselves a problem or need they hadn't previously recognized. In addition, you make the customers feel important. You show that you are interested in them.

Do not ask questions that can be answered with a simple "yes" or "no." Ask questions that challenge your customers to think. Ask questions about specific problems or needs. Ask questions directed toward specific buying motives.

## Build Confidence

It is important that your customers have confidence in you. When they are buying insurance, real estate, machinery, building supplies, or any other product or service, customers want to know that they can rely on the advice presented to them. There are many confidence-building techniques that you can add to your sales presentation.

**Be Honest.** Although it is important to show the benefits of your products, never exaggerate your claims. Stating a claim that can't be fulfilled to a customer is a sure way of losing all credibility. One untruthful claim is the same as one fly in an otherwise good bowl of soup; the customer is going to reject the whole bowl.

**Don't Criticize Your Company.** If you don't like the policies, products, or management of the company you represent, why should your customers have any confidence in your company?

**Let the Buyers Compare.** When it is feasible, let the buyers compare your products and competitive products. This is certainly possible with any products that are small and easily transportable. Food products can be compared easily, as can cosmetics, writing instruments, paper, paints, and many others.

*Tip   Deanna Delrio has developed an interesting way to have her customers try her product and compare it with the competition. Deanna sells syrup for a major food products company. Deanna carries a toaster and packages of waffles with her on sales calls. The toaster is used to heat the waffles, allowing her customers to try her product. The heated waffles allow Deanna to show how much thicker her product is than competitive syrups.*

**The Guarantee.**   If your company offers a better or lengthier guarantee on its products, make sure that this is stressed in your presentation. This can be a powerful sales aid, especially when selling a new product or selling to a new customer.

**Testimonials.**   These are statements from satisfied customers that can be incorporated into your presentation. Knowing that there are many satisfied users of your product will impress your prospect.

**Case Histories.**   Case histories are similar to testimonials— just longer. These are presentations of situations experienced by other customers or business firms that are similar to the present situation of your prospect. The case history relates how your product or service solved some kind of problem for a customer. Presumably, your product or service will do the same for your current prospect.

## Be a Good Listener

Listen to what your customers have to say. Don't listen only to the words but understand their meaning. Understand how your customers feel. You can win your customers' confidence by being a good listener. You can determine their real interests and needs by paying close attention to them. If a customer interrupts you during your presentation, pause to hear what that customer has to say. Give your full attention to what is being said. Direct your attention to those issues in which your customer is interested.

## Maintain Control

Although it is important to be a good listener, it is also important that you stay in control of the situation. You want to take the presentation in the direction you have planned. If there is a question or complaint, respond to it but move back to your planned presentation at the first opportunity. When customers digress from the topic, direct them back with appropriate questions.

Stay in control of visual aids and other materials that you use during the presentation. Many salespeople make the mistake of handing catalogues, brochures, and other materials to their customers, then start their presentation. When customers are look-

**Illustration 9-3    A good listener pays close attention to the points of interest for the customer.**

ing through this material they are not listening to what you have to say. If you wish to point out something in a catalogue, hold onto it, pointing to what you want to illustrate so that the customer is listening to what you are saying.

## Use Visual Aids

As you learned from a previous discussion, some presentations are built entirely around audiovisuals. All presentations can be enhanced through the effective use of such aids. They can often illustrate features that are difficult to describe. Commonly used audiovisuals include charts, graphs, photographs, catalogues, flip charts, manuals, films, slides, and tapes.

## Stress Benefits

Although your product or service may have many interesting features, keep in mind that your customers are not interested in the features; they want to know how the features will benefit them. Stress customer benefits, not product features in your presentation. Chapter 4 of this book described the process of translating features into benefits.

## Use Persuasive Words

Build your presentation around the use of persuasive words. A study conducted by Harvard University identified the following 16 words as very important in developing persuasive communication.[1] Use them frequently in your presentation.

| | |
|---|---|
| you | advantage |
| save | guarantee |
| money | security |
| health | discovery |
| easy | new |
| now | benefits |
| safety | positive |
| results | proven |

## Speed of Delivery

You do not want to talk too fast or too slow. Talking too fast will result in important points being missed. Talking too slow will bore your prospect. Gauge your speed of delivery to fit the prospect and the selling situation. You can tell how your presentation is being received by the questions asked, the responses given, or by the lack of response you are receiving. Complex selling situations may require a slower delivery pace, while less complicated selling situations may be enhanced by a normal conversation speed.

## Do Not Mention Competitors

It is generally best not to mention competitors in your sales presentation. Discussing competitors will only serve to confuse facts that you are trying to present about your offering. If a customer brings up a competitor, acknowledge the competitor briefly and return to the point you were making. If a customer insists on discussing the competition, be prepared to present a detailed comparison of your offerings versus competitive offer-

---

[1]"Sixteen Most Important Words," *American Media Eagle* (Des Moines, Iowa: AMI Press, 1982), p. 9.

ings. Be sure to concentrate on features that your competitors can't match.

When customers are satisfied with what they are currently using, you may be able to show how your product might be used along with that of the competitor. "I understand, Dr. Rafael, that you are happy with the medication that you are currently prescribing. However, do you have any patients who don't respond to this medication?" "Yes, I have," responds the doctor. "For those patients, Dr. Rafael, prescribe this medication; I think you will be pleased with the results."

## USE SHOWMANSHIP

To maintain the interest and attention of your prospects, it is often helpful to use a little showmanship as part of your presentation. Showmanship involves making a point in a dramatic fashion. Showmanship can be fun and can provide some entertainment for your customers.

There are endless ways in which showmanship can be used. Most effective advertising messages rely on showmanship. Many are familiar with the Bounty paper towel commercial that shows Bounty absorbing a coffee spill faster than ordinary paper towels, yet remaining strong enough to support a filled cup of coffee. Why do we remember this message? Because the commercial used showmanship to dramatize an important benefit of the product. An announcer might have just held up a package of Bounty and said, "Bounty is stronger and more absorbent," but this wouldn't have been as effective or memorable.

Think of ways in which you can use showmanship. A representative selling protective packaging showed that a special container with an egg inside could be dropped without breaking the egg. A salesperson for a protective covering material gave prospects a knife and asked them to try to damage the material. A sales representative handling a new adhesive glues a broken handle back onto a coffee cup while discussing the product. At the end of the presentation, the salesperson hands the cup to the buyer and challenges the buyer to break the handle off the cup. A salesperson for a company manufacturing unbreakable children's toys hands the buyer for a department store a hammer and asks the buyer to try to break one of the toys. These are just a few of many possible examples of how showmanship can be used to dramatize a point.

*Allstate Insurance Company*

**Illustration 9–4    Showmanship maintains both the attention and interest of the customer.**

The use of showmanship offers many advantages. Showmanship maintains interest and attention. Showmanship substantiates claims about a product that might not otherwise be believed. Showmanship can be used to demonstrate points that otherwise would be hard to explain. Finally, points made in a dramatic fashion will be remembered long after features merely explained are forgotten.

Although showmanship can be very effective, there are several cautions that should be kept in mind. Most prospects will enjoy your use of showmanship, but some may not, preferring instead a more conservative presentation. Make sure that your demonstration will work. After setting the contents of a wastebasket in a buyer's office on fire, one sales representative found that the fire extinguisher being demonstrated wouldn't put it out. Finally, demonstrations should be short and fresh. If a demonstration takes too long to develop, the prospect will lose interest. Furthermore, even though you may be repeating a demonstration for the one-hundreth time, make it appear fresh and exciting to your customer.

## LENGTH OF PRESENTATION

Your customer generally determines how long your presentation will be. The more interested the customer is, the more time you will get. Take as much time as allowed to make a thorough presentation but don't take more time than you need. Your customer's time is valuable. A presentation doesn't have to be long to be good. Abraham Lincoln's Gettysburg Address only contains 268 words.

## RESPONDING TO DIFFERENT CUSTOMER TYPES

The different types of people you constantly meet make selling interesting. However, this also adds to the challenge of the job. You must be able to adjust your presentation to satisfy all customers. Many customer types are described in Chapter 3; each requires a different approach. Some examples follow.

| Customer Type | Presentation Adjustment |
|---|---|
| 1. Silent type | It is important to get this customer to participate. Ask questions that require a lengthy answer. Attempt to find topics of interest such as sports, movies, family, etc. Get the prospect talking on this topic and then move back to business. |
| 2. Vacillating type | This type seems to wander from topic to topic. You must be firm and stay in control of the presentation. Whenever your customers start to stray, gently bring them back to your presentation topic by asking questions or making appropriate comments. |
| 3. Skeptical type | Support everything you say with facts. Rely on demonstrations, sam- |

ples, trial periods, case histories, research results, and testimonials.

**4.** Hostile type

Find out what has caused their hostility and try to solve it. Attempt to win them over with statements such as, "I know that I can't correct what has happened in the past, but I can assure you that there will be no problems in the future."

**5.** Closed-minded type

These prospects don't want to try anything that's new. Question them about the products they are using now. Find out what they don't like. Show them how new products you have to offer overcome these problems.

**6.** Know-it-all type

Let them do much of the talking. Ask questions soliciting their opinions. Compliment them on their knowledge.

**7.** Busy type

Many prospects have very little time available. Keep your presentation short. Select one major selling point and concentrate on it.

**8.** Indecisive type

Keep the presentation simple and provide many facts. Create a sense of urgency. Attempt to close very early.

**9.** Deliberate type

Present facts and support all of your claims. Slow down your presentation; give the customer time to deliberate.

**10.** Talkative type

Let them talk but take every opportunity to steer the conversation back to the point of departure.

**Tip** *Everyone wanted to know how Sam had done it. Sam had made a sale to Harper's Department store. Salespeople for Sam's company had been trying for years without success to sell to Harper's.*

*Sam sells shirts for a leading manufacturer of menswear. Like salespeople before him, Sam had not been able to get in to see Harper's buyer. The buyer was purchasing a competitive brand and was not interested in switching. Making one more attempt, Sam sent a note to the buyer* *asking for ten minutes of time "for advice on an important business problem." The buyer was curious and granted Sam an appointment. Sam showed the buyer a new line of shirts and asked the buyer what would be a fair price for the shirts. The buyer examined the shirts carefully and gave an answer. "That's interesting," said Sam, "we're selling these shirts for $10.00 a dozen less than the price you just set." Sam made a sale on the spot.*

## HANDLING INTERRUPTIONS

It would be nice if you could complete your presentation without interruptions, but this is rarely the case. The phone rings, a business associate drops in, or the secretary comes in with an urgent message. In a home presentation, telephones ring, neighbors knock at the door, and kids run through the room. These interruptions are generally beyond the control of either party. Although most interruptions are short, unfortunately they are normally long enough to break the train of thought that was developed.

### Continuing after the Interruption

How difficult it is to continue after the interruption depends on the length of the presentation and the interruption, the complexity of the presentation, and the interest of the buyer. If the prospect is keenly interested and has been following the presentation closely, the prospect will be anxious to continue. In this case, you should repeat your last few remarks and then move into new material. Statements such as, "As you recall, we were discussing the binding on the books," or "As you remember, we were just beginning to discuss the installation of the equipment" could be used. In complex selling situations, you may have to review material previously presented before you can move on.

If your presentation was not particularly effective before the interruption, or the buyer showed only minor interest, the interruption may provide an opportunity to change your approach. Introduce some new ideas. Talk about different features. Present a case history.

If interruptions continue, suggest continuing the presentation in a different place or at a different time. A conference room or a coffee lounge might be used. If it is almost lunchtime, invite the buyer to lunch.

### Forestalling Interruptions

You may know from past experience that there will be constant interruptions at a particular buyer's office. For important buyers, find ways to reach them when they aren't busy. You may be able to reach some buyers very early in the morning or later in the evening. You may be able to invite the buyer to your office or to a neutral location. You may take the buyer on a tour of your plant or to a facility where your company's equipment has been installed. With planning, you can find ways to get around many of the interruptions.

## COMPETING FOR ATTENTION

When making your presentation, you need the buyer's full attention. In some cases, buyers will tell you to "go ahead" and then proceed to read mail, sign letters, glance at reports, or make telephone calls. What should you do? Some salespeople fear offending the buyer and proceed with their presentation. This is a mistake. A buyer engaged in other activities is not going to hear your presentation.

You have several alternatives in this situation. One option is to remain silent until the buyer finishes whatever he/she is doing. Each time the buyer returns to some other activity, stop your presentation until the buyer looks up. Eventually the buyer will get the message.

Another option is to inform the buyer politely that what you have to say is very important and you can wait until the other business is cleared up. As a last resort, another appointment time can be suggested. "If you are too busy at the moment, Mr. Tisdale, what time tomorrow would be best?" In each of these cases, the buyer will generally get the message and give you full attention.

## CHARACTERISTICS OF A GOOD PRESENTATION

A number of important issues involving the sales presentation have been discussed. This section highlights the essential features of a good sales presentation. Ideally, your sales presentation should:

1. Arouse and maintain interest
2. Get to the point quickly

3. Be clear and complete
4. Anticipate questions and objections
5. Cover price
6. Stress benefits
7. Motivate the customer to action

It is important to gain the attention of your prospect quickly. A good approach, along the lines of those discussed earlier, should be used. Make sure you maintain the interest of your prospect after the initial approach. Use showmanship, visual aids, demonstrations, and get the prospect involved in the presentation.

Assume that your prospect does not have time to waste. Get to the point as quickly as possible and keep your presentation concise. Buyers will not appreciate your taking 30 minutes to say something that could have been said in five. Choose your words carefully. Use persuasive statements.

Your presentation must be complete. Cover all material in which your prospect would be interested. Support your claims with proof. Provide adequate detail. Be sure that the points you make are clear. Watch the prospect for any evidence that there is little or no understanding of what you are presenting. Don't be afraid to repeat material if necessary.

When planning your presentation, anticipate likely questions and objections. Work responses to such matters into your presentation. All prospects are interested in the price they will have to pay. Make sure that price, discounts, and terms of sale are part of your presentation. Don't make your customer ask about these concerns.

Your prospects are interested in knowing how they can profit by buying from you. Stress product benefits, not features. A feature is merely a characteristic, while a benefit is the satisfaction a buyer receives from that feature. You can clearly see the mistake of stressing a feature in the following exchange.

Salesperson: This model electric space heater delivers 5000 BTU's and has an automatic magneto and thermal control.

Customer: That's nice, but will it keep the room warm?

Finally, the ultimate objective of your presentation is to get your prospect to take action—to buy. If this is achieved, your efforts have produced the results desired.

# PAVE THE WAY FOR CALL-BACKS

Even the best of salespeople will not make a sale during every call. However, much can be accomplished during calls when no sale is made. You have had the opportunity to present a story that the prospect can now think about. You have had the opportunity to initiate or reinforce a working acquaintance. More important, you have had the opportunity to learn.

What have you discovered about the prospect and/or the prospect's business during your sales call? What needs and interests have you identified? These are things that can be used to improve your chances of success during your next sales call on this prospect. The importance of gathering and maintaining good customer records was discussed in Chapter 7. Make sure that you record all new information immediately after your sales call. This new information will now become part of your permanent record on this prospect to be reviewed before your next call.

## QUESTIONS

1. Identify the various types of sales presentations. What are the advantages and disadvantages of each?
2. Under what circumstances would each presentation type be used? Provide some examples.
3. Should a business card be offered at the start of a sales presentation or at the end? Give one good reason for each. In what type of selling situations wouldn't a business card normally be used?
4. What is meant by the approach? What is the purpose of a salesperson's approach?
5. Describe three different approaches. In what type of selling situation might each be used?
6. What are different methods a salesperson can use to build confidence during a sales presentation?
7. How does showmanship enhance a presentation? Develop an example illustrating the use of showmanship in a sales presentation. Are there any situations in which showmanship shouldn't be used?
8. Identify three different customer types. How would your sales presentation have to be altered for each of these types?

9. In some cases, you may find a busy buyer engaging in other activities during your presentation. How should you handle this situation?
10. What characteristics should a good sales presentation possess?

## SALES CHALLENGES

1. The opening statements of a sales presentation are often vital in determining whether a sale is made. You have resolved to strengthen the opening minutes of your presentation. Select a product and develop the opening two minutes of a sales presentation for that product. Keep in mind that you must gain attention and spark interest during these opening minutes.
2. Assume that you are a salesperson in a retail store that sells a wide range of personal and business computers. A potential customer has just walked into the store and greets you. "Hello. My name is Gorman Langer. I'm an accountant with my own private practice. As my practice has been growing, I find that I can probably use a small business computer. I know very little about computers and I could use some advice. I have to meet a client shortly so I only have about ten minutes." Your normal presentation on small business computers takes about 30 minutes. What should you do?
3. Leonard Kopnick sells heavy-duty commercial sewing machines and related equipment for the Delmar Company. Leonard has just entered the office of Rhonda Pawluk, owner of Milford Manufacturing.

**Leonard:** Good morning, Ms. Pawluk. I'm Leonard Kopnick from Delmar Company.

**Ms. Pawluk:** Have a seat. I'm very busy this morning. I hope you don't mind if I clear up a few matters while we talk.

**Leonard:** I could come back at a more convenient time.

**Ms. Pawluk:** *(While glancing through some papers on her desk)* No, go ahead with your presentation.

**Leonard:** Delmar has developed a new, fast-action sewing machine that I'd like to bring to your attention.

**Ms. Pawluk:** *(While moving from her desk to the filing cabinets)* What type of machine did you say?

**Leonard:** I have some brochures here that illustrate the new machine. Would you like to glance through them?

**Ms. Pawluk:** Yes. Let me take a look at them while I make a phone call.

What would you do at this point if you were Leonard Kopnick?

# CASES

### 9-1 Lounge Boy Lawn Furniture

Frank Durante is a salesperson for Lounge Boy Lawn Furniture. He is sitting in his hotel room reflecting on the day's events. It has not been a good day. Until now, Frank's sales trip through Illinois had been very successful.

Frank is concentrating his sales efforts on a new folding chair introduced by Lounge Boy. This chair uses wood slats instead of plastic strips. This makes the chair sturdier and more attractive, yet the specially designed thin strips of pressed wood are very light so the chair is easily portable.

Frank's first appointment in the morning was with the buyer for a large discount store. The buyer, who seemed to Frank to be very young (possibly a recent college graduate), met Frank in the lawn and garden section of the store. "Hello. I'm Greg Dudeck," stated the buyer. "I'm one of the assistant buyers in this department. What do you have to show me?"

The product approach had generally worked very well for Frank. Since the product was attractive and surprisingly light in weight, Frank had found that just handing the product to the buyer and letting the customer inspect it for a few minutes worked very well. So, Frank simply handed the chair to Greg Dudeck.

After examining the product for a few minutes, Greg asked, "What's the cost?" "The chair is designed to retail for $19.95. The cost to you would be $135.00 per dozen or about $11.25 per chair." "That's way too high," replied Greg. "I can't see it retailing for more than $12.95. I'd be interested at about $8.50 or $9.00 per chair."

"I can certainly see why you would want to retail this chair at $12.95," replied Frank. "That would be a great price. However, we can't sell it at $9.00. The material, labor, and delivery amount to that." "That's all I'm going to pay," repeated Greg. "When you're ready to talk price, come back to see me. Good day."

Early in the afternoon, Frank went to the buying offices of a large mail order company. Frank was escorted into the office of

Georgia Lazemby. "When are you going to learn that I don't see people on Wednesday afternoons?" was Ms. Lazemby's opening statement. "I'm sorry," said Frank. "I'm only in town for the day. I could arrange an appointment for next week. I'm heading back to the main office tomorrow." "Never mind," was the reply. "Let's see what you have."

"This chair has been selling extremely well in department stores all across the country," said Frank. "The Marshall Field store downtown has been selling more than 50 a month." "I don't care what Field's is selling," replied Lazemby. "Tell me about this chair and the price."

About halfway through Frank's presentation, Lazemby interrupted with the statement, "That's enough. I'm not interested." Frank attempted to ask a few questions but Lazemby sternly cut Frank off, "When I say I'm not interested, that's final. Now I have work to do!" Frank left quickly.

1. What do you think went wrong in these two selling situations?
2. What could Frank have done to avoid the unsatisfactory outcomes in each case?
3. How could Frank have better approached each customer?

## 9-2 The New Buyer

Larry Oneida sells men's slacks, shirts, sweaters, and related items for a leading clothing manufacturer. Larry covers part of several midwestern states. He is liked by everyone he serves in his area. Larry keeps detailed notes on each of his customers so he can inquire about their family, golf game, fishing, or whatever it is that the customers enjoy discussing. Larry is also very good at suggesting interesting ways in which his merchandise can be displayed and promoted in the customers' stores. Consequently, Larry has been quite successful.

On a particular call at Kern's Department Store in Detroit, Larry met Christine Esch for the first time. Christine was a new buyer who had been on the job for less than a month. Larry invited Christine to have a cup of coffee with him in the store's cafeteria so that they could get acquainted. Larry learned that Christine had been a salesperson in the clothing department before being promoted to the buyer's position. Although Christine had been successful in her sales position, she was unsure of herself as a buyer. She felt too much was expected of her too quickly in the buyer's job and that she hadn't been prepared adequately to assume her new responsibilities.

"I'm particularly concerned about our coming spring sale," said Christine. "I'm not sure what to order for the sale." Larry recognized this as his cue to go to work. Larry presented his company's new spring line to Christine. Larry also offered Christine some very attractive prices on merchandise that the company had overproduced. These, Larry pointed out to Christine, could be promoted as price specials during the spring sale. Finally, Larry suggested a few discontinued items and certain other items of merchandise that were on sale that month. These could also be featured at special sale prices.

Christine was a little concerned that the total order size was larger than those normally placed with Larry's company. Larry assured Christine, however, that the display ideas he had for the merchandise together with the special prices would guarantee a big spring sale success. Christine expressed her appreciation for Larry's assistance and stated that she hoped this would be the start of a long and rewarding business relationship.

1. List the outstanding features of Larry's selling job.
2. What characteristics has Larry shown in this situation that would demonstrate why he has been successful through the years?
3. Has Larry been too aggressive? Did he take advantage of an inexperienced buyer?

# 10

# MAKING EFFECTIVE DEMONSTRATIONS

A demonstration is a test-tube picture of your product in action. It shows what the product will do, how it will perform, and how it will fit the prospect's needs. It backs up the salesperson's story and makes it concrete. It informs, shows, and promotes interest. Because it attracts the prospect's attention, a demonstration can do in a few minutes what long explanations might take hours to accomplish. In many cases, the demonstration is the dominating influence.

The demonstration is not a crutch to be used instead of effective selling, but an aid to selling effectiveness. You can do a better job by using a variety of aids to pep up the presentation, to make it sparkle, to make it lively, to make it appealing. Consequently, a topnotch demonstration, carefully thought out and presented at the proper time, enhances the presentation.

A buyer also recognizes that a demonstration is helpful. However adequate descriptions are, they may not convey the entire meaning or the complete perspective that a buyer wants. However descriptive words may be, they still do not convey the same impression that a product does in operation. With potential appeal to sight, sound, touch, taste, and smell, the demonstration leads the buyer toward credibility and conviction. Prospects want to know as much as possible before they decide to buy; demonstrations help them make decisions.

The place of the demonstration in the stairway to sales success is shown in Figure 10–1.

**Figure 10-1**

## THE STAIRWAY TO SALES SUCCESS

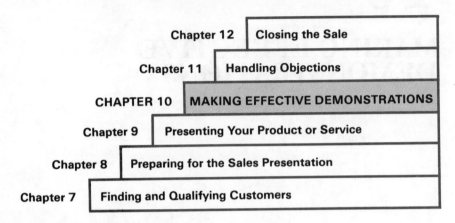

| | |
|---|---|
| Chapter 12 | Closing the Sale |
| Chapter 11 | Handling Objections |
| CHAPTER 10 | MAKING EFFECTIVE DEMONSTRATIONS |
| Chapter 9 | Presenting Your Product or Service |
| Chapter 8 | Preparing for the Sales Presentation |
| Chapter 7 | Finding and Qualifying Customers |

# DEMONSTRATION PREPARATION

One cannot say too much about the importance of advance preparation. Excellent demonstrations do not just happen; they are planned and rehearsed. A new ship is taken on a shakedown cruise to find any weaknesses before it is delivered. The same thing can be done with a demonstration. Many unexpected situations may arise when making a demonstration. Therefore, prepare by organizing and rehearsing your demonstration several times. The correct words of explanation, the appropriate introduction, and the right follow-up make this much like the production of a play. Each part must fall into place if the finished demonstration is to succeed.

## Organization

Some salespeople do not organize their demonstrations. Each demonstration is given in a different way depending on the efficiency of the salesperson. Although some variation may be permissible, too much indicates that a salesperson has not grasped the essential features of the demonstration.

Develop a strong and convincing presentation that applies to the situation. For example, a piano demonstration for a beginner would be quite different from a demonstration for an accomplished pianist. In demonstrating a tractor to a farmer who owns flatland, it would be unnecessary to demonstrate hill-climbing capabilities. Demonstrating a personal computer for home use would be quite different than demonstrating the same computer to an executive for business use. If you have a general-purpose product and a specialized product for sale, do not use the same demonstration for both. An orderly presentation must be suited to the needs of the prospect through an approach that can be understood and appreciated.

## Emphasis

Your product usually has a number of features superior to those of competing products. All these features, however, will not lend themselves well to demonstrations. Some are so unimportant that a demonstration of them is not warranted. Others are of such a nature that a demonstration would not be convincing. That leaves, then, only a few features—perhaps one, two, or three, that merit demonstrating.

A carefully worked out presentation proceeds step by step toward an ultimate goal. If only one feature is to be demonstrated, it might be well to use it and then to try to close immediately. If more than one feature is to be demonstrated, you might move immediately from one to the other; or, you may intersperse feature demonstrations throughout your presentation. If the presentation is long, it is often best to interweave demonstrations to hold interest.

Particular features of your product that may be interesting to one prospect may have little appeal to another. Thus, there is no need to demonstrate the high-speed potential of a car to an older person who drives conservatively. Neither is it necessary to demonstrate the tremendous get-up-and-go of a powerful outboard motor for water skiing to one who is solely interested in fishing. The small farmer is not so much interested in knowing that three, four, or five plows can be pulled by a tractor if the main concern is essentially with the motor's economical operation. In other words, demonstrating features that have little or no application to the prospect is wasteful. It is difficult for a salesperson not to demonstrate all outstanding features of the product. Yet you should refrain from doing so if some features have little application for the individual. *The buyer's interest, not the salesperson's, must always be foremost.*

## Condition Check

Can you imagine a customer being asked to try a piano that's out of tune? If your customer is going to use a handsaw, would

**Illustration 10–1    Target the demonstration to fit the needs and wants of the customer.**

you provide a soft pineboard or a knotty oak? If the customer wants to use a hammer, will you use soft wood in which to drive a nail or hard wood in which the user will bend nail after nail? If your prospect is to watch a demonstration, is the room hot or air-conditioned, well-lighted or dim, fresh or musty? If the demonstration is to take place in a room of your choice, the surroundings should be appropriate for your work.

If you are putting on a mechanical demonstration, do you have all necessary items? Are they in working order? Are they entirely suitable for the purpose you have in mind? In some demonstrations, it may be necessary to use a makeshift item, but that is uncalled for if you set up properly in advance. If you are using assistants, be sure that they are properly coached to do the right thing at the right time. When you transport your equipment long distances and use it constantly for demonstration purposes, considerable upkeep is needed. If you neglect this, you may be embarrassed to have equipment fail at a very inopportune moment, or it may look shabby when it should be bright and shiny.

# DEMONSTRATION TECHNIQUES

The aim of any demonstration technique is to bring the product or service alive for the prospect. It should make the customer understand its value and show how its unique qualities fit into work or leisure periods. In a sense, the demonstration is a pilot plan of operation for the real thing. The demonstration should give the prospect a taste of what will happen if the product is purchased. It should give an idea of how the product can be used and how it can make life more meaningful or more enjoyable.

## Sense Appeal

Although a demonstration frequently appeals to sight, do not forget that we have other senses as well. If you can also appeal to hearing, taste, and smell, your demonstrations will be more effective. For example, you would not want to introduce a new wine by just having the merchant look at it to appreciate the color; of much more significance would be the reaction to its bouquet and taste.

Appealing to the prospect in as many ways as possible will ensure a better presentation. A parachute jumper usually has an emergency chute as well as a main chute. If the first fails to open, the emergency chute should save the jumper. By appealing to a person in a variety of ways, you guarantee that one appeal will be effective. It is quite possible that what you consider to be a minor appeal may be the prospect's motivating force.

When appealing to the senses, make the demonstration correspond with the product's actual properties. It is self-defeating to advertise or to demonstrate falsely. To be of any value to you and the buyer, the demonstration must be realistic and credible. When a salesperson makes a presentation, it is not how much is presented that counts, but how much the prospect believes. A salesperson's statements may not ring true and may raise doubts in the prospect's mind. But if the demonstration confirms the truth of the statement, the prospect will develop greater trust in the salesperson.

## Product Testing

There are so many ways of testing products; dozens of ways can be devised to demonstrate particular features or points. Tests that appeal to the eye and ear are numerous. Testing a musical instrument for tone, testing a car for quietness of operation, testing an electric fan for sound are all illustrative. Many tests are effective because you see them in operation. Often, tests that are simple and easy to make can bring out the outstanding characteristics that appeal to the eyes and ears.

Tests can be physical and chemical. A store may retail two lawn chairs. One sells for $18, the other for $35. The $35 one is springier, has greater resiliency, and has heavier steel components. It is easy to see and feel what accounts for the difference in price. Fastness in color can be tested by exposure to the sun and by washing. High-speed tools may be tested under various conditions of use. A drawer in a piece of furniture can be tested for strength by pulling it out partway and standing on it.

Tests should be appropriate for the product. There are spectacular tests made that bear little relationship to the product.

Tests should not only be appropriate, they should also be sensible. The product may be suitable and highly accurate under normal conditions of use, but when it is subjected to unusual stress, it might be inadequate. Products should not be exposed to tests that reveal weaknesses. Leaving a product at a home, an office, or a factory for a trial is really a testing period. Frequently, however, supervision is needed to carry out the test under suitable conditions for which the product was constructed. Improper testing procedures may do much harm.

## Prospect Involvement

Frequently, a demonstration includes action that someone must perform. Whenever possible, bring the prospect into the act. If machinery or equipment is being demonstrated, the buyer will be intrigued by moving handles or pushing levers and seeing wheels turn. Operating intricate machinery can be fascinating. In the demonstration, the carpenter should try to saw a board; the prospect should drive the car; the office manager should run the duplicating machine; the dentist should try the drill; the mechanic should use the set of tools. By bringing the prospect into the demonstration, you can show the prospect how the product functions, note its efficiency, and explain its advantages. When it is not feasible for the prospect to participate in the demonstration or use the product, paint the prospect into your word picture.

Avoid having a prospect carry on a demonstration which requires skill without which the demonstration can fail. Not only

**Illustration 10-2** Whenever possible, promote customer participation in the sales presentation.

does failure damage the image of the product, but the humiliation can make the person lose face. Embarrassed, the person will be eager to get rid of you as quickly as possible. A sale will be impossible.

A delicate situation can arise in demonstrating a piano. Should the salesperson be able to play the piano well? If the potential buyer plays with confidence, no feeling of inadequacy arises if the salesperson also plays. Of course, some customers would have little regard for the salesperson who performs poorly. If, on the other hand, the salesperson performs superbly and demonstrates the piano beautifully, it may embarrass the mediocre pianist who wants a piano for personal pleasure. In that case, the buyer would be unwilling to sit down and try the piano after hearing a salesperson's polished performance. This illustration applies to many other products as well. *In any demonstration, the primary objective is to make the product look good.* If the customer is doing the demonstrating, the instrument should perform well. The better the prospect can tie in with the product, the greater are the chances of making the sale.

## Take Prospect to Location Where Product Is in Use

Many prospects desire to see proof of the salesperson's claims. They want to be shown that the product will do what the salesperson says it will. In fact, showing the prospect successful product applications is an effective sales device. People are more likely to believe and remember what they have seen than what they have heard.

Salespeople have many opportunities to show prospects their product in use. A salesperson for a construction company may take a prospect on a tour of previous buildings constructed by the salesperson's firm. An industrial equipment salesperson may take a prospect to a manufacturing plant where previously sold equipment is in use. Computer salespeople may take prospects to locations where their equipment is being used. There are endless possibilities. The greater the similarity between the prospect's operation and the situation where the salesperson's product is in use, the more convincing the demonstration will be.

## Plant Tours

A plant tour may often be used successfully. Salespeople may talk at great length about production techniques, production standards, and quality control, but not get their message across. In these situations, a tour through the plant will give the prospect first-hand knowledge of the manufacturing processes. Salespeople selling highly technical, sophisticated equipment may want to show prospects the quality control devices used in the manufacturing process. Salespeople selling food, beverages, or medical products may want to show the cleanliness of their production operations.

## Showmanship

When you hear the word "showmanship," you may immediately think of an actor who gesticulates and performs vocal acrobatics. Sometimes the performer's words flow in a steady stream; sometimes they are halting or jerky; sometimes low, quiet, and earnest. Different moods are suggested through word pace and intonation. All of these effects have one end—to stir the audience.

Now transfer this thought to those salespeople who are most adept in acting, the pitchpersons. Standing in a store or on the street, they will soon gather a crowd about them by what they say, how they say it, and the interest that they arouse. Like the medicine man of yesterday, they can move people emotionally. To avoid monotony, they talk fast, talk slowly, talk loudly, talk softly. They arouse interest, anticipation, challenge, and desire, and their audience breathlessly listens. Above all, they do not allow enthusiasm to diminish before they sell their goods. The successful salesperson should attempt to create this type of enthusiasm in the product demonstration.

## Group Demonstrations

Carefully handled demonstrations help to convince prospects. When demonstrating before a group of buyers or a committee, the interchange of opinions among the buying group and the information volunteered by the salesperson as the demonstration proceeds provide an interesting, informative conversation that develops depth of understanding for each member of the group. Questions arise and are answered. New ideas are evoked that focus on the product in new ways.

One might compare a demonstration before a group of people to a many-faceted diamond. As the diamond is rotated, each facet sparkles and emits a glow. In a demonstration, each member contributes either through knowledge or lack of it on the subject. Try this procedure: (1) make a demonstration to a member of a committee and record all questions asked, (2) repeat the process with each member of the buying group separately, recording the information that is requested and the questions that arise, (3) repeat the demonstration again to the entire group. Up to this time, no member of the group has seen the demonstration more than once. It may be old and repetitious to you, but to the buying group it will merely be a second going-over. Notice how many new questions arise because of the interplay among the group members. The interaction among group members has resulted in new questions and new insights.

### Demonstrating Intangibles

Up to this point, we have been talking about demonstrating a product. How can you demonstrate intangibles? Most salespeople feel that the best way is to paint word pictures. Many intangibles have some tangible features connected with them. In selling stock, for example, the prospect may be intrigued by an impressively designed certificate. Stock certificates are beautifully engraved (as are many other financial documents), to promote faith in the corporation. An unusual order blank can be a form of demonstration. As you fill it out, the customer is intrigued to see you put in measurements, draw in designs, or make special alterations. Blueprints and designs may also be used as a dramatic demonstration. Since it is difficult for many people to reason or think in the abstract, try to associate abstractions with some concrete realities. Often a picture of a burned home or company and a visit to the site to witness the rebuilt structure, can convince a prospect of the value of insuring with your firm. If you are selling liability insurance on a car, and someone is hesitant, arrange a meeting with a customer who has had an occasion to use liability insurance. If you are selling life insurance, you might mention a widow with several children who has been a beneficiary and has realized the value of the policy you sold.

*Tip  Demonstrating a service is often difficult. However, Jose Lamas, who sells a moving service, has developed a very effective demonstration that has helped him close many sales. Jose uses a toy van to represent the vans his company uses to move household goods. To demonstrate the careful handling the customer's furniture will receive, Jose carefully wraps and packs miniature furniture into the van. Once packed, Jose asks the client, "Wouldn't you like to be sure that your furniture is handled in such a fashion?" Few people can answer "no" to such a question, which allows Jose to move into his close.*

## DEMONSTRATION INGREDIENTS

There are four ingredients to a demonstration.

1. A salesperson to make the demonstration.
2. A prospect who listens to and watches the demonstration.
3. The tools used for demonstrating
4. The methods applied to the use of the tools.

## The Product Itself

For many demonstrations, the product is the best tool to use. There can be exceptions, of course. When a product is so complicated or technical that it would be better to have other devices that are simpler and more understandable, use the simpler devices to demonstrate the action. But when individuals see the product, observe it, examine it closely, see how it operates, see strong points, what can be done with it, and what ought not to be done with it, they gain a strong impression. Likewise, it becomes easy to bring a person into the demonstration to actually handle and use the product. After buying the product, the person will be able to use it because of the learning experience during the demonstration. When the buyer sees the care with which the salesperson handles the product, it creates an impression and tends to lead to similar handling after the purchase. Often, when you get a new item, you may not read the directions carefully, may skip over portions of the guarantee, and may be careless in reading about maintenance provisions. But if all of these factors have been explained during the demonstration, you will be more likely to remember them.

Avoid the use of illustrative material that has become soiled, torn, or dog-eared. When illustrations show signs of wear or discoloration, replace them. Usually, there is no great difficulty in obtaining reproductions to bring freshness to your demonstration.

**Illustration 10-3** Small scale models enhance clear understanding within the prospective customer's mind.

*photo by James Milmoe for Philip Morris, Inc.*

## Overlays

The overlay may be used as a series of transparencies in a loose-leaf binder. The first transparency, for example, may represent the base of a machine. After you and your prospects have studied it thoroughly, put the next overlay over the base. When you fit the second transparency over the first, a significant new part will be added, and its functions can be easily explained. Then put a third overlay on, and a fourth, and a fifth until at last you have the machine completely pictured. This permits you to study any portion of the equipment separately, in conjunction with any part, or in relation to the entire unit. When a product lends itself to this presentation, it is most effective. Advantages are simple to demonstrate, it is not expensive, and reproductions can be easily made.

## Display Boards

You are probably so familiar with the device of a display board that no explanation is needed. Salespeople who have learned to use chalkboards effectively may have a decided advantage in demonstrating how a particular machine works or fits into the prospect's needs. Interesting demonstrations sometimes involve magnetic boards on which objects like model automobiles are attached and moved about freely to illustrate particular points. To make an orderly presentation, fasten a series of pictures or objects on a cork board or a bulletin board. There are other types of display boards such as the one on which you can attach a heavy object by pressing against a special surface, and feltboards to which rough-back illustrations will cling.

## Charts

A variety of charts may be used for demonstration purposes. One of the better-known types is the flip chart. This consists of a series of illustrations in which salespeople can start with the first chart and, after describing the items on it, turn it over on an easel to reveal the next chart. As you explain the charts, you can use other devices such as the chalkboard to supplement your demonstration, and you can pass out models and samples to heighten interest.

A variety of illustrations may be placed on charts. Some are carefully made and reproduced to show an exact operation or present specific information. Some charts may be handmade to suit the needs of the particular demonstration. Charts may be constructed of a variety of materials and may be folded, rolled, or assembled in pieces. They may be in black and white or color; they may be large or small, bold or subdued, extravagantly designed or simple. They can be made in any way as long as the purpose of the charts is not forgotten; they should impress and enlighten.

## Graphs

Graphs are a particular type of illustration which can convey certain messages. The common graphs are line graphs, bar graphs (both horizontal and vertical), component bar graphs, and pictographs. The last-mentioned graph pictures actual objects for illustrative purposes. To keep symmetry and proportion, graphs are frequently drawn on a grid which may be lightly drawn in and later erased. Graphs may be drawn to scale. Graphs on semilogarithmic paper are quite descriptive but must be used with caution since the ordinary person can easily misunderstand them. We mention them here because they are excellent ways for demonstrating particular ideas when you are dealing with people who are well-versed in sales techniques. Care should be used in constructing and interpreting graphs. They can be tremendously effective, but they can also deceive the customer.

## Posters

Posters are pictures or illustrations on soft paper or on stiff board. They are often made in a series and can be shown one after the other; even better, they can be set up in array, side by side, one above the other, or in some such arrangement so that the whole group, taken together, conveys one impression. Using posters all displayed at once, salespeople can go from one to the other as they carry out their demonstrations. Salespeople who have a large number of posters available can use them all to convey a message, or they can select certain ones to bring out vivid impressions or convey precise ideas. They are able to segment their presentation by dwelling on certain posters and omitting others.

## Kits

"Kit" refers to a number of illustrations and devices which may be used in a demonstration. A kit might be a group of specimens, objects, or samples. It can be a combination of objects and of printed matter. It may be samples plus cutaway models. A salesperson can have a first-aid kit as a sample. The salesperson with cleaning fluids and brushes would have small bottles of fluids, soaps, and detergents together with assorted brushes. This material could be used for a demonstration in the buyer's home, office, or factory. The imaginative salesperson should be able to think up many types of kits or many products which might be placed in a kit to carry the message of the product.

## Portfolios

A portfolio is a case that resembles a large book cover or binder. It might be paper, plastic, or one made of more durable material. If you wish to create an exquisite impression, you might have one made of beautiful leather. It can be small or large. The person who sells advertising can use a portfolio to carry illustrations of subject matter. It may include a variety of advertising materials and pictures and, perhaps even premium suggestions. The portfolio is useful in showing previous advertising campaigns, and it is convenient in selling intangibles. The insurance salesperson, for example, will find it most helpful when giving vivid descriptions of the various plans that are available. The salesperson of securities finds a portfolio an excellent means of assisting in the presentation of material. The individual selling cemetery lots may find a portfolio of color illustrations helpful.

## Catalogs

A catalog is usually considered more of a reference volume than a tool for demonstration. Yet a catalog *can* be an excellent demonstration tool. A large catalog is an impressive means of demonstrating the size of your assortment and the volume of items you sell. It gives you readily available illustrations and descriptions of most of the items, and you can immediately turn to the right page. Catalogs can be large or small, loose-leaf or bound. In constructing a catalog, use a standard size such as 8½ by 11 inches. If you leave supplements with a prospect they can be filed more easily than if your loose-leaf is an odd size. The catalog, like any other tool of demonstration, should be clean, current, and accessible.

## Samples

Samples are one of the best ways of demonstrating a product. Samples of food give the prospect an excellent idea of quality, taste, size, and color. Samples of laboratory equipment are used to indicate table construction, corner construction, glueing construction, acid-resistant construction, types of materials used, and how the product will react under use. The house-to-house salesperson finds samples one of the best ways to introduce a product. Marketing research indicates that a prospect who has sampled the product is more likely to buy that product than if the appeals are directed only through advertising. Giving merchandise on a trial basis is really sampling. Over a period of time, the prospect can determine what the item can do. Many samples are small amounts of the product that the prospect can use. Other samples merely illustrate the actual product. For example, an advertising specialties salesperson leaves a sample calendar that shows how your advertisement would appear if you bought the calendars to give to your customers.

## Audiovisual Aids

Motion pictures, slides, projectors, phonographs, tape recorders, and other audiovisual devices are useful in conducting demonstrations. The motion picture is a continuous demonstration and represents one of the best visual aids available. Skilled actors can dramatize and carry out impressive techniques. Slides are particularly useful because the rate of presentation can be controlled. If a slide demonstration is accompanied by a tape recording or a phonograph record, the slide must be changed to fit the words on the sound track. Many times, however, salespeople use slides and furnish the explanations themselves. In that case, they can go as rapidly or as slowly as the situation warrants and can vary the length of time for each slide. Additional explanations can be used to clear up particularly knotty points.

*Tip* *Roslyn Aldrich has settled on the use of a slide projector as her chief tool in explaining the merits of her product. She has prepared a series of slides showing component parts of the lathe that she is selling. Roslyn frequently makes demonstrations to groups of three made up of an experienced lathe operator, the operator's supervisor, and the plant superintendent. Sometimes these group sessions include other interested parties in the firm including the purchasing agent or one of the purchasing agent's assistants. These demonstrations enable Roslyn to proceed at any pace she desires, to use a personal description of each slide, and to stop to answer any questions. Roslyn does not use a record or tape but does all the presentation personally. At the end of the presentation she has a number of slides that show the basic frame of the lathe and each succeeding slide shows the addition of one more component until the last slide shows the finished lathe. Roslyn has found that this method enables her to get opinions from each member of the group, to counter any unfavorable opinions by adequate additional explanation, and to get a group consensus that puts her in a favorable position when negotiating with the purchasing department representative.*

## DEVELOPING A POSITIVE DEMONSTRATION

To get the most out of a demonstration, be sure that you organize it properly. Attention to detail in advance ensures a far better demonstration. A superior demonstration can increase sales; a weak one can lose them.

### Have Respect for Your Product

Your attitude toward your product will help to establish the customer's attitude toward it. Have you ever noticed the choral director leading an audience in singing? The director sings the first verse with strength and fervor, and everybody joins in. A lower voice is used for the second verse. The members of the audience lower their voices. Notice how the leadership of one is instinctively followed by others. The same is true in your demonstrations. Merchandise should be handled with care and respect. Beautiful gems on a black velvet background are far more appealing than those displayed on a plain counter.

During a particular demonstration, something may go wrong—a part may become unmoveable. Do not angrily push or jerk, but use a gentle motion to relieve the strain. Carelessly handling beautiful objects or marring your product through indifferent care is a reflection on your character. The customer shudders to see a fine product abused and will form a poor opinion of the guilty party. After a demonstration, replace the equipment in the case or box as carefully as you took it out. Again, this shows the customer that you value your product. If you carelessly thrust it into its container, the customer will undoubtedly notice. Of course, you should not take valuable time that could be used for selling to pack your equipment. There is a difference between rapid but careful handling in storing equipment and carelessly throwing it together.

### Use Prospect Language

Use language with which the prospect is familiar. Words are your means of communication. They are not ends in themselves, nor should they be used to demonstrate your ability to speak, your vocabulary, or your brilliance. During the demonstration, you should talk to explain or clarify so that the prospect will be convinced of a need for your product. Communicate effectively! Use words that your prospect can understand and appreciate.

It is easy to forget, as you go from one prospect to another, that one may be highly trained, another poorly trained; one is a technician, the other a layperson. To one buyer, technical language is appropriate; to another, standard English is preferable. One buyer may need a detailed explanation, while another would be interested only in the highlights. A demonstration that proceeds too quickly for one person may be boring to another. That is why you change your style, your approach, and the way you talk to fit the needs of the listener.

### Maintain Prospect Interest

You have received advertising messages in the mail. You know that some messages will capture your attention while other messages lack anything of interest and are ignored. Look at an advertising message for a new perfume. You open the mailer to see a page of black on white print with the name of a new brand. This message will likely be ignored, and the perfume soon forgotten. What if the mailer that you open contains a full color illustration with a picture of the new perfume in an attractive bottle? You probably will pay more attention to this message. Finally, what if the mailer contains the full color illustration and is scented with the fragrance of the new perfume? This mailer will attract the greatest interest and attention.

Keep this example in mind when you are conducting a demonstration. When you tell your story, you are painting a word picture. The listener may be following you, but will not hear or remember all that you say. If there is strong interest, the listener may receive and remember 90 percent of what you say; if partially interested, half of what you say might register. However, if the listener has only a casual interest, as much as 75 percent of your presentation may be wasted effort.

Careful observation during your presentation will reveal this lack of interest. If, when attention wanes, you can bring in an interesting demonstration, you will notice at once that the attention of the individual becomes riveted to what you say and do. From a casual observation there develops strong attention coupled with interest. The demonstration adds action to words. It is something different; it tells something previously not known. It shows something not previously seen.

### Demonstration Effectiveness

Are your presentations getting across? Are the buyers following you? Do the customers understand what you say? Sometimes you can tell how well buyers understand by looking at them, but do not trust that method too far. The best way to know that your messages are clear and your demonstrations are effective is to check now and then to see if the prospects grasp what you say.

Sometimes the demonstration is so fascinating that the objective for giving it is missed entirely. Make the demonstration a device, not an end. When the prospect enjoys it as an end in itself, it is ineffective. To be sure of its effectiveness, use controlled questions that are pertinent to the effects you are attempting to create. For example, when demonstrating a machine, you can say, "Have you noticed how quietly it operates?" "Do you see how smoothly the gears shift?" to illustrate freedom of grinding gears. "Do you feel how cool it runs?" when you are stressing a cool operation. Use searching questions to find out whether the prospect understands the fine points.

If the product that you are demonstrating lends itself to entertainment, be sure to use this feature to the utmost. In demonstrating a musical instrument, it is far better to play a selection that is interesting to the customer than to play a series of notes and chords.

When demonstrating features of a game, try to have individuals participate in it. After a cooking or sewing demonstration, the guests in the audience are often entertained with a luncheon,

**Illustration 10-4**   Observe the level of interest in your audience to determine whether or not your message is understood.

style show, or music. In conducting a demonstration, the clever salesperson can so involve the people that they have a delightful time. Possibly, one reason why the home or party demonstration is successful in selling to homemakers is that it furnishes an evening of entertainment.

*Tip     Isabel Thorngren has been remarkably successful in demonstrating various sewing machines. Isabel works in an appliance store. She has studied each type of sewing machine in order to demonstrate its particular capacities. She has practiced sewing on each so that she can present the individual strengths of each machine. When a prospect walks into the store, she meets the customer graciously and tries to find out which type of sewing machine the person might prefer. Isabel demonstrates various types of sewing, explains various attachments, and invites the prospect to try the machine. Isabel is careful to steer the prospect to the machine's basic use that is easy to handle.*

*If the customer wishes to try some intricate sewing, Isabel will carefully demonstrate and then guide the prospect in using the machine. At all times Isabel attempts to keep the customer at ease and to make the entire demonstration enjoyable. Should the prospect ask about a special kind of sewing better done on another model, Isabel will move to the appropriate machine and demonstrate this particular feature. If the prospect seems to prefer the second machine, Isabel will demonstrate its features. As soon as the prospect appears satisfied, Isabel will attempt to close on either one of the machines by comparing them and will end by asking, "Which one do you prefer?" Isabel's product knowledge and demonstration ability have made her successful in selling sewing machines.*

If customers are watching a demonstration that is not pertinent to their work or one that they do not understand, little is accomplished. Thus, it would not prove particularly beneficial for farmers to watch a tractor demonstration on a crop they do not harvest. Many times we get lost in spectacular demonstrations that show how effective the product is in certain unusual applications, and we forget the prospect's particular needs. You may demonstrate to a farmer how a truck will go over rocks and deep-rutted roads without dragging, but the same demonstration would have little interest to a person who buys a truck for city deliveries.

## Avoid Demonstration Lag

Timing is important in making your presentation and demonstration. When timing your demonstration for an individual, set your pace to fit the listener. In timing for a group it becomes more difficult to determine how fast to go. Timing also depends on how important each individual of the group is in the buying picture. Unless you feel that certain people reacting slowly are relatively unimportant, it is wise to go slowly enough so that these people get a fairly good grasp of your demonstration. Others may detect a bit of dragging, but it will not bother them too much.

You can point out before making your demonstration that it has been your experience that in any group there are always some who grasp what you say and do faster than others, but that the ones who grasp information readily in one part have difficulty understanding another part. Consequently, to be sure that you are not offending anyone, you probably will pace the demonstration so that all will grasp what you are saying. This is merely an effective way of telling those who catch on quickly that you want your demonstration to apply to everyone in the group.

### Demonstrations Are No Substitute for Good Selling

Some men put talcum powder on their faces so that they do not have to shave twice in one day. Some people use powder or perfume instead of taking a bath. Some people think that cramming for tests is a substitute for regular study. There are many makeshift techniques used in every phase of life. There is nothing wrong with using talcum powder after shaving, or perfume or powder after bathing, but it is totally inadequate to use them to cover sins of omission. Salespeople who substitute devices, gadgets, tricks, and hocus-pocus for topnotch selling will be disappointed. If they think that a good demonstration will make a sale, they are wrong. If they think that a good demonstration will help to make a sale, they are right.

In most instances, depending on the demonstration alone to make the sale is dangerous. The skillful golfer has a bag full of clubs. Each club has a specific purpose, and no outstanding golfer would depend on one club for all shots. The demonstration is like a particular golf club. Most salespeople find that it has a specific place and a specific use. Yet, that does not mean that you cannot change its use, experiment with it, or occasionally substitute it for another sales tool as the golfer might substitute one club for another under particular circumstances. This indicates versatility, open-mindedness, ability to assess a particular situation, creativeness, and often expediency.

## DEMONSTRATION—A FINAL WORD

Learn to use the demonstration brilliantly and skillfully. Make your product come alive, stand out in the buyer's mind, and kindle buyer enthusiasm. In a demonstration, you can be dynamic because you are doing several things at once. You have a chance to show yourself at your best. You have a chance to shine as an individual; be spirited, eager, authoritative, confident. Here is a chance for you to master the situation, to control the interview, to dominate the group, and to show your strength. You can dazzle the intellect by painting vivid word pictures while your hands carry on the work of the demonstration. If the prospect participates, tie the customer into the demonstration so firmly, so graciously, so commandingly, so realistically, that at the end there is only one appropriate path to follow—purchase the product.

## QUESTIONS

1. To what extent can a demonstration make a sale? Are there limits to what a demonstration can do?
2. A demonstration should be confined to the requirements of the prospect. How is this often violated?
3. What are the dangers involved during a demonstration when the equipment has not been checked properly? Who is to blame?
4. To what extent can you involve a prospect in a demonstration? What are some of the inherent dangers?
5. Can demonstrations lend reality to selling intangibles? Explain.
6. In selling, how can you illustrate an abstract principle through a demonstration?
7. When should the product be used in a demonstration? When the product itself cannot be used in a demonstration, what is the alternative?
8. In a demonstration, why is it essential to use language familiar to the prospect?
9. Unless the prospect's interest is kindled by the demonstration, the final result is usually negative. Why?
10. The speed of a demonstration must be adjusted to suit the needs of your customer. How can this be done when the demonstration is being made to several prospects?

## SALES CHALLENGES

1. If you can apply your sales presentation to all five senses (seeing, hearing, smelling, tasting, and feeling) of a prospect, you have a greater chance of making a sale. Some products will have one outstanding appeal that can be exploited, others will have more. Some will have more than one appeal to the

senses but not in equal strength. You are to select five different products and, for each, try to appeal to each sense. (Your teacher may suggest five products for you to use.) Do not try applications that are not suitable. Many products can be judged by the ear and eye but may not be used for a taste test. For each product give one sentence of explanation for each sense applicable.

2. Discuss how each of the following can be used effectively in a demonstration: (1) pictures, (2) portfolios, (3) display boards, (4) kits, (5) projectors, (6) charts, (7) student suggests a different one.

3. "A spectacular piece of showmanship may result in a marvelous demonstration but still not convince the buyer." Discuss this statement bringing in such categories as the importance of a demonstration; salient features involved in the presentation; how pertinent the facts are to a sale; was it entertaining, instructive or both; and essentially what might it contribute or not contribute to facilitating a sale.

## CASES

### 10-1 Romeo Truck Distributors, Inc.

Mr. Bruster, the KRD truck salesperson, is talking with Mr. Noseda who is looking for a new pickup truck for use in his landscaping business. From their conversation, Mr. Bruster learns that Mr. Noseda will be the principal driver of the new vehicle. He shows Mr. Noseda some of the KRD V-8 engine parts mounted on a display board on the wall and then points to a large picture of a KRD pickup chassis hanging beside the display board.

Bruster: As you can see from the features I just mentioned, KRD pickups are not only engineered for the best transportation at the lowest long-range cost, but they're also smartly styled. The best way to get the total feel is to drive one yourself. I've got my demonstrator parked outside. Let me show you what I mean.

Noseda: No, I don't think I have the time right now. I think I'll just take that literature home and study it tonight. Maybe I'll stop back tomorrow if I'm not too busy.

Bruster: This will only take a few minutes, and I'm sure that you'll find it worthwhile. Actually, a short ride will tell you more about KRD pickups than you could learn from the literature.

Noseda: Well, OK. But I have only a few minutes, so we'll have to hurry. *(The salesperson and prospect walk outside the showroom and get into the truck.)*

**Bruster:** Notice the wide door, plus this low step. Makes it easier to get into and out of the cab. That's pretty important when you're climbing in and out all day.

**Noseda:** It's a lot easier than getting into my older trucks.

**Bruster:** If I had to describe this KRD in a few words, I'd say it's all truck. Take this inner door panel, for example; it's made of steel, not fiberboard. There's more resistance to scuffs and stains, and this means less maintenance. And inside the door itself, rust inhibitors in every nook and cranny, even between joints and seams. This gives KRD trucks longer life and better resale value.

*(Bruster starts engine, drives truck out of dealership lot.)*

**Noseda:** What engine does this have?

**Bruster:** It has the 5.0 litre V-8 engine. This engine is probably best for your needs because it gives you ample horsepower combined with good gas mileage. We also have an in-line six plus a high-performance V-6.

**Noseda:** The high-performance engine doesn't interest me. I'll bet it uses a lot of gas. As far as I'm concerned, operating economy and durability are most important. I want an engine that's built for hard service.

**Bruster:** The short-stroke engine design means economy in two ways: operating savings and longer life. There's less friction, less wear. The short strokes also give high power at low engine r.p.m.'s.

*(Bruster and Noseda drive past a used truck lot.)*

**Noseda:** I notice that there aren't many used KRD's on that lot.

**Bruster:** That's typical. Used KRD's are hard to find. And when they do appear, they're snapped up quickly. That means you can count on top resale value.

**Noseda:** What about the brakes? Can I get disc brakes?

**Bruster:** Disc brakes are standard equipment; they're self-adjusting so you don't have to worry about costly adjustments. Let me show you how they work. Just put the truck in reverse, back up, then apply the brake. That does it—automatically. In fact, this happens every time you back up and brake. Now let's head up this steep hill here. Feel how the rear suspension handles? Even on dirt, there's no rear-wheel hop. And the rear springs automatically adjust their stiffness to the weight of the load, so you get a top ride just like this, with any load on any surface.

**Noseda:** How does it handle on curves?

**Bruster:** Very well. I'll turn at this next corner so you can see how it handles. Feel how the front end takes the bumps even while turning? That's because of independent coil front suspension. It gives you better control for safety and longer tire life. And it gives more ground clearance, too. Here, try it yourself. Just slide over, I'll come around.

**Noseda:** I really should get back to work. Do you mind if I drive it back to the showroom?

**Bruster:** That's fine. The seat adjuster lever is on the side of the seat. Notice how you sit straighter; your back gets better support. And all the controls are handy and easy to read. The glare-proof dash design gives you better visibility and greater safety. Speaking of safety, this year's models include many standard safety items that were extra-cost options last year. We turn right at the next corner to get back to the dealership. Isn't that power steering terrific? Conventional steering also uses the same KRD recirculating ball system. Both give you the easiest handling pickup on the road. *(Bruster and Noseda return to dealership.)*

**Noseda:** Do all KRD's have this big rear window?

**Bruster:** That's optional. It gives you better visibility for backing and for checking your load. Let's get out and take a look at the pickup box. Notice the wood floor. All KRD pickup floors are made of chemically treated wood to resist wear and moisture. There's no rust problems and none of the drumming noises you get with a metal floor. Of course, we can equip your pickup just about any way you'd like—radio, heater, even air conditioning. But first, Mr. Noseda, let's go inside and decide on the axle and transmission combination that's best for you.

**Noseda:** Why don't I just get some literature to take home tonight? Then tomorrow I'll stop back and see you.

**Bruster:** Why don't we just go inside, and I'll price out a truck for you just the way you'll want it. It will take just a few minutes, and it might even save you a trip back here.

**Noseda:** Let's hurry.

**Bruster:** Considering your business, you'll want a 1002 Powerflow with the standard 5.0 litre engine, heavy-duty springs, and larger tires. Now, how about the transmission? What kind do you have now?

**Noseda:** Three-speed, but I've had a lot of trouble with it recently.

**Bruster:** I'd recommend a four-speed transmission. It's more rugged and better suited to your job because you probably drive off-road quite a bit. Not only that, the deep first-gear ratio will mean less clutch wear and longer life. Now, you showed quite a bit of interest in power steering, power brakes, and the full-width rear window. These items make driving a fully loaded pickup as easy as driving your personal car. They'll pay for themselves in the added convenience alone, and of course, you'll want a heater and de-froster—the deluxe one is best for the winter weather we have here. Was there anything that I missed? How about the custom cab? That includes a chrome front bumper and grille, chrome hubcaps and side trim plus special seat fabric, right-hand sun visor, left-hand armrest, and a color-coded floor mat. It's well worth the cost because it dresses up the vehicle and the seat is more comfortable and durable.

**Noseda:** How much does it cost?

**Bruster:** $412 for the whole works. It's a real bargain because if you bought all the items separately, it would cost $470. And you'll get more at trade-in time.

**Noseda:** OK, put it in. But I think that's everything I'll need. Why don't you give me the full price so I can think it over?

**Bruster:** OK. With everything we've talked about, the full, delivered price would be $12,992. That's for a 1002 Powerflow with four-speed transmission, radial tires, heater and defroster, radio, custom cab, and the full-length rear window. And don't forget all the standard features that you'll find only on KRD's: dual headlights for better night vision, printed electrical circuits to eliminate wiring problems, independent front suspension and progressive leaf rear suspension for a comfortable ride at all times, and the famous KRD V-8 engine. You know, a truck engine has to be built for long, trouble-free service, and that's what you get from this V-8. You will find that this engine is used in the big two-and-a-half ton trucks that are used by bottlers, furniture stores, and many others. So you know that it's sure to hold up in your operation. I get so wound up over this engine that I could talk about it for hours. But honestly, I feel that it is the best engine you could get for your job. I have this type in stock in red, blue, or green, and we can have it for you first thing tomorrow. So why don't we write up an order right now? We can arrange the financing almost any way you want. What color do you like: red, blue, or green?

**Noseda:** I think I like red best.

**Bruster:** Fine, I'll write up an order for the red one. Let's see. The total price is $12,992. Mr. Noseda, just sign the order and then we can work out the financing. This will only take about ten minutes. Then we'll be all set, and I'll see that your truck is ready first thing tomorrow morning.

1. Comment on Mr. Bruster's presentation and demonstration.
2. Should Mr. Bruster have given a more thorough demonstration?
3. What are the advantages of a demonstration-in-use approach?

### 10-2 Chippewa Board of Education

The members of the Chippewa Board of Education had just seated themselves in the boardroom at 8:00 p.m. Greg Faigle of the Veselica Corporation arrived to demonstrate a Model No. 21 projector.

A month before, Greg had called on the school superintendent, Theota Ocampa, to sell his new projector. Ms. Ocampa showed interest and carefully followed Greg's presentation. Greg offered a demonstration to Ocampa at that time, but Ms. Ocampa declined. She told Greg she had seen the projector in use previously and liked it. Since this projector sold for $1,575, Ms. Ocampa was hesitant about placing an order until the school board had seen it and was willing to approve its purchase. If the board members found the projector satisfactory, they probably would order two. Ms. Ocampa arranged to have Greg demonstrate the projector to the board members a month later at 8:00 p.m.

Greg had finished his last call at 5:30 in Keystone, a town ten miles from Chippewa. Since his demonstration was at eight that evening, Greg decided on a leisurely dinner at Russel's Steak House, a well-known restaurant on the outskirts of Keystone. He drove to the restaurant and sat down to dinner at 6:00 p.m. At 7:00 p.m., he left the restaurant to drive to Chippewa. When he got to his car, he saw he had a flat tire. His spare was flat so he couldn't just change tires. Fortunately, there was a gasoline station a block away, and Greg was able to get a person to repair his tire. By the time his tire was repaired, it was 7:30. Greg drove hurriedly to Chippewa. On the way, he was held up at a railroad crossing by a long freight train. Greg managed to get to the meeting just at eight.

Ms. Ocampa introduced Greg Faigle to the school board members. Ms. Ocampa mentioned that since they had discussed various projectors at several meetings, she had invited Mr. Faigle to demonstrate his projector this evening. Then, turning to Greg, Ms. Ocampa said, "The meeting is yours, Mr. Faigle."

Greg thanked Superintendent Ocampa and the board for permitting him to give the demonstration. Then he spent 15 minutes explaining his projector to the board. He mentioned several unusual features of his machine that made it far superior to any other machine on the market. After his presentation, he asked the board's indulgence while he set up his equipment. Since he had hurried in at the last minute, he had not even unloaded his equipment.

Greg went out to his car and brought in his equipment. He looked around the room and saw that he would have to place his projector in the back of the room. He looked around for a suitable table for his projector but found none. So he asked Ms. Ocampa if he could borrow a table. Obligingly, Ms. Ocampa, accompanied by Greg, went looking for a table. They found a suitable table in a room down the corridor. The two carried the table back, and Greg set up his projector.

Schools usually have projector screens either on the walls or on tripods. Greg Faigle had never had any trouble getting one before, so he had not brought his own along. Unfortunately, there was no screen in the boardroom; Greg asked Ms. Theota Ocampa if she could locate a screen. The two of them went to the equipment room. Greg found a suitable screen. He returned to the boardroom and set up the screen in front of the room.

He looked for a wall receptacle to plug in the cord. Most rooms have receptacles in both the front and back of the room. But in this room there was none in the rear. Since Greg did not have an extension cord long enough to reach the front, he was forced to ask Ms. Ocampa for one. Visibly irritated, Ms. Ocampa went to the equipment room and came back with an extension cord. Finally, Greg was ready for the demonstration. It was now 8:45 p.m.

Greg switched on his machine and began his demonstration. He showed several slides, explaining features as he demonstrated. The machine brought out each slide beautifully, too well in fact because some of the slides were dirty, and the dirt showed up clearly. Greg apologized for the dirty slides. He said he had used them the night before and had not had time to clean them.

The tension created by the difficulties of setting up the equipment had eased, and except for some dirty slides, everything was fine.

Finally, Greg said, "I have reserved a few outstanding slides to demonstrate two particular features of this machine that are unique." Then he attached a piece of equipment and turned on the projector. It lit up for a moment and then went out. A tube had blown out. Hurriedly, Greg took off the top of the machine and removed the tube. Then he reached for the spare tube. It was not in the case. "Sorry, folks, I'll have to step out to the car for a moment to get another tube."

Greg dashed out to the car, rummaged around in a bag, and soon found the other tube. He hurried in, inserted the tube, closed the machine, and snapped the switch. Nothing happened. Then Greg remembered. Several weeks ago he had burned out a tube and had used the spare. He had dropped the old tube in the bag, fully intending to stop at a store to get a new tube. However, Greg had been very busy lately and had forgotten to get a new tube.

1. What should Greg do now?
2. How many mistakes did Greg make?
3. How can you meet such unexpected contingencies?
4. Can Greg still make the sale?

## 10-3 Doubleman, Inc.

Sylvia Delavara sells demonstration equipment in the Southern California market for Doubleman's Inc. Sylvia's firm offers a wide range of visual aids, cameras, films, slides, projectors, records, cassettes, phonographs, film and recording equipment, and tape recorders. In addition, other demonstration equipment such as kits, boards, charts, graphs, portfolios, brochures, and special items can be designed and produced for business customers. Sylvia's firm is able to meet most demands for demonstration equipment.

Sylvia's customers rely heavily on her advice. Customers will often describe their needs to Sylvia and ask her to develop an appropriate demonstration package for their sales force. If the customer likes what Sylvia develops, and the price is acceptable, Sylvia has a sale.

Sylvia's sales have ranged from $50 to $50,000, with most of her sales being in the $3,000 to $25,000 range. Considerable experience, training, and ingenuity are required to prepare a complete package for customers. Presently, Sylvia has been asked to prepare demonstration packages for three customers. This equipment will be carried by salespeople in their cars and set up and used on the buyer's premises.

a. The Zephyr Company manufactures and sells industrial vacuum cleaners and floor cleaning equipment for commercial establishments and offices and desires a package that their sales force can use to demonstrate the Zephyr equipment.

b. Terasuler Fromer, Inc. produces flatware, serving tables, equipment, chairs and tables, dishes, and other items to equip cafeterias. The company does not produce kitchen and dishwashing equipment. The owner of the company would like to have a complete demonstration package for the sales force to use when calling on potential new accounts.

c. The Sullivan Furniture Company manufactures and sells specialty furniture to churches, lodges, public buildings, institutions of various types, and all other customers that have special furniture needs. Most orders are for a relatively small number of units but some orders are quite large. Customers normally describe their needs to a Sullivan salesperson who will sketch the desired item. If the sketch and price are acceptable, a sale is made.

**You are to prepare a demonstration package for one of Sylvia's customers. Identify exactly what will be provided to each of the salespeople and how the equipment will be used. Remember what the purpose of the demonstration package is and that it must be transportable.**

# 11

# HANDLING OBJECTIONS

An objection is an obstacle, and, if not handled properly, may prevent you from concluding the sale. To remove objections, you must understand them. Do not assume that objections are bad. Objections pinpoint what is on the prospect's mind and how close you may be to closing a sale. As shown in Figure 11-1, a skillfully handled objection may lead right into the close of the sale.

## REASONS FOR OBJECTIONS

There are many sound reasons for customer objections. Prospects may not understand what you are saying. They may be unfamiliar with your product or they might not understand its operation. What might be relatively simple to you may be quite complex to them. Objections may indicate the need for further explanation. Although prospects may be genuinely interested, they may not understand your product's functions.

Prospects may object to purchasing a product because their needs are minimal. They have no real objection to any feature of the product, nor do they think the price is too high; they merely cannot justify the expenditure. They may be able to satisfy their needs by renting equipment or by hiring someone to do the work. Farmers, for example, frequently borrow equipment or pay someone to come in and do the needed work. Sometimes they will trade work with one another.

Sometimes a person may object to buying because there are penalties attached to the use of a product. A person may hesitate to buy a dog because of neighborhood resentment. An individual

**Figure 11-1**

## THE STAIRWAY TO SALES SUCCESS

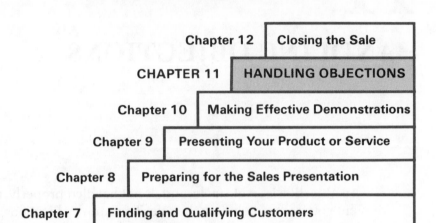

| | |
|---|---|
| Chapter 12 | Closing the Sale |
| CHAPTER 11 | **HANDLING OBJECTIONS** |
| Chapter 10 | Making Effective Demonstrations |
| Chapter 9 | Presenting Your Product or Service |
| Chapter 8 | Preparing for the Sales Presentation |
| Chapter 7 | Finding and Qualifying Customers |

may think twice about making a purchase because of fear of ridicule, cost of upkeep, difficulty in making repairs, changes in family that might develop, loss of prestige if it proves unwise, and many other reasons. Timid people are reluctant to buy if they feel there are definite chances of unpleasant repercussions.

Some prospects object to a product because it is too expensive for them. The product may be something of superb quality, such as furs or jewelry, or a product that is too luxurious, such as a large cruising boat compared with a smaller boat with an outboard motor. The product might be entirely beyond the prospects' reach. More likely, though, they could buy it if they wished, but then would have to curtail spending in several other areas having higher priority. Many people will buy items beyond their means to their own misfortune; some will buy and mortgage their future for years. Industrial buyers are quick to shun extravagant purchases unless they can justify their actions in terms of cost. Unwise buying of this nature by purchasing agents will soon have them job-hunting.

Then there are always some people who will object for no apparent reason. They have a negative attitude and seem to feel that their most important duty is to find fault. Such people can be sold a product, but it is useless for a salesperson to try to discover their reasons for objecting—it is simply the individual's disposition.

## PROPER ATTITUDE

Take objections in stride and handle them in a logical fashion. An objection should not be a high wall to stop you, but rather a hurdle to take in stride in your presentation. If a number of objections are raised in a presentation, you should take them as a runner meets hurdles. Some objections are minor and will be low hurdles; some objections are major and will be high hurdles. You need different degrees of effort to overcome them, but do not let them stop you.

Neither belittle nor magnify an objection. If you belittle it, you hurt the prospect's feelings; if you magnify it, you erect a stumbling block that may be impossible to move. Objections that are given too much attention raise barriers that were originally insignificant. You can raise an imaginary barrier so high that you cannot knock it down.

Whether the objection is real or trumped up, at no time can the salesperson's attitude be disinterested or disparaging. The salesperson must be pleasant, sympathetic, interested, and should adjust to the mood of the buyer. The salesperson indicates that the prospect's ideas are wise, statements perceptive, and actions carefully planned. Prospects resent a salesperson's careless or flippant attitude; that shows little consideration or respect.

An objection indicates unwillingness to act favorably toward your proposition, at least for the moment, and requires you to start probing by asking questions. It is important that you ask the right questions at the right time if you want helpful answers. "When prospects feel free to reveal feelings, current situations, finances, needs, and desires, the salesperson knows how to help them, service the business, write additional business, and obtain referrals."[1] Have a questioning plan as well as a questioning strategy. As you continue to probe, attempt to move from general to specific questions to gain a better idea of the customer's thinking, reservations, hindrances, and any particular problems or lack of information.

---

[1]Anthony J. Alessandra and Jim Cathcart, "How to Ask the Correct Questions," *Banking Today*, Vol. 12, Issue 2, Copy No. 118, (February 1985), pp. 15, 16.

# RECOGNIZE AND UNDERSTAND REAL OBJECTIONS

When a prospect has an objection, be sure that you understand it. Before you answer, repeat it, or pause to think carefully. If you and the prospect are not on the same track, the answer might be objectionable. You may be trying to answer a question that was never asked. You may be trying to refute an objection that was never raised.

Is your prospect's objection real, or is it merely an excuse? If it is a sincere objection, you must handle it one way; if it is merely an excuse, you can handle it in a casual fashion or brush it aside. Many people raise excuses to see how easily you can be stopped or how readily you can be thrown off track. Maybe they are trying to get rid of you. Perhaps their minds are on something else, and they want to be alone. You may, at the moment, be little more to them than a talkative nuisance. If the prospect is truly busy or troubled by a pressing problem, offer to come back at a more convenient time so that your presentation will receive the person's full attention. If you perceive that you may be able to capture the prospect's attention, make your presentation so lively and interesting that it overcomes the prospect's distraction and causes the prospect to listen.

## Hidden Objections

Hidden objections can be difficult to uncover. A prospect's stated objections may be superficial and may hide really significant problems. As you struggle with such a situation, seemingly getting nowhere, you soon realize that the objection is superficial and that something prevents the prospect from making a decision. Hidden objections may be the ones that would embarrass the prospect if they were known. For example, their earnings may be insufficient to buy easily, or the operation of a piece of equipment may seem too complicated to master. Prospects may want to buy the product, but because they know their social group might be critical, they hesitate to buy. When business buyers suggest that you return later, or that you leave your literature, or that they are not in the market now, it might be because they are not authorized to buy.

Hidden objections (especially if they're major objections) must be uncovered and handled before you get anywhere. You can use several methods to uncover hidden objections. Start to pack your equipment and casually say, "Apparently, Ms. Edding, there is some reason why you don't want to buy today, or there is something I have omitted. If you would just mention it, maybe we could clear up the problem." Or say, "Since the proposition does not appeal to you now, perhaps we can get together sometime in the future. Would you mind telling me why you were not interested today?" At this point, the prospect might give you the real reason, allowing you to answer the objection and swing back into your sales pitch in an attempt to close. Or you might say, "Ms. Edding, I've laid all my cards on the table, but they didn't seem to make the right combination. Apparently, there is something missing that I haven't been able to supply. What is it?" A perfectly frank approach sometimes brings out a hidden objection. Or list a number of common objections and say, "Certainly one of these prevents you from buying today. Would you mind telling me which one?" If necessary, list the objections on a piece of paper.

## Objections Are Never Trivial

If you suspect that a customer is hesitant to bring up an objection because it is trivial, say, "Mr. Elliott, objections may be trivial, or they may seem so small that a buyer would hesitate to mention them to a salesperson; but what may seem small to one person is important to another. If there is any problem that concerns you, even if you feel it would look small in the eyes of someone else, don't hesitate to mention it." The major objection is the one that appears large to the prospect, not necessarily to others. If you can get on common ground and discover where the problem lies, you can go ahead easily. Do not diminish the importance of the prospect's objection.

*Tip    Mina Moskovitz is an expert salesperson of women's clothing at Dressers Fashions, a high-class women's apparel shop in one of the major resort areas in Florida. Early in her career, Mina learned each customer's differences and treated them accordingly. Through repeat purchases from steady customers, Mina has been able to develop a strong following from customers who rely on her for suggestions and for notification of new shipments of merchandise.*

*As soon as Mina learns of a new quirk or difference about a customer, she tries to adjust herself to help the customer select new clothes. Customers know that Mina keeps to herself any confidences they give her. They also*

*feel at ease with Mina because she never belittles them,
their ideas, or any objections or questions they voice.
Mina reassures them that each person has individual
desires that are important. As a result, Mina has established a deep rapport with each of her customers, assisting
them in selecting apparel and leaving them feeling at ease
and happy after each transaction. These customers are
satisfied and continue to buy from Mina.*

If you are having a particular difficulty with an objection,
you might stop and say to the prospect, "Miss Ludwig, I wonder
if we are talking about the same thing. Let's check to see if we
understand one another." Or say, "Miss Ludwig, it seems that we
may be talking at cross-purposes. Perhaps I don't understand
your viewpoint. Let's compare notes." The purpose of all of
these approaches is to get your prospects to reveal any hidden
objections that they might have.

## MEETING OBJECTIONS

The skillful handling of objections is an absolute necessity to
complete a sale. To meet objections satisfactorily, anticipate
what objections may arise so that you can be ready with
convincing responses. Preparation and practice are the keys to
handling objections. The salesperson who is prepared can take
objections in stride. For the salesperson who is caught off-stride,
these objections become obstacles that are difficult to overcome.
The sooner you make up your mind to master the art of overcoming objections, the sooner you will have a stronger presentation and be able to strengthen your sales performance.

### Direct Denial

The direct denial of an objection is a dangerous technique
and should be used sparingly. People object to being told bluntly
that they are wrong. An awkward situation develops when prospects are put on the spot. Even if they are proved wrong, they
are not going to admit it gracefully and then buy. They have
been exposed and put into an unhappy situation.

Instead of saying, "You're wrong on that, Ms. Osborn," you
might say, "Ms. Osborn, some authorities feel that ours is the best
approach to this situation." Or say, "Our previous experience
indicates that the following result occurs." Instead of saying, "I

don't see, Ms. Osborn, how you can reach this conclusion when the facts clearly demonstrate the opposite," you might say, "Ms. Osborn, I can understand how you reached your conclusion, yet a close study of the facts by experts has revealed that a somewhat different approach would be more suitable."

Avoid angry responses to your prospects. A statement may upset you because you know it is absolutely wrong. If you must use a direct denial, push it aside deliberately as you would push aside other obstacles in your way. Do not be too abrupt, however. You can pound a stone away with a fierce thrust, or you can roll the stone away with a firm movement. Both approaches can be direct and to the point, but the latter is more acceptable. No one likes to be contradicted abruptly and roughly.

### "Yes, But" Method

The "yes, but" method of handling objections uses an indirect denial, which is more palatable to the prospect than the direct denial. Seldom does a prospect make a statement or raise an objection that does not have some element of truth in it, although basically it may be unsound or essentially false. By acknowledging the truth in a statement, you do not offend the speaker. By countering the false part of an objection, you can also open up a new theme.

Suppose that the prospect says, "Your car is so heavy, it takes a lot of gasoline to run it." You can reply, "Mr. Dolvin, it is true that some people who must do a lot of stop-and-start driving in the cities have found this car is not as economical as others; but once you get the car rolling on long drives, the amount of gasoline used varies little from most cars in similar driving. And the additional comfort of the heavier car on long trips such as you take will be important." To the farmer who says, "Your smaller trees won't bear as much fruit as these large ones," you reply, "It's true that each tree doesn't bear as much fruit. Yet, farmers who have orchards of both sizes of trees find that the yield per acre is about the same since you have more smaller trees than you do large ones. The advantages of the smaller tree is that you can prune it and pick the fruit easily."

You need not always use the words "yes, but"; that is the technique. The approach can be varied by using a number of similar words that carry the same meaning. This provides a graceful transition that should easily lead from the prospect's objections to your reply without antagonizing the prospect.

## Turn Objections to Advantages

The alert salesperson frequently turns an objection into a sales advantage by rearranging words or stating the objection in a slightly different way. To the prospect who says, "Your shoes won't last as long as others I have seen," the salesperson replies, "That may be true, but ours are inexpensive. That enables you to have two pairs instead of one, keeping each looking new longer." Or to the objection, "I can't afford such a large house," the salesperson replies, "With your large family, Mr. Rourke, you can't afford not to have a large house. A smaller one would cramp you, make you uncomfortable, and interfere with your work. Here you can have your own room or study in which you will not be disturbed." To the customer who says, "It's a nice suit, but I can't afford it; it's too expensive," the salesperson replies, "Mr. Zamba, that's the reason why you should have this suit. It looks good on you, and your type of work demands an immaculate appearance. You can't afford not to look your best."

Take the objection of the prospect and turn it into an advantage. If a prospect complains about high price, you can point out how long the product will last, that it will not need replacement, or that its style is outstanding. If the prospect says that the product is flimsy, say, "Because of the lower cost, you can replace it easily and have the advantage of a new product more often."

## Ask Questions

In many situations, objections can be handled by throwing them back into the lap of the prospect by asking questions. If prospects object and you answer, "Why?" they are forced to do some thinking before answering. If there is a legitimate objection, their answer will be helpful in completing your sale. If their objections are trivial, their reply will reflect insincerity. This will help you to determine what type of follow-up to use. A series of probing questions may be beneficial to you and the prospect. This forces prospects to give careful thought to their problems and why they think that your product is unacceptable. They are compelled to focus attention on their own problems; and as they answer questions, they may reveal some of the issues that face them. This, in turn, may lead to greater revelation and possibly a substantial order.

**Illustration 11-1    The effective salesperson is able to turn objections to advantages.**

If prospects say, "I can't buy this now," answer "Why?" They might say, "Not only do we have an inventory in the store now but large stocks in our warehouse that we have to sell before buying any more. As a matter of fact, we've gotten a bit careless and some of our stock is getting old." This information gives you an opportunity to point out how the buyer can put up special displays or run special sales. Not only could they sell a lot of this item, but to do so they would bring out their entire warehouse stock and possibly supplement it with some new stock for the big show. This could necessitate an immediate order to supplement the stock on hand. Another buyer might say, "No, I don't think I need any more at present." Further questioning reveals that they are considering dropping your line and replacing it with a competitor's. The buyer feels that sales of your product have been slow and the new product of the competitor seems to be moving better. This information is priceless. It may open the eyes of your company to the fact that it needs to do more research and development on the present product line to bring it up to date. Prospects' objections inform you of what your customers are feeling or what is bothering them.

## The Boomerang Technique

This technique involves turning objections into reasons to buy. If handled properly, this technique can be used to move directly into the sales close. For example, the prospect might state, "I can't afford to buy right now." To this you can reply, "Miss Shen, you can't afford not to buy. You need the product, and in this day of rising prices, can you afford to wait?" If the prospect agrees to this, all you need is a pen for the order form to be signed.

## Admit and Counterbalance

In some cases the prospect's objection is valid and cannot be denied directly. However, a counterbalancing reason might be given to offset the objection. Notice the following: "This equipment is too heavy." "It is heavy, Mr. Capaldi, but that makes it stronger." "This material is too dark." "It is dark, Ms. Krasky, but it won't show spots." "This color doesn't seem so sharp." "It's true, Mrs. Sherif, but that enables you to wear the hat with many kinds of clothes." "This car seems so small." "Because of its compactness, Mr. Neeme, it enables you to get through traffic easily and to park readily." "This house seems so far away from town." "That's why it's quiet around here, Mr. Plosz. It's away from people and traffic."

## Forestalling Objections

A salesperson soon learns that a pattern of objections normally develops during the course of a presentation. With experience one can almost tell at what moment particular objections are going to be raised. Since an objection is an interruption, there are times when it would be preferable to answer it later. To avoid early standard objections, it is easy to incorporate answers in a presentation to prevent these objections from arising. For example, a prospect may object to the color of the container. You anticipate this by saying, "Mr. Ipso, our glass container is brown instead of clear. This brown prevents chemical action that weakens the solution." "Miss Crane, the surface of our product is rough instead of smooth. We have found that a rough exterior helps the user to get a firm grip." "Mrs. Rzonca, the color of our numbers may be different from those you have been using. Our experience shows that often these numbers must be read in partial darkness. When we hold our numbers in a darkened area, they glow so that you can see them easily."

Many salespeople find the technique of forestalling objections very useful if price objections are likely to occur. For example, you are trying to sell a product that is new to the prospect who has no idea of what the price will be. You might forestall a possible price objection by building up a high price expectation through the way you present the material. As you explain what you have, how it operates, what its features are, and how customers appreciate its use, you can interject the statement, "Would $35 sound too high for this product?" After further presentation to impress the customer that the price might be $35 or more, you finally add, "And as an introductory price, we are giving customers our special rate of two units for $19.95."

If it is a relatively expensive product, you might say, "Would you think $2,500 would be too much for it?" Later you could say, "This product for which many customers are willing to pay $2,500 is now selling for $1,995." Many people have no idea about prices when they encounter a new product or request a service that they have not used before. If salespeople mention a price, you fix it in your mind as the price that they are asking. Then, if they quote a lower price, you are pleased.

## When to Handle the Objection

In timing the answer to an objection, at least three possibilities arise. The first would be to answer the objection immediately but not abruptly. You might pause for a moment or two, rephrase the question, ask a question or two of your own, and then give the proper answer.

A second approach is to recognize the objection by agreeing that the prospect has raised a legitimate point, but indicate that you will answer it later in the presentation. You might say, "Mr. Liang, that is an excellent question you have raised; however, I think you will find that it fits very well into my presentation at a later point," and then go on to assure the prospect that you will handle the objection later. You might even jot it down. Both of you can then forget it for the time being because both know it will be easily recalled. This approach may have added merit if the question is new to you or opens an area that needs some extra time to come forth with a satisfactory answer. In some cases, a question may be asked for which you have no reasonable answer. You might try to sidestep the question if you feel that it is inconsequential or inform the prospect that you will have to investigate the issue raised and respond at a later time.

A third approach is to ignore the objection entirely because you feel that it is not genuine or that the prospect might forget it. In this case, go on with your presentation or demonstration without directly answering the objection. Only if the prospect repeats the objection will you answer it. If it crops up a second time, it shows that the question is still on the prospect's mind. Then, most of what you are saying does not penetrate because your prospect is so busy thinking about the objection that there is no time to hear what you are saying. Generally, the sooner you handle an objection, the better off both you and your prospect will be.

*Tip  Sumio Isobe had studied prospects over a period of time and was almost able to anticipate the exact time or points where certain types of objections would arise. Through experience, Sumio had identified most objections, developed effective answers for them, and set up a pattern as to when he would give these answers. Some he would answer when the questions were raised, some (minor points) he would evade and answer only if they persisted, and some he would record on paper to ease the prospect's anxieties, promising to answer them later. This procedure enabled Sumio to give a smooth, well-developed presentation. To offset a number of common objections, Sumio anticipated them by having answers as part of his presentation.*

*Sumio has been very successful in selling boats and motors to a varied group of buyers. He has effectively used objections as selling points. However, Sumio (as well as anyone else) can never be totally prepared for new or unusual objections. Nevertheless, Sumio's thorough preparation permits him to handle, and if necessary juggle, these unusual objections until he can think them through and prepare a satisfactory answer.*

*Since each year brings variations in the products he sells and the customers he sells to, it is essential to rework his objections list regularly. Sumio is successful in sales and enjoys these constant challenging changes.*

## EXAMINING OBJECTIONS

If you sell for a period of time, you will hear many types of objections. The more of these you can catalog and develop answers for, the better off you will be. If you have ready-made answers for standard objections, you can concentrate on problems of the moment; your presentation, interruptions, and other factors that demand your attention. If you anticipate objections and have adequate answers, you can proceed smoothly and with assurance. Most objections that you encounter will fall into one of these categories:

(1) objection to need for the product or service,
(2) objection to product or service,
(3) objection to source,
(4) objection to price,
(5) objection to buying now.

### Objection to Need

A business person will frequently express objections to need. This is often the result of being currently overstocked with too much merchandise or too many lines, or a lack of demand for the salesperson's product. In other situations, prospects will express objection to need in terms of being "just not interested."

**Too Many Lines.** Too many lines is one of the frequent complaints of buyers. On the shelf of a small grocery store, you see six or eight brands of coffee when two or at the most three would be sufficient; in a small men's store, you see two lines of belts when one would be sufficient. Walk into a machine shop, and you may see several little-used, special-purpose machines that could be replaced by one general-purpose machine that would be adequate for all needs.

Although a prospect may feel that another line is not needed, the extra line may mean extra sales. If the shoe dealer tells you that an excellent line of winter boots has already been delivered, with a little probing you might discover that it is an

**Illustration 11-2** Objections, such as too many product lines, may be overcome by stressing the importance of variety.

*photo courtesy of Owens-Illinois, Inc.*

expensive line of rubber footwear. To this you can respond, "Don't you think that boot sales would increase if you also had an inexpensive line? Many people use boots infrequently and prefer the lighter, inexpensive ones."

A store carrying several lines may be persuaded that, by introducing your wider line, the four present lines can be eliminated. If a storekeeper is reluctant to take on your line, you might point out the rapid turnover of your line and high profit margin. Show that sales and profits per linear foot of display space are much greater with your line than with any other. If the prospect says that carrying your machines would mean carrying an additional stock of parts, indicate that carrying replacement parts for your machines is not necessary because they can be ordered directly from the factory and fast service is guaranteed. Be sure to stress the advantage of your line.

The objection that a person "can't buy everything" frequently is given to salespeople who talk to wholesalers and retailers. These buyers must reject numerous items because they do not have room for them, they do not think that your item complements their regular lines, or they may offer other reasons. It would be impossible for these customers to begin to buy all products that they are asked to consider. And yet, many do buy items they had not planned to acquire because some thoughtful salesperson has pointed out opportunities or developed methods that permit the prospects to handle these items satisfactorily and profitably.

**Insignificant Product Demand.** Many of today's successful products once experienced little or no demand. Personal hygiene products such as soap, deodorant, and mouthwash were once in this position. Air travel and automobiles once were in little demand. Through vigorous selling efforts, these products and services today have achieved heavy demand. When products or services are in a no-demand situation, it is the salesperson's job to stimulate demand.

Drug salespeople, as an example, often find that there is no quick demand for new drug products. When they introduce a new drug to physicians, they want pharmacists to stock the drug so that prescriptions can be filled. When calling on druggists, however, they often hear, "I'll wait; there is plenty of time. When prescriptions come in, I'll get your product." Even more resistance may be encountered when attempting to put a new product on the shelf. The druggist will say, "No one has asked for it; it won't sell." To counter such statements, indicate how the new product can be sold. Point out that your firm is going to support the new product with a large advertising campaign. Identify other dealers who have introduced the product successfully. Eye-catching displays can stimulate sales.

If your product is used in a potential customer's manufacturing process, offer to provide a free trial amount so that the customer can make a comparison with what is currently used. You can't expect the manufacturer to accept your product without giving it a thorough trial. The customer must have confidence in the reliability, durability, performance, and safety of your product. The creative salesperson can devise many ways to stimulate demand in a no-demand situation.

**Not Interested.** Have you ever thought about going to see someone who's not interested in seeing you? Would you want to discuss some topic with a person who's not interested in listening to you? Would you want to persuade a person to take action on a matter they're not interested in? Probably not. Yet these are situations that are not uncommon to some salespeople, such as insurance salespeople. Most people are not interested in talking about or buying insurance until the consequences of being uninsured are pointed out.

**Illustration 11-3  Suggest eye-catching displays to promote your product to its best advantages.**

Each of us has used the "not interested" excuse during our lives and all salespeople have heard it. The salesperson's response should be "Why?" or "Why aren't you interested?" The prospect's reply will enable you to launch into your presentation again with more interesting selling points. The buyer may not be interested because you have not marshalled enough facts to strike a responsive chord. Somewhere along the way, if you make a proper presentation, there must be some point that will be attractive to the listener. If you hear the same objection again, ask yourself, "Is interest lagging because I'm not interesting enough?" Maybe the fault is with you, not with what you are selling. Paint word pictures about your product that appeal to the buyer.

### Objections to Product

A prospect may object to the product by saying that it does not fit present circumstances; that the product currently being used is satisfactory; that a friend used and was disappointed with your product; or if the prospect is in business, that your product is not profitable to stock.

**Doesn't Fit.**   When prospects say that your product does not fit, ask them why your product is so different from similar ones manufactured by others. Why won't your product work for them? If they are retailers, why won't their customers buy it? If your product is more expensive or cheaper than the one they handle, agree and say, "I'm sure, Mr. Ruel, that there are many people who would appreciate a product at our price and quality. Seldom will one brand satisfy everyone's demands." Often, the real answer to many prospects' objections is that you have not completely sold them, and it is up to you to do a better selling job so that they will see the value of your product. If a problem in construction is revealed, it might be possible to make a slight alteration in your product.

**Satisfied with Present Product.**   Many people are content to stay with merchandise they are presently using because change upsets present procedures. Doing something different or doing the same thing in a slightly different way requires additional effort. Why bother to change when everything seems satisfactory? This is often the attitude of prospects who are satisfied with present merchandise.

You can agree with prospects that many of the items they handle are undoubtedly satisfactory and that it might seem unreasonable to change. However, they should recognize that there is a steady stream of new products, and old products that are being modified. Ask your customers to look at their stock and see how products have changed over the past five years. When they think about it, they will be surprised to note many changes. Those who are slow to change miss excellent opportunities to get in on something new, something better, something that will move rapidly and prove more profitable. Business is filled with illustrations of how a product has been outmoded by a new item that better performs the same function.

No enterprising manufacturer can ignore a new material. Cheaper substitutes or better substitutes are being developed; if they are not incorporated into the product, they will force the manufacturer into a weaker sales position. At one time, carpeting was made wholly of wool. When wool was in short supply, prices skyrocketed; manufacturers began experimenting with synthetics and other materials. Now carpets are made of a variety of materials, only one of which is wool. In the automobile market, there is a constant struggle among suppliers of steel, aluminum, magnesium, plastics, zinc, copper, precious metals, and paper. When a new item can be substituted to do a job better or do the same job less expensively than the present one, complacency becomes dangerous. Any alert salesperson can show the value of new ideas, materials, and products.

Most buyers want to examine a new product before placing an order. The chance to examine or use the product in advance gives the purchasing agent an opportunity to determine that your product will perform successfully. Without advance use, assurance that the product will perform satisfactorily can be established through testimonials, guarantees, and demonstrations. Few salespeople are willing to guarantee that their product will work successfully as a component of another product without a proper trial, not only in the manufacturing process but in all uses. Failure could be damaging to the manufacturer using the product and disastrous to its producer. If you are confident that your product will perform satisfactorily for the prospective purchaser, prepare a convincing presentation. If the prospect says, "I want to check it further," ask, "What would you like to check? Maybe I can help you." This may uncover any hidden objections that you can handle easily.

**Product Disappointment.**   Imagine selling an item house-to-house and having a homemaker say, "I don't want it. A friend of mine bought it and was disappointed." How do you feel when a purchasing agent tells you, "We don't want it. I talked with a friend at lunch yesterday who said your product didn't perform as promised." Or how do you feel when a druggist says, "I don't think I'll add this item to my stock. We druggists had our regular meeting last night, and one who stocked your product said it didn't sell as expected." These are samples of replies that indicate that friends of the prospects have found your product unsatisfactory. Perhaps it wasn't designed to meet certain needs of the disappointed user, or poor results came from improper use. Occasionally your product may have a defect that causes it to malfunction. If this occurs, repair or replace the product promptly so that the customer knows you will stand behind your product.

Ask the buyer to give you the name of the disappointed user. Tell the customer that you would like to correct the problem. If the prospect refuses to give the name, you may assume that this is a trumped-up excuse and that you need to sell harder. If the objection is sincere, your willingness to correct the problem will impress the prospect. If the prospect happens to know the problem, you can explain how it might arise and how to avoid it. By following instructions carefully, the prospect might never face that problem with your product.

**Profit Margin.**    The objection that goods do not carry enough profit margin is being seriously shaken today. Rapid turnover, lower inventory, narrow lines, specialized goods, branded items, and a host of other features tend to wipe out the gross margin factor as the important one to consider. For example, an unknown product with a wide margin may not be nearly as profitable as a well-known branded item that is highly advertised and has a narrow profit margin. The latter may outsell the former ten to one with the net result that the latter is far more profitable.

To the merchant who says that your product is not profitable enough, point out that profit can be secured on large dollar sales rather than on a large gross margin and few sales. The advertising and sales promotion activities of your firm can be important for increased profits. Merchants who tie in with cooperative advertising get the entire benefit of the sales efforts of your firm.

*INTERNATIONAL MULTIFOODS CORPORATION*

**Illustration 11-4  A product's sales promotional activities should be coordinated with the sales force effort.**

## Source Objections

When prospects object to the source, they may be objecting to the salesperson's firm or to the salesperson. Prospects may say that they do not like your firm, that your firm's service is unsatisfactory, that they are satisfied with present sources of supply, that they do not buy from strangers, or that they do not believe what you are saying.

**Dislikes Your Firm.**　When buyers say that they do not like your firm or someone in it, find out exactly what they mean. If they say that your firm does not live up to its promises, find out exactly where your firm failed. Then tell them that you will do all in your power to correct whatever is wrong. If they have some personal gripes against one of your firm's officers, point out that your relationship is a business one and that you are selling a product that will help them. Do not under any circumstances agree with the prospect's criticisms of your firm. Get their minds off personalities and on your product's advantages. Sell your product's uses, guarantees, price, value, and delivery. Positive ammunition overcomes unpleasantness.

**Unsatisfactory Service.**　If prospects say that your service is unsatisfactory, ask them why. On what do they base their claims? Do not argue with them. If they do not have a valid criticism they will evade the issue. Then go on with the presentation. If they quote one or more valid instances, acknowledge the possibility that such instances have, unknown to you, occurred. Point out, however, that such is not your firm's policy. Whenever such unfortunate incidents do occur, tell your prospects you are glad to learn about them because that enables you to tell your firm so it can avoid such occurrences in the future. Show them you appreciate this information, and then continue to sell your product.

Tell them that if at any time they receive unsatisfactory service, they should tell you; and you will make amends immediately. They know that most firms have problems, that difficulties arise, and that misunderstandings are bound to occur. But when you indicate that these difficulties must be rare because you had not heard of them previously and that you are ready to correct them, they will be more inclined to listen to you.

**Present Sources Satisfactory.**　Some buyers are loyal to salespeople and are reluctant to make changes. Yet, professional buyers depend on their skills and abilities in product purchasing to hold their jobs. When you encounter this objection, reply, "Mr. Shippee, I appreciate the loyalty you are showing, yet this loyalty may be dangerous for you. You may be deliberately overlooking opportunities or closing your eyes to developments that are taking place. No one firm has a monopoly on all ideas or the best products. As an enterprising business person, you can't afford to pass up new opportunities."

**No Buying from Strangers.** Homemakers often say that they do not buy from strangers. A homemaker may be impressed with your product, but because of many instances in which people have been defrauded by house-to-house salespeople, there is hesitation in buying. It may be that the homemaker has been defrauded by a previous salesperson. Under these circumstances, if you have made sales to satisfied customers within the area, mention such sales as examples. Many salespeople carry some kind of identification that lends credibility to their firms and their products.

If professional buyers raise the same objection, you can easily refer them to one of the standard rating books or to other accessible financial data sources that rate your firm. In most instances, this is a weak excuse and should be treated as such.

**Does Not Believe You.** Some of your statements may seem so far-fetched that a prospect will not believe you. When this situation arises, go through your presentation carefully again. Go slowly, add more illustrations, feed-in testimonials, cite examples, try to give information that can be checked if so desired.

If possible, demonstrate your product. Perhaps you can give the prospect a sample that can be tested for quality and durability. Suggest the type of test that will best demonstrate the quality of your product. If you test your product in the presence of the prospect, be sure that the reason for this test is clear and point out how it is meaningful.

If your prospect shows disbelief, try the "order book influence." If you can open your order book and show sales to people in the community, to neighbors, or to influential people, the prospect will gain confidence. This method is especially effective in a small town where the banker, the mayor, the car dealer, and other business people have given you signed orders.

## Objections to Price

Since price objections are the chief stumbling blocks for many salespeople, careful study should be made to see how these objections can be overcome. Price objections can arise from a variety of causes. The price may be greater than the prospect expects to pay, or the prospect might not be able to afford it. Sometimes your product is priced higher than competing products.

**Price Too High.**  Price is neither too high nor low; it is a relative factor. It is high or low only in relation to the value the customer expects to derive from the product.

If the price is only slightly too high for the prospect, you may not have much trouble in explaining the difference. A slight difference can be justified by availability, selection, services offered, convenience, and many other considerations. Sometimes prices advance rapidly beyond your control, and potential buyers might not have caught up with that fact. When they shop around, they soon learn that prices have changed.

If customers resist you because they think the price is too high, point out values one after the other to justify the price. Not long ago, one of the authors of this book bought a pound of cookies. The clerk took a large number of cookies in one hand and put them on the scale. Then, by adding two or three cookies at a time, the pointer approached one pound. Finally, the clerk added only one cookie at a time until the pointer indicated the desired weight. Selling a pound of cookies for a specific price meant adding cookies until they justified the cost. There is a comparison with your customers. They see a price tag or hear a price quotation. At first they think the price far overbalances the value. Then you start piling on value, adding up qualities, giving comparisons, showing special features, demonstrating particular advantages. Soon you have piled up so much that the pointer swings over the agreed amount and customers feel that they are getting full value if not more. Whether this should be cookies on a scale, or ideas in a discussion, the result is the same. Purchases are not made until buyers are convinced that value warrants the price.

**Can't Afford It.**  When the prospect says, "I can't afford it," you can often answer, "You can't afford to be without it." At this point, let me relate a personal story. When I was in college, I read a well-known insurance company's advertisement on how to retire at the age of 65 with an adequate income. I had always had the idea of protecting the future by setting aside something during one's working years. I filled out the coupon and mailed it for further information. Imagine my surprise when, a week later, a well-dressed salesperson, a representative of this insurance company, came to see me. I was flabbergasted. Here I was, a college student, working my way through school. Dressed in old working clothes, I was beating a rug in the backyard of an Ann Arbor home when the representative, responding to my inquiry, came to help me provide for my future. I do not recall the words of our conversation. I pointed out, however, that all I wanted was information. I was working my way through college. I had no money; I had no idea of buying insurance of any kind. I could hardly make ends meet as it was. The salesperson appreciated my position, left a calling card, and said that I should call when I was in the market.

That same evening I bought a $15,000 policy from an agent representing another firm. I could not afford it; I did not have any money; I was not interested, yet I bought it. Why? I was borrowing money from people who had no security or protection except my promise. I needed to protect these people, and I bought a policy with life protection, with an income in case of disability, and with a retirement provision. The second agent qualified me by discovering my immediate need and convincing me not to put it off. The first salesperson observed the immediate situation and concluded I was not ready to buy. The second salesperson studied the entire situation and showed how I could meet my need at that time.

There are many ways of working out programs that will enable buyers to afford what you are selling. Many salespeople sell merchandise with high price tags. The real estate salesperson deals in thousands of dollars; the car salesperson deals in thousands of dollars; furniture salespeople deal in hundreds or thousands of dollars. When you notice a customer hesitating because of the magnitude of the price, break it down into smaller units. Suggest a small amount down, plus easy monthly payments over a period of years. The cost per day will not be large when analyzed in this fashion.

What holds true for the consumer may also be true for the manufacturer. When you say $90,000, $175,000, or $260,000 to a manufacturer, the price might stagger the business owner. But when this overall price is presented in terms of years of use with monthly payments over a long period, the cost seems lower even though the final total is greater. Just as distance is covered one step at a time and a job is completed one unit or task at a time, so may a large sum of money be paid over a period of time by breaking payments into manageable amounts.

**Cheaper Product Will Do.**    Two items side by side may look alike, yet one can sell for $5 and the other for $10. The customer wonders why. Although some products may be priced out of line, you will usually find that there is a reason for the difference in price between similar products. If you have any doubt about this, go to a clothing store and try on a suit for $150, another for $300, and a third for $465. The most expensive one may not wear any longer, but as soon as you put it on, you know that there is a difference.

Sometimes the prospect may find a cheaper product satisfactory. For example, the ordinary individual doing some painting at home need not have as expensive a paintbrush as a professional painter. The new piano player does not have to practice on the most expensive piano. As a matter of fact, the beginner would be unable to appreciate its fine qualities until considerable skill had been reached. But in too many cases, the prospect buys the cheaper product because some salesperson is not showing the greater advantages that would result from having the better product. Salespeople are often careless or prone to overlook the many additional qualities of their product that might be appreciated by a customer.

**Cheaper Elsewhere.**    No matter how hard you try, no matter how low you set your price, you will often find a competitor who will sell at a lower price. Price competition has been common for many years and has healthy aspects because it forces high-cost firms to discover new economies and to keep their prices competitive. Some firms are willing to cut prices severely and try to operate on smaller margins, others reduce quality to lower their prices.

When you meet price competition, stress value, services, reputation, guarantees, delivery dates, durability, trouble-free operation, and safety. Even in competitive bids, many buyers do not take the lowest bid because they consider factors other than cost. If buyers like you, they may give you an order at a higher price. They justify this action because of certain factors not covered by price. If they do not like you, they do not dwell on those factors, and you lose the order. Many times, firms have obtained orders on low bids, have substituted inferior materials, and have gotten away with it. Such occasions remind you that you cannot win them all. Some salespeople are extremely price conscious and seem to think everything hinges on price. If they cannot be low, they do not know how to sell.

We frequently hear the saying that "all things being equal, prices should be the same." Yet it is rare that all things are equal. Qualities may vary, deliveries may be fast or slow, installation may be prompt or otherwise. There can be so many variations that the alert salesperson can easily demonstrate that a seemingly high price will, in the end, be lower. You do not buy clothes, machines, or equipment; you buy satisfaction.

*Tip   Norma Laskowski has heard the "all things being equal" statement many times. She has never let this response from a customer discourage her, however.*

*Norma represents a firm that sells parts for industrial machines. In some situations, Norma's price may be $100 or more higher than a competitor's. Norma does not get into a price battle. She stresses service—speed of response and delivery—as her major sales appeal. Norma has many examples to relate about business firms that purchased from a competitor to save $100 on price, only to experience a two- or three-day delay in receiving the necessary parts and incur down-time costs of $1,000 or more. In extreme emergencies, Norma has loaded parts in her car and driven 200 miles to satisfy a customer's need. For most customers, she is able to circumvent the "price only" factor by being alert to other opportunities to help the buyer.*

## Objections to Buying at the Moment

Sometimes when salespeople attempt to close the sale, buyers will object to buying at the moment by saying that they must think it over or that they must talk it over with someone. Sometimes, particularly in industry, buyers will object by saying that they will wait for the price of the product to come down.

**Think It Over.** Find out why the buyer wants to "think it over." You could say, "Ms. Bard, I appreciate your wanting to think this proposition over. However, in a situation like yours, you will be losing a wonderful opportunity by delaying. If you tell me what you'd like to think over, perhaps I can give you the data you need to make your decision."

When the objection is an excuse, brush it aside and continue with your selling. Bring up vital points to close the sale. You might say, "Ms. Bard, I appreciate your desire to think it over, but we've had many instances in which other people have done the same thing. Later, they've come back, bought, and were sorry that they waited. Usually, the reason for delay is some slight difference that can be cleared up readily if we know what it is." Either way, whether dealing with an excuse or a legitimate objection, try to uncover the client's reasoning and cope with it immediately.

**Talk It Over.**  "First, I must talk it over with my wife, my husband, my partner, my friend." This is a common objection, and often comes up. An appeal to ego is sometimes successful in overcoming this objection. A husband makes many purchases that he does not talk over with his wife. The wife makes many purchases that she does not talk over with her husband. Many a person making important purchases would never dream of talking them over with a business partner. Often, then, this excuse is merely a stall. Usually, it arises in major purchases involving considerable sums of money.

One way to overcome this excuse is to dwell on the confidence that the other partner has in your customer. The other individual has trusted your customer in the past and undoubtedly will in the future. If it is a major purchase, try to make it look minor. Instead of talking about the total purchase price, talk about payments in terms of months, weeks, or days. You might say to a homemaker:

Salesperson: Do you have any quarters around the house?

Homemaker: Yes, I probably have a few.

Salesperson: Could you find 8?

Homemaker: I think so.

Salesperson: You know that's not very much. You need only 8 quarters a day and we will move this new refrigerator into your house. Your spouse wouldn't object to having a trouble-free refrigerator that offers the best food protection available.

To the factory owner who says, "I can't afford $40,000 for the machine," you might say, "How much is the present equipment costing you now?" He might reply, "Nothing, I've got it all paid for." Then you show him that because of breakdowns, repairs, delays, and slow operation, the increased production of the new machine would be 50 percent greater than the old one. You might say, "Mr. Oso, in wages alone, your new machine will save you $50 a day—that's $250 a week—$1000 a month—$12,000 a year. Let me show you some of the additional savings." And soon you come up with a grand total of $16,000 a year. "Over a period of five years, Mr. Oso, you save $80,000 by buying the new machine. I understand you have charge of production in your firm, and your partner, Ms. Garcia, handles sales. Probably each time you've consulted her, she's ended up by saying, 'Well, I'll leave it up to you.' Don't you think when she comes back from her business trip, and you tell her about this new machine, she'll say, 'Well done, Tony,' or 'That was a good move on your part.'?" Talking it over with someone else indicates that the individual lacks confidence. Try to reassure the prospect.

**Wait for Price to Drop.** When you hear this objection, bring up instances in which other people did the same thing only to have the price go up. Price changes are not on a one-way street. Many may have assumed they must inevitably come down, but actually the opposite may happen in an inflationary period. People who have waited to buy land have often watched the price rise. Others who used this excuse found the best homes and lots were snapped up, and the ones remaining at lower prices were much less desirable.

Another way of attacking the lower-priced objection is to show that while waiting, one is being deprived of the pleasure of using the item. People have been known to wait for years for a price to come down. By the time they buy an item at the lower price, they do not have much use for it.

Still another approach is to mention that when price comes down, the quality often goes down with it. For example, people who patronize end-of-season sales for reduced prices find soiled, torn merchandise that is not the color desired, not the style hoped for, and usually not the right size.

Paint a vivid word picture of the losses involved during the waiting period—losses in pleasure, comfort, safety, security—all are costs of waiting. Demonstrate to your customer that waiting for the price to come down is not a method of buying cheaper because the worry and loss of use more than make up for the difference in price.

# QUESTIONS

1. What are the advantages of objections raised during a sales presentation?
2. How can overlooking a hidden objection prevent a sale? Is this carelessness by the salesperson?
3. When a prospect makes a statement that is wholly incorrect, how should the salesperson respond?
4. Must a salesperson always handle objections in the same order that they are raised by a prospect? Explain.
5. When people say that they are not interested in an item, can you accept this as an honest expression?
6. How does one meet claims of unsatisfactory service from a product? Can the user be at fault? Explain.
7. What are the ways of counteracting loyalty to a competitor?
8. Is the price paid the only true cost of a product or service to a customer?
9. Are there easy ways of determining whether a prospect can afford the product you are selling?
10. How should the salesperson handle a customer who must "talk it over" with others?

# SALES CHALLENGES

1. Your firm expects to market a new model of car weighing about 2,000 pounds to a mass market. It will be smaller than the "standard" car but not smaller than a mini-car. The four-door sedan will handle four passengers comfortably and have a roomy trunk for luggage, packages, or recreational equipment. It will handle two sets of golf clubs easily, an outboard motor with a gas can and fishing equipment, or several suitcases. It will be economical to operate compared with other cars even though that does not mean cheap operation when compared with the smallest subcompacts.

   Your assignment is to anticipate and list a number of objections (not fewer than 7) that could arise when selling this car and briefly tell how you would handle each objection.
2. A major problem results when a poor sales representative has preceded you in your territory and has sold your product based on promises that were greatly exaggerated. You are finding great resistance from many homemakers who have been told by disappointed users not to buy your product. Actually,

the vacuum cleaner you are selling is superior to competing ones. After listening to a number of users, you discover the leading causes for dissatisfaction are:

(a) It is too noisy.

(b) A former salesperson used a trick demonstration that showed results the homemaker finds impossible.

(c) Several of the accessories were too expensive and not useful in normal cleaning situations.

(d) It is difficult to fit payments into their spending.

(e) The salesperson made statements and promises that weren't true. These were not major, but small, irritating items that had been completely ignored after the sale.

You are to answer each of these criticisms in a manner that will dispel fear and overcome negative thoughts as you deal with each new prospect.

3. How would you answer each of the following objections:

(a) "I'll wait until prices come down."

(b) "Your delivery service is slow and not dependable."

(c) "Your selection is too wide. I already have unsold old inventory of your stuff."

(d) "Your directions for setting up and operating the machine are too complicated. I'm not getting good results. Your machine's not dependable."

# CASES

## 11-1   Joiner Sales Ltd.

Mary Mantez had just completed the demonstration for her vacuum cleaner. She had gone over the outstanding features carefully. Step by step, she had shown the advantages of the water bath to catch dirt and had shown its superiority over bag-type cleaners. Using an ordinary vacuum cleaner of a well-known brand, she had cleaned the carpet. Then, following with her own, she showed how much dirt her machine picked up from a supposedly clean carpet. Each accessory was used in an effective way to bring out its advantages and importance to the homemaker. During the demonstration, conversation had been easy and informal. There appeared to be no tension or hostility. Both Mr. and Mrs. Barba had asked a number of questions that were answered to their apparent satisfaction. From time to time in the demonstration, they had operated the machine and several times tried the attachments on different jobs.

To be sure of making an effective demonstration, Mantez had chosen her prospects carefully. She felt certain there would be no financial problem in paying for the cleaner, even though it might be considered expensive. She had made the appointment a week in advance at the convenience of Mr. and Mrs. Barba.

In the step-by-step approach she had been using successfully, Mantez brought out her order pad and began filling it in, asking the Barbas which attachments they thought were necessary at this time. Mrs. Barba spoke up and said that before they made any purchase, they would like to think about it. Skillfully, Mantez conducted the conversation to try to get the Barbas to commit themselves as to what they wanted to think about.

After about five minutes of probing, Mantez detected signs of irritation. Realizing that she would lose the sale if she persisted, she agreed that it would be wise not to act immediately. She did, however, get permission to call back the following Monday evening for the Barbas' decision. She then gathered her equipment and in a spirit of cordiality bid the family good evening.

When Mantez got home that evening, she tried to analyze why she didn't make the sale. Everything appeared favorable. There were no loose ends in the presentation. The "think it over" statement was either stalling by the Barbas, or there was some real reason that had not been answered satisfactorily.

1. Did Mantez make mistakes in her presentation?
2. Was the "think it over" reply genuine?
3. Was the close attempt handled properly?
4. What preparations are necessary for the following Monday evening?

## 11-2 Strong Calculator Company

The Strong Calculator Company has been in business for years, and its products have a good reputation. About one year ago Strong introduced its printing calculator; since then, its sales have increased so rapidly that presently it is challenging the company's standard calculator for the lead in sales. Since the profit margin on the printing calculator is considerably higher than on the standard calculator, the company's salespeople have been urged to push the new calculator.

Dorah Galitz has recently come to work for the Strong Calculator Company as a salesperson. This is Galitz's first job since graduating from college. The only prior experience she had in selling came from working part-time in a clothing store while attending school. Since joining Strong, she has undergone training in selling and has spent one week at the manufacturing plant studying the company's products. She has also spent time accompanying experienced salespeople on their calls to observe their sales techniques. For the past three months, Galitz has been calling on prospects by herself. Her sales, however, have been disappointing.

The following are excerpts from some of Galitz's sales calls.

**Interview 1**

This sales call was made on a small manufacturing firm with approximately 200 employees. As we listen, Galitz is talking to the purchasing agent, Ms. Feldstein.

**Galitz:** You've probably heard about our new printing calculator, the Strong Deluxe.

**Feldstein:** No, I can't say that I have.

**Galitz:** Well, we introduced it a few months ago. It operates electronically and has many features including the display feature and the new printing tape.

**Feldstein:** We only have a couple of calculators in the place, so I'm not too familiar with them. What's a printing calculator?

**Galitz:** A printing calculator does everything the old-style calculators do, with the added feature that it prints all the figures on a tape to give you a permanent record.

**Feldstein:** That sounds pretty good. How much are they?

**Galitz:** Only $450.

**Feldstein:** Only! That's pretty expensive for a calculator.

**Galitz:** But this is a printing calculator.

**Feldstein:** That's still too much money. The last two calculators I bought cost $275 each. They were used, but they work just fine. I bought two of them for the price of one of yours.

**Galitz:** That sounds like a good price. What kind are they?

**Feldstein:** Oren.

**Galitz:** When did you buy them?

**Feldstein:** Seven or eight months ago.

**Galitz:** Had any trouble with them?

**Feldstein:** No, they're working just fine.

**Galitz:** That's good. Oftentimes you have problems with used equipment. Now, with our calculator, it is easier to check back on your figures because you have a record on the tape just like an adding machine.

**Feldstein:** Sorry, we don't need any calculators now. Say, do you carry adding machines? I sure could use another adding machine.

**Galitz:** No, we don't, but you could use our calculator not only for adding and subtracting but for many other operations as well.

**Feldstein:** I know, but that would cost too much. All I need is an adding machine. But leave me some literature on you machine, and if the need ever arises, I'll give you a call.

**Galitz:** OK. Sorry you can't use a calculator today. Here's a brochure describing our calculator, and here's my card. Be sure to give me a call when you need a calculator.

**Interview 2**

In this sequence, Galitz is calling on a large accounting firm that employs about 150 accountants and clerical workers. Galitz has just finished explaining the features of the calculator to Mr. Fadel, the buyer.

**Galitz:** And so you see, Mr. Fadel, the advantages the Strong Deluxe has over old-style calculators.

**Fadel:** Your talk sounds good, but I hope you've improved the quality of your machines.

**Galitz:** Why do you say that?

**Fadel:** Well, about six years ago we bought 20 of your calculators, and several of them have broken down.

**Galitz:** I'm sorry to hear that. Our machines are quality made and operate electronically. Consequently, we seldom have trouble with them. Maybe the machines you bought were abused or something. Sometimes the employees can be rough.

**Fadel:** I'm sure our employees aren't hard on the machines. Besides, the Orens and Nationals we have don't give us trouble. The service we got on your machines wasn't very good either. It took the repairer two or three days to show up. During that time two employees had no calculators. That costs us money, you know, when we have to wait like that. Can't you people improve your service?

**Galitz:** Well, those things happen occasionally. That was before my time, anyway. We're trying to improve our service all the time, but we can't always get the service department to cooperate. They've got their problems, too. But you won't have any problems with this printing calculator.

**Fadel:** That's not what I heard. I heard that these printing calculators are nothing but trouble.

**Galitz:** What do you mean, trouble?

**Fadel:** They're always breaking down, the tape gets stuck, etc.

**Galitz:** That's not right, we don't have any trouble with our machines. One of our competitors, maybe.

**Fadel:** No, it wasn't one of your competitors. Orens seems to have a real good printing calculator on the market now. I'd like to see theirs before I make any decisions. Besides, theirs doesn't cost as much as yours.

**Galitz:** I want you to be satisfied with your choice, but no one makes a better calculator than we do. Granted, theirs does sell for a few dollars less than ours, but this difference in price is really insignificant when you compare the two machines. We use nothing but the best materials in our calculators which, together with the fine workmanship employed in their manufacture, enables us to offer you the finest calculator on the market today. Why don't you buy four or five to begin with? See how much better they are than what you are using now. Once you have satisfied yourself, I'm sure you will want to replace all your present machines with Strongs.

**Fadel:** No, I'm not going to buy any more Strongs until you people improve your service and quality.

**Galitz:** I guess I can't convince you by talking, Mr. Fadel, so here's what I'd like to do. Let me leave you one of our new Strong Deluxes to try for a week or two. After you've used it for awhile, you'll see that what I'm talking about makes sense. That's fair enough, isn't it?

**Fadel:** Well, I'll use your machine for a week, but I won't promise anything.

## Interview 3

In this sequence, Galitz is calling on a small engineering firm. As we listen, Galitz has just finished describing the new calculator to Miss Meldrum, the engineer who doubles as office manager for the firm.

**Meldrum:** That sounds like a real nice machine you have, Ms. Galitz. How much is it?

**Galitz:** This calculator sells for $450.

**Meldrum:** Wow! That's a lot of money. We're a small company. . . and we can't afford to spend that much money for a calculator.

**Galitz:** That's not so much. Rather than looking at it as an expense, consider it an investment. You do a lot of work with figures on your job, and you must be accurate. Right?

**Meldrum:** Right, but. . .

**Galitz:** If you make a mistake in your figures, it could throw the whole job off, couldn't it? And this could cost your firm a lot of money, couldn't it?

**Meldrum:** It sure could.

**Galitz:** To help ensure against this happening, you need the Strong Deluxe in your office. With all the figures in front of you on the display board and on the tape, your likelihood of making errors is greatly reduced. The cost of this calculator is quite modest when compared with the money you will save.

**Meldrum:** You're making it sound like we make a lot of mistakes.

**Galitz:** No, that's not what I meant at all.

**Meldrum:** OK, I like your calculator, but before making a purchase of this size, I have to talk it over with the boss who is out of town this week.

**Galitz:** That sounds fair enough to me. Tell you what—in the meantime I'll leave this machine for you to use until your boss returns. This way, you'll have a better idea of how the calculator works, and you can demonstrate it for your boss. Then you'll give me a call?

**Meldrum:** Yes, I will. Thanks for leaving the machine.

Comment on Galitz's sales presentations and her ability in overcoming sales objections. Can she improve in this area?

## 11-3 Overcoming Objections

### Situation 1

Roland Epperman, who covers the Lake area, is attempting to close a sale to Brekla's Department Store for computerized cash registers and related equipment to handle cash receipts, check payments by mail, credit card charges and payments, inventory control and updating, and record sales by product line. Roland has outlined a program to implement the new equipment. His program has been accepted by Amir Brekla II, president of Brekla's and Regina Brekla's son, as well as Amir Brekla III, vice president and grandson of Regina Brekla.

Regina Brekla and her late husband Amir founded the store in 1940. The original store opened in a small building one block from the current Brekla location. Through hard work and long hours, Regina Brekla and her husband developed the store to the point where it was necessary to construct a new, larger facility at the present location where Brekla's has been for the past 20 years. Ownership of the store is entirely in the hands of Regina Brekla, Amir II, and Amir III, with Regina having 51 percent ownership. Sales of Brekla's last year were $6,995,642.

Regina Brekla has final control on all decisions requiring major expenditures. Most of the time she accepts the advice of her son and grandson. When Regina examined the program outlined by Roland Epperman, she was impressed. When she heard that the new program would cost $200,000 to implement, she balked. Regina said that was too much to spend as the store was getting along all right with its present system.

Roland Epperman, together with Amir II and Amir III, tried to convince Regina of the merits of the new plan. Regina admitted that the plan looked "pretty good" but not "$200,000 good."

How can Roland convince Regina that the new plan is worth $200,000?

### Situation 2

Marta Cabrera was convinced that she should add a new line of merchandise in her boutique. Her store was doing enough business to give Marta an income to meet her needs but not enough to build up much of a savings. Marta owned a nice home, a small car, and rented her store facilities. Her merchandise was priced from medium to high and appealed to above-average income customers.

The new merchandise that Marta was interested in was a line of cosmetics and related items that had been brought to her attention by Miquel Cruz of LaVerne, Ltd. It was a well-advertised line with considerable market acceptance. The customers patronizing Marta's boutique were the type that would use the LaVerne products.

In order to take on the new line, Marta would need extra space. A jewelry store next to Marta's boutique had just closed. This store could be rented at a reasonable rate and a connecting passageway could be opened. Marta could use the additional space for the LaVerne line as well as have room for other merchandise additions. Marta would need about $50,000 for the expansion. The bank representatives that Marta spoke with wanted security for any loans. It was suggested that Marta could mortgage her home. However, ten years earlier Marta had done something similar, but made a bad decision, and had lost all of her savings. She had vowed never to take such chances again.

Miquel had every confidence that Marta would be successful if she engaged in the expansion. However, Miquel's firm does not finance their customers and, at this point, Miquel has not been able to convince Marta to mortgage her home for the expansion.

What should Miquel do now?

# 12

# CLOSING THE SALE

The closing of a sale can be compared with the final act of a dramatic production. Just as a play builds to a climax, so does a good sales presentation. An appropriate background has been constructed, characters introduced, information presented, questions answered, and now the play reaches the conclusion. If all has gone well in the dramatic production, the curtain will fall and the audience will leave with a satisfied feeling. If all has gone well in the sales presentation, the buyer will be satisifed with what the salesperson has presented and demonstrated and a sale will be completed. The final step on the stairway to sales success is the closing of the sale, as illustrated in Figure 12–1.

## ATTITUDES TOWARD THE CLOSE

Picture yourself as the salesperson who is ready to close. You have worked hard. You have finished an excellent demonstration. Your presentation has been outstanding. You are certain that the prospect needs your product. You know that the price is competitive, and the quality of the item well worth the cost. Now comes the time to get the *yes* answer. This is when you show whether you are a good salesperson. If the sale is of considerable size, you will naturally be apprehensive, for it may be impossible to determine how the buyer will react. What will the buyer finally do?

Put yourself on the other side of the desk. The buyer has a problem; the right merchandise must be purchased at the right price. Picture the department store buyer of dresses. Are the dresses the right styles, the right colors, the right prices? Will they sell? How many in each size should be ordered? Is there a

**Figure 12-1**

## THE STAIRWAY TO SALES SUCCESS

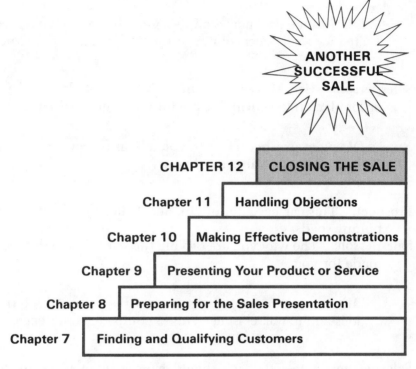

better source? Many thoughts leap into the buyer's mind. The buyer's job depends on making the right decisions. Will it work out?

If you were a customer, you would have many questions. "Have I done all right with the old product? Have I done all right without this item? Can I get along without it now? How will I meet the payments? Am I sure I cannot do better? Am I being unduly influenced by a good sales talk? Can I afford it? Should I look around some more? Should I wait a little longer? If I don't buy this item, what other things could I buy?"

Both of you sit facing each other. You wonder, "Have I done everything possible to convince this person to buy my product?" The prospect thinks, "Am I sure that I am not being influenced by the salesperson rather than the need for the product?" Remember that, although you do have to sell yourself as a reliable person, it is the product that must be promoted and sold to the prospect.

# MANAGE THE CLOSING

Throughout the sales presentation, you must manage yourself properly. Impress buyers by dwelling on your strengths and compensating for your weaknesses. How can this be done?

> **DO** arrange products, samples, models, order blanks, pens, etc., for ready accessibility at the time of closing the sale.

**Salesperson:** Mrs. Mayer, the sample is for you to keep. I have the order blank filled out and ready for your signature. Here is a pen.

> **DO** paint prospects into the picture as if they already own the product and are enjoying it.

**Prospect:** This car has a lot of zip, and I sure like the way it takes bumpy roads.

**Salesperson:** The way you are driving this car tells me this model is made for you.

> **DO** arrange to meet in a private office to avoid interruptions and to talk closing terms in complete confidence.

**Salesperson:** I feel that we should have a quiet place to discuss details in finalizing terms that are agreeable to you.

**Prospect:** I feel more at ease in a private office. When people dash through and interrupt our conversation, I get distracted and that adds uncertainty in making a decision. Disruptions bother my thinking.

> **DO** engage the prospect actively in the demonstration.

**Salesperson:** The way you operate this copier shows that you have a genuine appreciation of what it will do.

**Prospect:** Actually, I'm surprised myself. At first I thought it would be hard to learn to operate.

> **DO** act as though closing were a customary procedure.

**Salesperson:** Many of our satisfied customers appreciate the same features that you do. They find its ease of handling, its smooth response to acceleration, its attractive furnishings, and its ease in getting in and out of tight parking spaces are genuine advantages. Now it is just a matter of writing up the order, and you can be driving this car home, Mr. Osaka, this afternoon.

**Prospect:** I feel so relieved when I make up my mind. You made everything so easy, and I feel sure I'll like this car.

**DO** assume the prospect will buy: Provide trial closings in your presentation.

**Salesperson:** Miss Onada, we've gone through how this machine will meet your needs and at a price you can afford. Let's now work out the terms of the purchase.

**Prospect:** Hold on! Not so fast! I'm not ready to buy yet. What about this expensive feature?

**Salesperson:** Miss Onada, we have thoroughly covered the feature you questioned and agreed that you would find it useful. Now that your questions have been answered, let's finalize the details.

**Prospect:** The machine looks OK, but how would I meet your schedule of payments? I'm strapped right now.

**Salesperson:** Miss Onada, we were discussing our regular payment terms. However, there are alternatives. You tell me how you would like to pay, and I'll see how close we are to a final agreement.

**Prospect:** OK. If you can figure out how I can pay for it, you've made a sale.

**DO NOT** apologize for your product, your firm, or your price.

**Prospect:** I think your price is too high for the quality.

**Salesperson:** I think we both recognize, Ms. Jackson, that you need this product in your work. What we should consider is, does this product meet your need at a suitable price? In your work you want a product to perform in a satisfactory fashion at a reasonable price. Our price is representative of and often better than other sources. We both know there is a wide variation in prices depending on the quality. In your case you would have great difficulty in finding a product of comparable quality—the quality suitable for your use—at a price significantly less. When the product suits your needs buy now and begin to enjoy the benefits.

**DO NOT** apologize for taking the prospect's time.

**Prospect:**  I'm glad I had the opportunity to hear your presentation. So many salespeople fail to realize that we need your services just as many others do.

Salesperson:  I know that your time is important, and I appreciate your taking a few minutes to visit with me. Realizing your need, it is an opportunity for me to tell you about the service.

**DO NOT** question a prospect's need for the product or ability to pay.

**Prospect:**  You have convinced me we need your product. I have never considered that we could afford this luxury but when I see what it will do for my family I'm sure we can work out suitable payments.

Salesperson:  It's only a luxury if it is not necessary; however, you can see the benefits your family will receive by buying the product now.

**DO NOT** put barriers in front of the prospect: Pointing out the dangers of using your product may discourage a sale.

**Prospect:**  I am aware that this product must be used with caution.

Salesperson:  I appreciate your knowledge of the product. My explanation of its use will guide you in using it without any fears.

**DO NOT** make promises that you know you cannot fulfill.

Salesperson:  You can depend on our delivery date since we allow for unexpected contingencies.

**Prospect:**  I'm glad you guarantee your delivery date. That will give me the opportunity to use your product in an important conference we have scheduled for that week.

> **DO NOT** betray confidences: Avoid talking too much and passing along a juicy bit of scandal.

**Prospect:**  Have you heard about the troubles Brown Company is having? Rumors are flying thick and fast about them.

**Salesperson:**  I called on the purchasing agent of Brown Company last week. As usual I was welcomed by the purchasing agent who gave me a nice order. As far as I know, their operations appeared normal.

## DECIDING WHEN TO CLOSE

As you approach the close, you must sort out several issues. There are several possible paths you might take, several alternatives available. Of the several alternatives, which one is best? End, once and for all the idea that there is only one time to close a sale. There may be many opportunities to start your close. The problem is to recognize the *best* time in *each* sale.

### The Early Close

There are as many examples of salespeople who failed to close early as there are of salespeople who succeeded in closing early. Never forget that the purpose of your presentation, demonstration, and of all your efforts is to close the sale. If you find it unnecessary to go through all of your presentation, be prepared to stop whenever you see an opportunity to close the sale. Perhaps the prospect had been looking at your particular item for weeks or months before you came; there was just one more question to be answered. The salesperson cannot know how much a prospective buyer knows about a particular item, and there is a danger of oversell.

Some prospects require considerable time and demand much information before they decide to buy. What may be an important purchase for one individual is a casual purchase for another. Some will quibble over the difference of a few cents in one item and think nothing of paying many dollars for another. If the person is a repeat buyer who is familiar with the product,

**Illustration 12-1    Avoid the dangers of oversell.**

very little selling may be needed. The individual comes in, asks the price, and buys it. Another person who is a first-time purchaser may consider it very carefully.

### The Part-Way Through Close

You have completed the early points of your presentation. You notice that the buyer is interested, but you continue your sales talk because you sense there is not a readiness to buy. Halfway through, you detect signs that the person may be ready to buy. This is the time to attempt a close. Since it may be hard to detect the exact time, try several closings along the way. Otherwise, you may pass up the best time. In taking pictures, how many times have you waited for a better opportunity only to find that the best opportunity has gone? Do not be afraid to attempt to close as often as it seems right.

### Close at the End of the Presentation

When you are presenting and demonstrating a product to a homemaker, or showing a new machine to a professional buyer, or selling a new line to a store buyer, it is probably desirable to go through your entire presentation before trying to close.

Essentially, you are presenting something new, and it is necessary that the buyer be convinced of all the merits of your proposition or product before acting.

When you have made your presentation and demonstration, when you have handled objections and have done whatever you think is necessary to clear up any problems or any questions, you *must* close. Many salespeople dawdle around because they do not know exactly what to do and are afraid to close.

**Tip** **Many salespeople falter when it comes to closing the sale because they are afraid of a "no" response. This was the case with Lola Utech who sold for the Power-Vac Company. Lola resolved to overcome this fear by cold canvassing. Lola selected a sunny Saturday morning and went door-to-door with the Power-Vac products. By the end of the day, Lola had never heard so many "no's" in her life. It became almost a game and the negative responses began to give Lola a chuckle. The day of cold canvassing cured Lola of her fear of a "no" response. Now Lola skillfully and with confidence moves into her sales close with prospects. As a result, Lola has become a leading salesperson with Power-Vac.**

True, there are rare occasions when you put the close off until you make another call when it seems to be a better opportunity. But many salespeople who defer the close would be far better off if they were to make it during or at the end of the presentation on the first call. If you must make another call before closing, set a definite time for your return visit.

### How Many Times Should You Try to Close?

There is no set number of times to try to close. The only universal generalization about it is that most salespeople do not try often enough. They give up too easily.

Salespeople may use from one to a dozen attempts to close the sale before they either make the sale or leave. Statistics show that most sales are made after several attempts to close. It is not unusual to try four, five, or six times before you close. Some salespeople may try as many as 20 times. Possibly, sales that are made easily or quickly may be potentially dangerous. If the buyers make up their mind so easily, they can change it equally fast and cancel the order or bring the purchase back for exchange or refund.

## Look for Closing Signs

What are some of the closing signs that indicate a prospect is ready to buy? Can you identify the time? The answer to the latter question is "maybe." The best you can do is to follow identifying signs. If you succeed in your attempt to close, you have chosen the right time; if you do not succeed, back up and start over again.

When a salesperson is making a car presentation to a couple, and one asks the other, "What color do you like best?" that is a signal to close. When a person trying on a coat says, "I certainly could use a coat like this," it is a signal to close. When the shoe buyer says, "These shoes certainly would go well with my new dress," close. When the prospect asks, "How long will it take to deliver this car?" close. "How does your guarantee work?" is a closing indicator. When the real estate salesperson hears, "This is the best-looking house we have seen yet," move in to close.

Many times, you can tell by the prospects' actions when they are ready. Many who study people soon learn that under particular situations they have certain expressions. Boxers review films of opponents to see if there are any mannerisms that tip off what the opponent will do next. The boxer may discover that a particular opponent will place his feet one way when preparing to throw a right and another way before a left jab. There are many revealing signs that the alert boxer can detect. The alert salesperson soon learns to detect the signs—facial expressions, nervous movements, eye changes, or hand movements. Such actions show tensions or desires that indicate the individual is ready for the close.

## Trial Closes

The trial closing, which is an attempt to close, may be used to determine if a customer is close to a buying decision. Some salespeople are willing to try more than others. Some try once and give up. In selling, do not fear trial closes. When you are sharpening a knife, you often test to see if it is sharp enough. When you taste soup, you try it carefully to see if it is too hot. The trial close is basically the same thing: a testing of buyers to see if they are ready to make the commitment to buy.

This can be the turning point in your selling career if, as you read this, you make up your mind to try to close. Tell yourself, "I am going to try to close; I will try over and over again. When I

**Illustration 12-2** Watch for verbal and non-verbal indicators to close a sale.

do not succeed, I will study my failures to see where I went wrong, to see where I can improve. Then, when I have made careful preparation, I will try again. Whenever I fail, I will study and try again." Do this, and you will not fail.

You should be warned that blind trails may not lead very far. They show that you have perseverance, but what you need in addition is intelligence. Carefully work out trial closes; carefully think out procedures; thoughtfully work out approaches.

**Tip** *Sometimes differences in price may not really be in the product but in the mind of the buyer. Nita Kroope learned that the time she closed early in her presentation. In one instance a customer came in and procrastinated in buying because the furniture polish she wanted was priced* *at $4.95, and she had seen the same item in another store for $4.79. After a lengthy discussion, Nita was able to sell the customer the item. On the way out of the department the customer saw some lounge chairs and stopped to examine them. Nita hurried over and showed her a new chair that had just been received and explained its advantages. Then she called the customer's attention to a nice chair on sale and explained its qualities. Nita particularly stressed the sale price of $550, a markdown of 40 percent. The customer, holding her small purchase, tried out both chairs carefully, stood silently for a few moments, and then said, "I'll take this new chair,"—price $900. Nita learned that she could not equate her thinking with the price-value thinking of customers. She spent 15 minutes to convince the customer to pay $4.95 and only 15 minutes more to sell the $900 chair. What Nita didn't know was that this customer had shopped for a chair for months, and as soon as she saw this one, knew it was what she wanted.*

## METHODS OF CLOSING

A number of closing methods may be used. As the occasion demands, you can use one or more methods until the sale is made. There is no one best method. Start out by using the most effective one that you know. If unsuccessful, try a second close using another approach.

### The Assumption Close

Assume the prospect will buy. You have made the presentation, the demonstration has been completed, objections have been answered, and the choice has been narrowed. At this point, the next logical step would be to make out the order form or to settle on some minor details. "Will Thursday of this week be all right for installing your furnace?" "We'll put on the whitewall tires and have the car ready for you tomorrow afternoon." "You can register for the course tonight and make a down payment of $20, with the remainder payable the first night of class." These are positive statements that are just one step removed from signing the order.

While you are talking, you can be drawing up the contract or agreement or filling out the order form so that it is ready for the buyer's signature. Handled properly, the buyer will not feel forced; it will simply be an indication that you are reaching a natural conclusion from a pleasant experience. Do not hesitate to use the assumption close because it is too bold. It is used successfully on many occasions.

### Summarizing the Advantages Close

After a lengthy presentation, it is not likely that the prospect will remember all the selling points. Therefore, it would be wise to summarize them at the end as a part of your close. Perhaps you brought out points that were not applicable to the prospect. When you summarize, concentrate on those points pertinent to the prospect, and omit the ones that do not apply.

Do not become too formal or too stiff in your summarization. Do not talk as if you were hammering your arguments home point by point. Summarize in a pleasant, cordial way that invites agreement as you go along. "Mr. and Mrs. Vocamp, you agreed, didn't you, that you wanted a big house? You agreed that you wanted sliding closet doors. The hardwood floors were the ones you liked. You wanted a full basement that could be converted into a recreation room. You wanted a double garage attached to the house. The lot has a number of trees for shade. The house is on a street where there is little traffic." Notice how you are recalling important features one by one. If any particular feature was unusually appealing, stress that a little harder. The review and summarization of points rapidly outline the outstanding features of the product and enable the buyers to see clearly and quickly the overall picture.

As soon as these important points have been planted in their minds, try to close. If your presentation has been well done, your prospects should have become so interested that they are ready to buy. Summarizing merely gives the clinching data that firm up the prospect's resolve to buy.

### Direct Close

One of the bluntest ways to close is to ask for the order. The bluntness may be tempered, however, by the skill with which you phrase your question. The way questions are used and the strength with which they are asked often are the influencing factors and become the determining methods in picking your close.

You may say, "Ms. Rosaldo, I know that in our discussion you have been in full accord with the facts, and you have agreed on respective points along the way. You have definitely agreed that this product would fit into your line of merchandise. As I write up the order, please give me the quantities, sizes, and colors."

Notice the directness of the following: "Mr. Stertzenheimer, we have completed our demonstration. You have driven the tractor, and have seen how it performs. You have said that it has many fine features that would be useful to you. We have agreed on the amount of trade-in for your old tractor. Now, tell me how much of a down payment you would like to make, and we can draw up the papers."

Speaking to a purchasing agent, you say, "Mr. Himler, you have seen how this equipment performs. Your chief engineer has seen it in action and feels it will be quite satisfactory. The operator who used it in your factory was enthusiastic about it. Sending in your order today will enable us to deliver this machine in a month. A few days after installation, you will be turning out parts more accurately, faster, and at a lower cost than you have ever done before. As I write up the order, will you tell me which accessories you would like to have?"

## Dispose of the Obstacle Close

You have made your presentation, shown samples, answered questions, and are leading up to the close, but you find an obstacle remaining. The couple buying carpeting likes the material and the texture; they approve of everything but the shade, which is not quite what they want. The new car buyer wants a light blue shade and yours is dark blue. The woman tries on the new blue dress, likes it, but wants a green one. The couple has gone through the house with a California redwood exterior. One is ready to buy now, but the other still wants a brick house. The buyer had wanted a one-story warehouse, and the one you are showing has two stories. Outside of that, it meets all specifications. As far as can be determined, there is only one obstacle remaining in each instance. If that particular point were satisfactorily cleared up, there would be no hesitation in buying. To reinforce this idea, ask the prospect in each situation if this is the only objection. If this objection were removed, would they buy?

Once you have gained an affirmative response, the skillful salesperson can work to demolish the objection. Point out that the "obstacle" is an advantage or that the feature will do no harm, or that it is not easy to get a similar product with as many desirable features. No single product will have everything. In this situation, the strong features more than offset what appears to be a disadvantage. The salesperson need not worry about doing a disservice when overcoming an objection. Most objections are minor. The customer benefits more by having the product than by doing without it because of some inconsequential weakness.

## The Choice Close

The next time you have an opportunity, watch a skillful salesperson using the "choice" method in selling shoes or clothing. After showing a customer several pairs of shoes, the salesperson tries to detect which one the customer likes best. Then, quietly, the salesperson will start removing shoes in which there is little interest. Finally, the selection remaining is down to two pairs, or three at the most. These are the ones the customer finds most attractive, most comfortable, most desirable. So, it becomes a matter of picking one without being distracted by multiple offerings.

Watch department store salespeople selling appliances. Usually, the store will have several brands and several kinds within each brand. Since they are not particularly concerned which brand a customer chooses, they narrow the choice to a couple that seem to appeal. Finally, the salesperson will say, "You will notice that both of these have very fine features. It just becomes a matter of personal preference. Since you can't go wrong with either, which refrigerator would you like delivered—X or Y?"

Notice how easily specific examples can be used. In selling hats: "Would you want the wide brim or the narrow brim?" In selling shoes: "Do you prefer the black or the brown ones?" In selling gloves: "Which do you prefer, the lined or the unlined ones?" In selling mosquito repellent: "Would you like the stick or the liquid?" In selling bath powder: "Will the regular or the economy size prove most convenient?" In selling lamps: "Which one appeals to you the most, the one with the side adjustment or the one that adjusts vertically?" In selling insurance: "Would the monthly payment or the semiannual payment be preferable?" In selling casting rods: "Which one feels better, the five-foot or the six-foot rod?" In selling bedroom furniture: "Which will look better in your home, the mahogany or the walnut?"

Although this method is applicable to personal buying, it can also be useful with industrial equipment. You will have different sizes and horsepowers in motors. There are special features that can be readily added. Many products are sold in combinations so that the buyer can have the entire package at once or buy it piecemeal by getting the main unit first and then adding elements as needed or when finances are available. Whatever the buying decision of the prospect, the alternatives are such that the salesperson wins. There are two or more possible choices from which the prospect may choose. To say "no" requires much more effort at this juncture. When the need exists and a convincing presentation has been made, the logical decision is to choose the best alternative.

## The Final Detail Close

You are ready for the close. Everything has been going smoothly, and you feel the prospect is ready to buy. You sense that the decision has been made. But you need one more effort to nudge the prospect over, so you casually bring in one more suggestion as an incidental feature. Yet both of you recognize that it really means that the person has decided to buy. The actual item you bring up may be unimportant but one that you would ask about only when you feel the time has come to act. You say, "We have now gone through what this machine will do for you, how it is made, and what you can expect of it. You will notice it comes equipped with two styles of levers. Which one of these do you prefer?" "This coat fits you well. If you tell us where you want the additional button, we'll put it on now."

As you think of any specific product or service you are selling, your mind soon becomes filled with details, small advantages, and minor decisions that can be suggested to make the buyer act. These details are transitional. They take the individual from a passive listener stage, through an interested prospect stage, to an active buying position. Nowhere do we suggest that you stop abruptly and start again. Rather, in each case there is a normal transition.

## The Emotional Close

Many people fail to move or perform unless motivated by emotional conflict or desire. Since they regulate our lives in so many ways, emotions can be put to work to bring about a desirable close. In selling protective equipment or services, you may relate stories or situations in which people have suffered because they failed to act soon enough. If you are a tire sales-person, you ought to know of situations in which people have been injured or killed because of smooth tires that could not stop the car. Or, you may know of cars that have been thrown off the road by blowouts on badly worn tires. Emotions are often more significant than the intellect.

**Illustration 12-3 The emotional close appeals to the prospective customer's sense of well-being.**

Be prepared to accept resentment from some prospects when you use this type of close. They sense what you are doing and they object. Granted, this is a negative approach. Because you have probably failed to close with other words, you now turn to this approach. When using the emotional closing method, be sure that you have informed the prospects thoroughly about your product, what it will do, and what it will offer so that once they accept, there are no bothersome details to clutter up the close. They know what your proposition is; they are partially convinced that they should buy; they can see the merits of it; but they are not thoroughly convinced. Hopefully, the emotional close will convince them to buy.

### The Standing-Room-Only Close

If ten items will supply the usual needs of a group of individuals, and if they know that these articles are available, they will show no haste in securing them. Nor will they willingly pay the going price. Should these people find out that 11 items instead of ten are available, they will recognize that there is a surplus, and they will be slow to buy. Even if the price goes down, they will probably not act because they know many are left. On the other hand, if these same people discover that ten items are needed and only nine are available, they may rush to buy the available items. If the seller holds off, the price may increase and the buyers may offer a much higher price, even though being deprived of the article would cause little inconvenience.

Many people want what they cannot get. The more difficult it is to get the more they strive for it. Being aware of this human frailty, alert salespeople can adopt it in their close. When you challenge the buyers in this way, their interest is aroused, their tenacity asserts itself, and their bulldog persistence sets to work. "No one is going to stop me from getting this," they think. "If it's that hard to get, I'd better buy it now." "If I'm the only one in town getting this offer, maybe I'd better snap it up."

The standing-room-only approach can be particularly useful when you can honestly tell the customers that you have only one item left and that you do not know when you can get delivery on another. Or, if wanted on time for a certain event, the customer had better get it now. If you are sincere and later events prove that you were right, people will gain confidence in you. If, however, this is merely a scare technique to get action, people will soon discover you, and sales will suffer. This method would not be considered the normal one to use under many circumstances; it is not to be used as frequently as other methods that we have discussed. Rather, it is a method for special occasions when the time is appropriate and the statements you make are truthful and can be verified. Buyers who have unwittingly been misled by this method will resent it, and they will not forget. Others who have followed your advice and succeeded in getting merchandise they need badly will be happy that you gave them the opportunity.

## Special Concession Close

Buyers are always looking for a special deal, a better discount, a larger portion, or better delivery dates; they want something extra over the regular deal. Sometimes the salesperson can make a special concession to the buyer to close the sale. Unfortunately, many buyers have learned that if they hold out long enough, they can get special concessions or inducements that other buyers do not receive. In price-cutting and discounting, it is not uncommon for the astute buyer to get a better bargain than the one who buys without dickering.

**The Combination Offer.** A combination offer or a tie-in will often close the sale. Think of many television commercials that you have seen. A kitchen utensil may be offered at a particular price. After the sales pitch and demonstration, another item is added still at the original price. As the commercial draws to a close, you are told that if you order today, yet another item will be included, still at the original price. In this way, the buyer seems to be getting something for nothing and goes for it.

Many magazines use the special deal to get subscriptions. "Send in your subscription now and get this free book." Introductory offers to retail store buyers are often made with a free deal attached.

**Special Discounts.** In the course of your day's work, you will meet buyers who insist on special discounts. If the price has not been announced, a salesperson occasionally increases the original price and then gives discounts that bring it back to the regular price. If a piece of equipment has extra parts, some of these may be removed and the base equipment sold at a lower price. Once the sale is made, you may try to increase it by adding features that were originally omitted.

Introductory prices will sometimes feature special discounts that permit better prices to customers. Special allowances are sometimes given for large quantities, old models, or special occasions. Legitimate price concessions can be made in such a way that the list price is not lowered. A lower price may be offered because added features are included that customarily are sold at reduced prices. If special customer discounts are requested and you cannot give them, tell the prospects that your firm does not permit price deviations.

**Be Careful When Giving Special Concessions.** A salesperson may have considerable leeway in quoting prices. As a matter of fact, price may have many components. There may be a cash price, a time price, different discounts if paid within certain periods, special quantity allowances, rebates for performance, special dating, and many other permissible deviations. Sometimes you are allowed to meet legitimate competitor prices. Avoid getting entangled with typical price hounds who always insist on a better price than anyone else. Once you give in to them, there will be a perpetual price battle. Some salespeople become known as price-cutters. If your product is priced right in the beginning, you should be able to justify your price.

The price-haggling tactic may be worthwhile for buyers, but salespeople soon find out about such prospects. When salespeople know what to expect, they can prepare accordingly. Many times, they approach the price-cutter with a special price so that they can "give-in" when the buyer becomes insistent. In that way, they seemingly reduce their price without actually doing so. What they may have done is to start with a higher price to suit the buyer who insists on having some concession.

When the bargaining gets hard, many salespeople may be tempted to offer a personal attraction to the buyer, or the buyer may ask for something from the salesperson. This may appear harmless, but it is the beginning of bribery. Salespeople who rely on buying their customers rather than selling their products to the customers soon find that they are driving down a rocky road. Once you have whetted the appetite of the unscrupulous buyer, demands are insatiable. The salesperson finds that other salespeople who are bidding on the order are using the same tactics. Finally, the whole corrupt procedure is exposed. The buyer is discharged from the purchasing job and the salesperson who participated in the activity is also out of a job. Those who build on the sure foundations of value, quality, service, honesty, and integrity, find—as the years go by—that selling becomes easier, customers become more friendly, the job becomes more pleasant.

## What to Do If You Cannot Close the Sale

When you have tried several closes and have been unsuccessful, prepare to leave. (This does not indicate that you have given up!) As you prepare to depart, review silently and rapidly the various closes you have tried to see whether you have left something unsaid or undone that would interest the prospect.

**Try to Find Out Why You Could Not Close.** There can be many reasons why a buyer decides not to purchase your product. If your prospect decides not to buy, your job is to find out why. If you ask frankly, the prospect may give you the answer. If the prospect objects that it is not advantageous to buy, quote a similar case in which the reaction was the same, but when the other person bought, the results were outstanding. If you cannot uncover the real reason for not buying, you might ask as you leave, "Was there something, Ms. Lokam, I said or left unsaid that made you decide not to buy?" If she replies to this question, she will give you another opening to continue your presentation.

**Reopening the Presentation.** If you sense a chance to reopen the presentation, you may digress into some general conversation as if preparing to leave and then adroitly swing back to the original topic and begin your presentation in another vein. By this time, you may have thought of another idea or there may have been a change of mind. With the new approach, it can become an entirely new presentation and the buyer may see it in a different light and buy. Timing is important. What a person would do one day might be considered foolish the next day.

You can always attempt to reopen the sale by indicating, as an afterthought, that you probably should have covered one portion of the demonstration better, that you failed to give complete information, or you did not cover fully some phase that was of paramount interest to the buyer. In none of these suggestions are you repeating yourself; you are simply trying to present all of the information that you have available. Offer something new, something additional, something appealing.

Although you could return some other time, you may never find the individual in a favorable frame of mind again. You may sense that the buyer is almost convinced; should you come back later, you would have to repeat a lot of the presentation. This may be the time to ask if you have omitted anything, if you have failed to make yourself clear, if there is any particular problem. As this casual conversation goes on, some clue may be dropped that will enable you to reopen the sale on another theme. A quick-thinking salesperson finds many opportunities to introduce material that may again quicken the buyer's interest and lead to a sale.

**Offer the Buyer a Trial Order.** If you feel that the buyer is satisfied in most respects with your product and sales proposition, but you still cannot close the sale, you might try the technique of offering a trial order. A salesperson with a new product for industry must have the product proved in use. Seldom will a purchasing agent switch from a satisfactory product to an unknown one, even though the price appears advantageous, unless there is assurance that the new product will perform as well as, or better than, the old one. At the same time, the purchasing agent does not dare to let opportunities go by. Therefore, you may be able to get a trial order to see how your new product works in this situation.

The trial order is often used to introduce a new line in a store. Buyers may be reluctant to purchase a large quantity until they see how it sells. The danger of buying too small a quantity, of course, is that it will be hidden on a shelf and no one will push it. The product does not get the exposure it should have, and the salespeople do not feature it. Many times, an otherwise perfectly good product fails because of the lack of promotion. When a customer wants a trial order, be sure to give enough of the product for a fair trial.

**Leave the Door Open, Even When You Don't Close.** Do not let yourself get "no'd" out of the office. This becomes so final that your chance of getting back is rather slim. If you perceive that the sale is not progressing well and that chances of closing are slim, try to exit gracefully, closing with an agreement for a return call at a later time. Set a specific time for the return visit. In itself, that move indicates that the buyer has sufficient interest to see you again.

It is wise to make the second call if you met constant interruptions or the buyer had been preoccupied during the first call. If your talk is not registering, it is no use to go on. Better try another time when you think your chances are better. Sometimes, more than two calls may be necessary. In each case, arrange your calls so that others may follow if deemed advisable. This means that at each call you should have something new, fresh, worthwhile, and specifically applicable to the sale. Do not expect the buyer to listen patiently if you drag out old material that has already been used. You were given another chance because you were expected to give something new or different. You may find it advantageous to bring the boss or another salesperson along with you on a call-back to create fresh interest.

A salesperson expects to make several calls on the industrial buyer or the professional buyer before making sales. Close business relationships are not cemented overnight. If you have trouble selling retail buyers because they think your line is too expensive and you cannot convince them the first or second time that they should stock it, do not give up. Continue to call. Each time you call, discuss some new reason for stocking your

**Illustration 12-4  Bringing a boss or colleague on a call-back visit may be advantageous.**

product. Eventually they will hear so much about it that they will try it. Also, on repeat calls you will meet the buyer in different moods. One day the buyer might be much more receptive than on another day.

## HANDLING THE THIRD PARTY

When two people enter a retail store and you notice that one is to do the buying, separate the nonbuyer from the buyer. It is much more difficult for two people to make a decision than it is for one; it is impossible if one is a bystander. Unsolicited comments can frustrate the customer so that all thoughts of buying disappear. Show the bystander some other article to divert attention; if possible, call in another clerk who will show other items of interest.

When selling to a group of people, experienced salespeople find it helpful to call on each individual beforehand and go over details. If possible, try to get a commitment to buy before the meeting at which the decision is to be made. This approach will enable you to size up the various individuals and sense what their feelings are toward you.

## SUGGESTION SELLING AND TRADING UP

For many products, you will have the opportunity for suggestion selling or trading up after you have closed the sale on the primary product. In suggestion selling, you may try to sell more items by promoting a larger quantity of the product the customer has chosen or by promoting related items.

Suggestion selling is very successful. When a car is purchased new, many people are responsive to additional items to dress the car up or make it more comfortable to use. Suggestions are also successful in apparel sales. Once the basic garments have been purchased the buyer will frequently welcome help from the salesperson to add accessories to complete the wardrobe.

Suggestions may be made skillfully, courteously, and helpfully without arousing antagonism. Many people who disapprove of having additional items forced upon them are happy to listen to a discreet presentation of additional merchandise. If you try to step up sales from the customer's viewpoint rather than your own, your suggestions will probably be well received. People resent sales pressure when there seems to be no need for the product. However, the customer will welcome suggestions for additional items that will more adequately take care of demonstrated needs.

**Tip** *In selling computers, add-on sales are really significant. Placido Italiano, a salesperson for Computer Expanded, Inc., was a follow-up salesperson who spent all his selling time in increasing sales to present users. Once the original computer had been installed and was operating fairly well, Placido would call as a representative of his firm, study the use of the computer in the purchaser's firm, and originate new applications that would require both hardware and software additions. Such additional sales would increase overall sales significantly each year for Computer Expanded.*

*Trading up* refers to promoting better quality than the customer would otherwise have purchased. Since quality is a relative term, usually there is ample opportunity to step up the quality of the purchase. Many times customers are intent on buying an item at a certain price. But once they have seen a similar item of higher quality, they recognize the value and transfer their attention to the better one. The quality item attracts more attention because it looks better, perhaps feels better, works better, lasts longer, gives trouble-free service, and has many other features.

## ENDING THE INTERVIEW

Even if you have closed the sale successfully, this does not relieve you of some important tasks: reselling the buyer on the product just purchased; and taking your leave gracefully.

### Post-Sale Goodwill

Do not leave abruptly. The buyer, Ms. Crowe, has been agreeable and considerate; she has given you her attention, and she has given or will give you money in the future. Be courteous and leave her with some reassuring words. In no way should you convey the idea that you got the better of her. Reassure her that she has made a wise decision that will help her firm in the future.

Tell the homemaker that the product will add pleasure to housekeeping. Point out to the young couple how the acquisition of a new home will mean much in their lives. Tell them that making the right start, such as they have made today, will lead to a happier future. When a customer has decided to buy there is a feeling of having done the right thing. The purchaser is proud of this action. Fan that pride into a glow of satisfaction. Develop the feeling of soundness in the decision.

### Taking Leave of the Buyer

When you have completed your call, leave! After the sale, there might be a tendency to relax and spend some time in general conversation. What a salesperson forgets is that the individual has given courteous attention for a prolonged period. It has taken time and concentration that that individual might have used elsewhere. Now that the interview is over, the buyer wants to get back to other activities.

In taking your leave, you should not be abrupt or hurried, but neither should you linger. You should act in a calm, collected way; in a businesslike manner you should assemble your equipment; in a sentence or two you should resell, as previously explained. Then thank the customer politely, and leave. Lingering may give the buyer an opportunity to reconsider or to wonder about the wisdom of the purchase. If the buyer should have a change of heart, it is easy to cancel the order if the salesperson is still present. All of us are familiar with people who say that they must leave and then keep talking on and on, never quite making the break. As a host, we have stood courteously talking with such people in the cold, waiting for them to start their cars and be off. Do not be guilty of such an exit. Make a few brief remarks and leave promptly.

## THE TREE OF ACCOMPLISHMENT

The tree of accomplishment in Figure 12–2 portrays the steps involved in making a sale and the preparation demanded of the salesperson to complete a sale successfully. Study the steps of the sale. Learn how to make each step effective. Practice each step until it becomes a part of your selling process. You must learn and perform so well that each step blends smoothly and almost unconsciously into the next step. The sale is segmented into these steps for instructional purposes. In applied selling, all steps are blended and used almost instinctively in the correct pattern and with sufficient intensity to meet the particular selling situation facing the salesperson.

As a background to effective selling, the selling tree must have a strong, live, developing root structure to nourish the salesperson's efforts. This root system must be fortified, extended, strengthened, and fed to keep it vigorous in supporting the sales effort.

## A SUMMARY

In the preceding five chapters and in this one, you have covered the steps that go into making a sale. The material has not been arbitrarily chosen by the authors, nor is it the product of any one individual. Rather, this information has been developed by many successful salespeople who, through years of experience, have discovered workable methods.

What you have read is not untried. It is a series of practical, applied, commonsense approaches to the task of selling. They work because they have been tested repeatedly. The sensible approach is to profit from the knowledge and experience of others. Learn as much as you can from them. Use methods that

**Figure 12-2**

## TREE OF ACCOMPLISHMENT

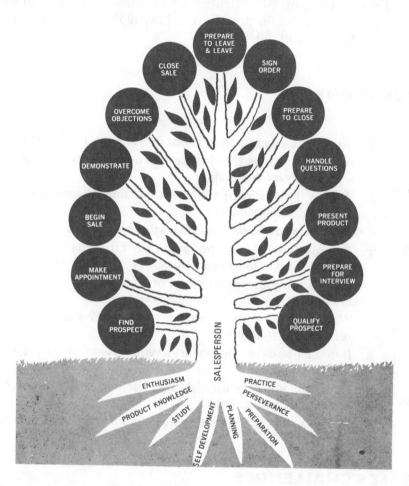

they have found successful. Refine them to meet your particular needs. Apply them consistently.

When you first try some of the suggestions, they may not work well. Before you condemn them, see if you are using them effectively; then, ask yourself if you are choosing the best methods for each situation. Of the many methods and approaches that you have been given, some will be better adapted to particular needs than others. Like any tools, these methods must be used properly for the greatest benefit. Challenge yourself now to become an outstanding salesperson by preparing yourself, and by carrying out the selling task with tools that have been used successfully by many others. Do not think you or your product or your firm is different. Basic principles remain the same. Modifications may be necessary to make them directly applicable, but the fundamentals remain. Always remember you sell to people.

## QUESTIONS

1. Should a salesperson attempt more than one close? Explain.
2. Are there signals that indicate you should attempt to close? Indicate several signals.
3. Why is it significant that summarizing advantages is often essential for closing?
4. Asking for the order can be a stumbling block. Why?
5. An emotional closing has significant drawbacks. How might this method antagonize a prospect? Give details.
6. Why is it important to close on the first call? Why not just make a return call at some later date?
7. What are the purposes of a trial order? Point out several reasons for trial orders.
8. If a call-back is necessary, what steps should you take immediately?
9. What do you accomplish by reselling a customer before leaving your sales call?
10. How do you terminate a sales call and leave your customer?

## SALES CHALLENGES

1. Emily Lauger found that in making sales, the close was much easier when the customer was given an extra, small discount. This approach was used successfully with a number of regular customers, but there was always the temptation to reward the customer who wanted a greater discount. Increasingly, Emily was troubled by this problem, but as long as her employer let her "get away with it" she continued these discounts and her sales increased each year.

   After several years Emily got an offer from another firm at a higher salary and additional benefits, an offer she accepted.

In this new job Emily began using the same discount technique she had used previously. Since the sales were much larger in this firm and competition was keen, her new employer learned early about these special discounts and deducted them from Emily's salary. She was told that it was not the custom of the firm to offer discounts and whenever she did so it would be charged to her personally. Emily knew, of course, that she could not afford this arrangement and that discounts would not be accepted by the sales department. If she was to retain this new job, which she liked, she would have to discontinue these discounts. The question was, HOW?

You are to develop a plan that Emily can use to eliminate these special discounts without losing customers and, at the same time, satisfy her employer. Put yourself in Emily's place and answer "How can I do it?"

2. Ronald Cuzo sold recreational equipment and supplies to sporting goods stores catering heavily to fishing enthusiasts, backpackers, hikers, and campers. Competitors were heavily entrenched and there was never an easy sale. Since most of the sales were in well-known advertised products, it was essential for Ronald to use personal efforts of various kinds to get and hold business.

Ronald was well-liked and got along well with buyers. His main problem was gaining acceptance of new products among his buyers. Since his buyers were often caught with new items that did not sell well and had to cut prices substantially to move such inventory, they were very cautious about buying. However, some of these new items sold well and the store suffered if it did not have adequate inventory. The question arises, how do you sell items with new brand names to your customers?

Your assignment is to develop, in dialogue form, an approach to sell successfully one new item; you may choose the item. Keep in mind the kind of products Ronald Cuzo sells.

3. Up to this time you have failed to make the sale. However, you have not given up hope of finally selling this prospect. Several times in trying to close you sensed that the sale was almost made. Your mind is groping for some kind of clincher before giving up. As you casually prepare to leave, you sense that if only you were given time the prospect would buy. However, now the prospect is getting impatient and starting to fidget. Your only possibility is to get a call-back. That will give you a fresh start, open up new avenues, and perhaps touch some responsive chord that will lead to a sale. You know the

prospect needs your product and is financially able to buy. There just seems to be some lingering doubt that you feel could easily be handled if discovered. The only present recourse is to get permission to come back—the sooner the better.

You are to prepare a dialogue for the closing moments that will touch the prospect in some way so that you are granted another interview.

## CASES

### 12-1   The Sportsman's Shop

Oren Pringle works as a salesperson in the tent department of Sportsman, a large sporting goods store. Oren has been running tent and tent equipment ads in the city's largest newspapers the past week, so a large section of floor space has been devoted to this merchandise.

On Thursday afternoon a prospect enters the store and begins to examine the items. Oren approaches the potential customer:

**Pringle:**   Quite a few tents here. We hope to meet the needs of most people in the city.

**Prospect:**   This is the biggest selection of tents I have ever seen.

**Pringle:**   Thank you. Shall we look at some of them? Do you mind telling me how you expect to use the tent?

**Prospect:**   There are five people in my family. That includes my wife, two sons, ages 5 and 11, and a daughter who's 9. We need a tent for a two-week vacation. We expect to stop several times as we travel—probably moving the tent every other day.

**Pringle:**   That means you want a tent that's easy to handle, and easy to put up and take down.

**Prospect:**   That's the general idea, and I don't want to pay too much either. Raising a family these days is expensive.

**Pringle:**   You're quite right Mr. . . . ?

**Prospect:**   Spencer is the name.

**Pringle:**   Yes, Mr. Spencer, Pringle is my name, Oren Pringle.

**Spencer:**   Can you show me some tents that are easy to put up?

**Pringle:**   Surely, Mr. Spencer. Here is a wall tent for a family your size. It will sleep five people comfortably. Note that the material is light in weight but guaranteed to be waterproof. The window on the right side can be opened easily for light and ventilation, yet the screen keeps out the mosquitoes. The floor is made of a strong canvas cloth, which takes considerable wear. It's waterproof so your feet won't get wet when it rains. To erect this tent you follow the easy instructions provided. Follow the directions carefully and you won't have any problems. In taking it down just follow the directions again. After putting it up once, it will be easy for you to do it again.

**Spencer:** It does seem simple after watching you do it. How much is it?

**Pringle:** This is modestly priced at $250.

**Spencer:** Costs money, doesn't it. How much is this round tent over here.

**Pringle:** Our round tents are made by one of the top companies in the business. This size, suitable for your family, is priced at $300. It is a top quality tent with some features that I showed you in the first tent. Its advantage is that it is a bit easier to erect, which is helpful if you have to set up the tent alone. Also some prefer a round tent. Personally, having used both kinds of tent, I found both easy to assemble and have enjoyed them both.

**Spencer:** Well, I wouldn't be alone, so setting up the wall tent would be no problem; besides I can use the $50 for something else.

**Pringle:** You have made a wise decision. As I write up the order tell me how you want to pay for the tent.

**Spencer:** I'll pay cash. By the way, did I see some sleeping bags on display?

1. What do you think of Pringle's efforts in making this sale?
2. During a presentation, would it be wise to include more accessories or try to increase the size of the sale? Discuss possible implications involved.
3. Once the primary sale is completed, is it wise to follow with an additional attempt to increase the sale or to try to sell a different product? Would you introduce the customer to another salesperson to attempt a sale of another product? Explain and defend your position.

## 12–2 Selling Shoes, Inc.

### Situation 1

Ardis McAlpine is busy assisting a customer. This is the summer sale period when prices are reduced. The customer has tried on a number of shoes varying slightly in style. The customer prefers several styles but unfortunately the right size is not in stock. The only solution seems to be a couple of less desirable styles that fit well and look exceptionally flattering.

As the customer hesitates, Ardis explains that although these styles were introduced later in the season they are well accepted. They had been reduced in price, but Ardis points out that not only are the shoes suitable for the remainder of the season but undoubtedly could be worn next year as well. At prices of $29.50 and $32.75, they are exceptional buys, expecially since these same shoes are expected to sell for $75 and $80 next season. The customer bought one pair of each style.

Develop a dialogue that would have led to a sales close in this situation.

## Situation 2

As Arthur Parrington arranged a new shipment of boots that had just been delivered, a man walked in and sat down to be fitted. Arthur looked up and approached the man immediately, opening the conversation with a cheery "Good morning." The man was looking around from where he sat but responded with a pleasant reply. He was wearing a pair of well-worn boots with rubber bottoms attached to leather uppers that reached to his knees. His shirt and heavy jacket framed an "outdoor face."

The prospect told Arthur that he had a small farm ten miles out in the country bordering a stream where he fished and trapped during his spare time. His primary work, however, was farming. He needed a new pair of boots and wanted something like, if not identical to, the ones he was wearing. The boots had to be roomy enough to wear two pairs of heavy socks. They also needed to stand up under rough wear. He said he did not want all-leather boots because they often leaked unless carefully treated, and he did not want boots he had to fuss with.

Since the store catered to people who enjoyed outdoor activities there was a wide selection of boots—leather, rubber, and leather and rubber. There were low, medium, high, and waders in various colors. Arthur brought out a couple of styles varying slightly from the ones the customer was wearing. The price for each pair was the same—$60.

However, the store had just taken on a new line of all-leather boots in both medium and knee lengths. They were of softer material but very sturdy, and were guaranteed to be waterproof. These were priced at $125.

After the customer tried on both of the first pairs, Arthur asked permission to bring out the new line. The customer readily assented and gladly tried on the new boots. They felt good and were comfortable to wear with either one or two pairs of socks. Arthur guaranteed that they would keep water out as well as the other style of boot. The customer wavered for a minute or two and finally bought the old-style boot. He commented, "These new boots sure look nice, but $125!"

1. Do you think Arthur would have sold the new-style boot if he had tried harder?
2. Do you think price was the main stumbling block?
3. Did Arthur exhibit weakness in his selling effort? Keep in mind that Arthur knew nothing about the buyer's family, income status, or living standards. How could Arthur have corrected this lack of knowledge?
4. Did Arthur do the best he could "under the circumstances"? Answer in detail.

## 12-3 Aspinwall and Ziegler, Inc.

Cyril Blankenship is one of three salespeople with Aspinwall and Ziegler, Inc. This firm furnishes a variety of sales services to its clients including the selection of salespeople. That is, Aspinwall and Ziegler will recruit and screen new salespeople for its clients. Aspinwall and Ziegler, Inc. is proud of its record in securing successful sales personnel for a number of companies.

The sales force selection is handled by Aspinwall and Ziegler in one of two ways. First, Aspinwall and Ziegler will recruit and screen a number of potential candidates and select one for their client to hire. The fee for this service is $1,000 regardless of whether the client actually hires the person recommended by Aspinwall and Ziegler. If the person recommended is not hired, Aspinwall and Ziegler will provide additional names at a fee of $1,000 per person. Under a second approach, Aspinwall and Ziegler will recruit and screen applicants and submit three names to their client from which the client will hire one. The fee for this is $2,000.

Cyril Blankenship has just completed a presentation to the president, sales vice president, and personnel manager of the Andrews and Pearl Corporation. Cyril has explained the procedure used by Aspinwall and Ziegler to recruit applicants and how they are screened to meet the needs of each client. The presentation went well but each of the listeners expressed some reservations. The president felt that the screening techniques used by Aspinwall and Ziegler might not be appropriate for the Andrews and Pearl Corporation. The vice president casually mentioned that Andrews and Pearl had "unsuccessfully" used other firms in their sales force recruiting in the past. The personnel manager mentioned that even the most advanced recruiting and screening techniques sometimes provide only mediocre results. The personnel manager concluded by saying, "It's easy to pick salespeople for routine selling jobs, but try to pick quality salespeople to sell expensive industrial equipment where customers must be cultivated over long periods of time."

Cyril admitted that sales jobs spanned a wide range of difficulties. However, Cyril insisted that his firm could do a good job for Andrews and Pearl. Cyril agreed to provide the three executives with results that Aspinwall and Ziegler had achieved for clients with difficult selling jobs. They agreed to meet again in one week.

1. What type of information is needed for Cyril to be convincing?
2. If you were in Cyril's shoes, how would you convince these three executives that Aspinwall and Ziegler can do a better recruiting job than Andrews and Pearl could do for itself?
3. What alternatives are open to Andrews and Pearl besides using Aspinwall and Ziegler?

# PART FOUR

## INCREASING YOUR SALES EFFECTIVENESS

The preceding chapters have provided a thorough overview of all aspects of the selling process. The final two chapters of this book bring all of this information together to show you how to achieve the maximum effectiveness in selling. Chapter 13 examines ways of using your sales knowledge to work more effectively with your customers; to be of more assistance to them. Chapter 14 covers the topic of self management—how to manage your time, territory, and financial resources effectively.

# 13

# MAXIMIZING CUSTOMER RELATIONSHIPS

Your future in selling will be determined in large part by the relationship between you and your customer. You know that you should remain friendly with customers and be willing to help them, but few salespeople really appreciate the depth of the relationship nor understand just how far to go in building goodwill. Sometimes salespeople become so self-oriented that they forget to be customer-oriented. They forget that they need the buyer's cooperation, and they take their customers for granted.

To build an effective relationship you must be able to "put yourself in your customer's shoes." When you do this, you help determine the kind of impression that you make, and you develop a better understanding of your customer. Gather the following information about your customer:

* name,
* date and place of birth,
* name of school attended and year of graduation,
* fraternal memberships,
* business affiliations,
* name of spouse,
* date of marriage,
* number and name of children,
* hobbies and interests,
* positions held in various companies,
* organizations and club memberships.

Most people give lip service to their willingness to see the other side of the picture, but how many can actually put themselves in the customer's shoes and learn the customer's likes and dislikes? Nevertheless, that is what you must do. To work effectively with customers and to serve them better, you must go beyond the normal requirements of your job, look ahead, and understand the effect your product or service will have on the user.

## SALES EFFORTS EXAMINED

In striving to establish the most effective working relationship with customers, it is wise to begin with an analysis of your current sales efforts. Perform the analysis with this question in mind: What can I do to make myself more valuable to my customers?

### Analyze Each Sale

The sale has been completed, and you have left the buyer's office. Review the steps of the sale to see where you were strong and where you were weak. Study each detail of your presentation and evaluate it critically. This is the time to analyze what you have said to see where you can improve. Among the questions you might ask yourself are:

- What might I have done better?
- What did I say or do that I wished I had not?
- Did I discuss topics that were not relevant to the sale?
- Did I venture into subjects that could have led to an argument?
- Did my talk stray from the purpose at hand?
- Did I talk too much?
- Could I detect that my prospect became weary once or twice when I belabored a point?
- Did I interrupt or cut the customer off during the discussion?
- Was the presentation too one-sided?
- How could the sale have been increased?
- Could better quality merchandise have been sold?
- Could my presentation have been more persuasive and the sales results better?
- Did I listen to what my customer had to say?
- Did I present my product in terms of customer needs?
- As I talked, was I thinking of the customer?

- Were the suggested applications interesting to the customer?
- Whose real interest did I have in mind?
- Will I be welcome on my next call?

## Look for Behavior Patterns

You should dissect a number of your successful and unsuccessful sales efforts to detect behavior patterns you have developed. Usually there are underlying strengths or weaknesses that can be isolated. The salesperson with a series of successes will do certain things right consistently, while the salesperson with a number of unsuccessful attempts will neglect certain essential features. The differences may sometimes appear slight, but they are significant enough to win or lose sales. Too often people look for big differences in performance when actually small differences are the deciding factors.

Break down a number of sales into their component parts and critically study each part. In some instances it may be necessary to break parts into subsections to isolate certain areas. List the significant points on a chart or set them up in a series of dots. Place the dots at different heights over a base line to indicate the importance of each sales point, the time spent, or some other measure of magnitude. Connect the dots with a line. The progression of a sales presentation would thus be indicated by starting the line at the left margin of a sheet of paper and moving across the page to the right. This gives you a sales profile that shows a sale from its beginning to its conclusion. Do this for a number of successful sales as well as for a number of sales failures.

Figure 13–1 illustrates the use of this technique. Assume that you have just completed a sales call. You can now graph each part of the sales call showing your deviation (positively or negatively) from normal or average performance. Doing this for a number of sales calls allows you to see what aspects of your sales presentation require improvement.

In evaluating sales profiles, it is necessary to engage in some careful introspection. Two salespeople may have similar sales profiles yet one may be successful and one unsuccessful. Much of this difference may be traced to each salesperson's behavior when talking to a buyer. Neither salesperson is unpleasant, each tries to please the buyer, but each salesperson is an individual and affects the buyer in a different way. Salespeople, because of individual differences, cannot simply imitate other successful

**Figure 13-1**

## ANALYSIS OF A SALES CALL

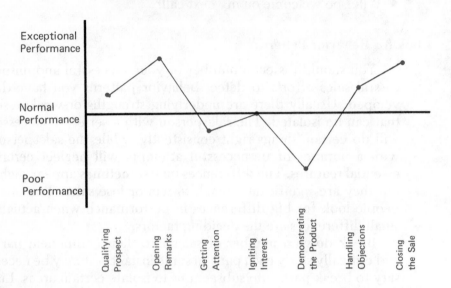

salespeople. Rather, as a salesperson you must marshall your strengths in a way that maximizes your own assets.

## THE "THINKING" SALESPERSON

Enough cannot be said for the importance of serious thinking. Creative salespeople are thinking salespeople. You must review to see where you have failed, what you have done wrong, and what has been omitted. You must rehearse your pattern of action, your procedures, and your behavior. If you sense that you have offended a customer, you need to analyze your weaknesses. You must try to develop new methods and unique approaches. You should continually try to do your job better and to become more convincing. Once you concentrate on your job, ideas will begin to come and you can develop new procedures.

As a successful salesperson, you must think of new ways to build sales, to get new customers, and to find new avenues of approach. You must think of selling in broader terms than merely making a sale. You must think of the market of tomorrow. You must plan to change procedures, to incorporate new and better methods. Since the products you sell today may be outdated tomorrow, you may have to change products or shift emphasis.

Are you aware of studies on consumers? Do you know what motivates customers and how to persuade them to buy? Do you take advantage of the multiplicity of sales aids available? Do you use them effectively? Do you experiment with them, and are you willing to try new methods that will eventually supplant present ones?

Salespeople who are content to keep on going in their usual ruts will soon regret their carelessness. If their work consists of mechanical ordertaking, they will be supplanted by catalogues and self-service, which are cheaper and equally effective. If they fail to develop into effective, dynamic, creative, assertive salespeople, there will be no room for them.

## CUSTOMER SERVICE—A MUST

Always be willing to serve your customer to the fullest extent. When a customer asks a favor of you, try to do it. Even when the request is to perform a menial task, do it. Do not confuse this attitude with self-abasement; you can serve your customer and still retain self-respect. Respect increases when others see that you are willing to do things for them. Go even further; try to anticipate things that your customer likes and do them without being asked. The customer will appreciate your thoughtfulness. As one druggist said about a particular salesperson, "Mr. Kimura does so many nice things for me, I just can't refuse to give him an order."

Customer-service training cannot be a half-hearted effort; it must be a genuine willingness to serve customers who trustingly give you their orders. Once recognizing these demands, the willing salesperson will make the sacrifices involved. Yet, these demands bring their rewards. A good customer relationship is established because you are doing your utmost to serve the interests of your customer.

### Customer Problems Require Your Attention

Solving customer problems is an area of major importance, and it calls for serious concentration on the part of salespeople. Problems may arise with the performance of your product or service, or they may arise in areas of your customer's business, such as in advertising, shelf displays, or inventory control. Many salespeople are unaware of the importance of looking at a customer's problems as though they were their own. Yet, that is

**Illustration 13-1 Anticipate your customer's wishes before being asked.**

what they are. Unless customers succeed in business, the salesperson cannot succeed in selling.

Keep your customer's loyalty by helping to find the best solution to a problem. Make every attempt to agree as to what is to be done. Point out the disadvantages of an unpopular decision and promote the advantages. This will temper original disappointment and direct attention to the reality of the situation. Be very careful not to magnify the problem by initiating hasty action.

Sometimes a salesperson can make a study of the customer's present operations to find ways for improvement. You may find that the location could be improved. Perhaps the right merchandise is not being stocked for the community. By talking to people in the area, you may discover wants that are not being met. Perhaps store hours are not the right ones for the neighborhood.

Your customer will appreciate your taking an interest in finding an agreeable solution to a problem. Be careful, however, that you do not poke your nose too far into someone else's business. If you can demonstrate how certain changes will increase sales, your suggestions will probably be considered—if not welcomed. Often, merely discussing product or service problems will bring an awareness of new approaches and new methods for finding amicable solutions.

Anticipate, if possible, the direction of your customer's business. If you can foresee developments that will help the business, mention them. If you see clouds on the business horizon, point them out as possibilities, not as certainties. Mention future conferences and meetings that may be beneficial. Introduce the customer to people who can be of assistance, directly or indirectly. Give aid in securing positions of influence for your customer. Secure books, magazines, and other literature to increase information on business opportunities.

If the customer has other needs aside from those connected with your product or service, be reluctant to offer solutions. You may not understand the situation well enough to give good advice. If a customer has a particular problem and asks for your opinion, you may not be able to give much help, but you might suggest some source where help is available.

When you do not have a solid suggestion to help solve a customer's problem, refer to a source that might be able to help. If you answer questions that are not in your area, you are an amateur instead of a professional. As an amateur your advice might be dangerous. In areas outside your field, be supportive, but do not try to answer questions that you are ill-prepared to handle. By stepping outside your professional competence, you do a disservice to yourself, your company, and above all, to your customer. Be willing to serve—but serve within your capacity.

## Give the Customer New Ideas

The most important challenge of your retail customer is to increase sales. You will be welcomed if you can make this happen. The salesperson who calls on retailers has any number of opportunities to be of service. The retailer, constantly within the confines of the store, surrounded by familiar merchandise, talking to regular customers, gets in a rut. Other businesspeople in similar circumstances are operating in much the same way. This leads to a deadly uniformity that needs attention. You, an outsider, visiting many stores, talking with many retailers, and having information that your firm is constantly gathering, should be able to contribute helpful ideas.

Suggest different store window displays, a new way of merchandising, different tie-in sales, a variation in hours of opening and closing, a change to self-service, the use of holiday promotions, emphasis on some special events—you could name dozens of suggestions that might be useful to a retailer. It is also helpful to pass along suggestions of what your other customers in other localities are doing. If you sell supplies to a summer-resort operator, for example, mention what other resort operators are doing to bring in more people. Tell how some operators are enticing people to come back year after year. Mention that some operators have increased their business by offering a greater number of services and variety of entertainment, appealing to a wider range of guests.

With a factory buyer, you might show how your product can serve better, how to use less of it and still get satisfactory results, or how to use it more profitably. Factory owners and managers look for new ways to manufacture, produce new products, and find solutions for their problems. By stressing service, you may overcome prejudice that may have developed toward you or your product.

### Provide Maximum Satisfaction with Your Product

Always be sure that the buyer receives not only the physical product but also other valuable extras, particularly in applications of the product and how to use it to derive the greatest satisfaction. Instead of saying, "Here it is," say, "Here it is. Now let's see how we can get the most out of it for you." The buyer will sense the difference at once. When you complete the sale, you make your profit, but the buyer's opportunities and problems begin when your job is "done." If you think you have finished your work by completing the sale, you are wrong. Your long-run success will be measured by the degree that you assist your customer.

Be sure the proper applications of your product are understood. If your customer is a farmer, precise applications of your product will hold interest. If you are selling fertilizer, suggest the correct applications for maximum results. If the product is a weed killer, the farmer will want to know the exact amounts to use without harming other plants. If you are selling to the homemaker, show the best way to use the article or the material. You can explain how your product will give greater value if it is used correctly.

Another way of ensuring that the customer will get maximum satisfaction is to recommend the right quality, the right quantity,

**Illustration 13-2** Proper application of the product, as well as point-of-purchase display, make sales more effective.

*IU International Corporation*

and the right selection of merchandise. This must be done if you are to act as a professional salesperson looking after the needs of your customers.

Although your reward may not be immediate from maximizing your customer assistance, the long-run results will definitely be to your advantage and to your customer's benefit. You could lose many of your new as well as your regular customers if you are unwilling to exert additional effort. The competition might win them away from you by doing the extra things you are unwilling to do.

### Sales Promotion Geared to the Customer

You have already learned the importance of sales promotion in many types of business activity. Offering assistance with the customer's sales promotion activities can be an excellent way of building an effective salesperson-customer relationship.

**Tip** *Janice Tessier is a salesperson for Flavorful Mints. One of Janice's customers is Farmer's Groceries, a small chain of four supermarkets. Janice had noticed that purchases of Flavorful Mints by Farmer's had been declining. When inquiring about this with Christine Farmer, the owner, Janice was informed that Flavorful Mints simply weren't selling well in the Farmer's stores. Knowing that Flavorful Mints should be selling better, Janice decided to investigate.*

*Upon examining the display of Flavorful Mints in the four stores, Janice found that inadequate and poor shelf positioning was being given to Flavorful Mints. She asked for permission to move a table into an aisle near the front of one of the stores. She placed the table in a strategic location and set up an attractive candy display. In the course of a week, this store moved more mints than the four Farmer's stores had the previous month. Because of such favorable results, Christine Farmer provided more and better shelf space to Flavorful Mints at all Farmer's stores, resulting in profitable sales for Farmer's and a big commission for Janice.*

Many manufacturers produce great quantities of materials to help sell their products at the point of purchase, the retail store. Examples of these point-of-purchase materials are materials for floor, window, and counter displays: posters; banners; and permanent fixtures, such as signs and clocks. As a salesperson, you can help retailers if you persuade them to use these aids wisely. Most salespeople whose firms offer point-of-purchase materials help the customer in setting up these materials in strategic locations in the store.

*IU International Corporation*

**Illustration 13–3   Part of the salesperson's job is acquiring good display space.**

Some manufacturers also make cooperative advertising arrangements available to retailers, and salespeople can help in setting up such arrangements. In cooperative advertising, the cost of advertising the manufacturer's products on the local level is shared by the manufacturer and the retailer. The advertising materials are drafted by the manufacturer and made available to the retailer.

In addition to explaining any cooperative advertising program to retail customers, you can also provide assistance on the advertising and promotional activities that retailers undertake themselves. Sometimes, too, you can pass along tips on how to improve the performance of the retailer's salespeople.

## Dealing with Customer Complaints

The way a salesperson deals with customer complaints affects future relationships with that customer. When a complaint is registered, you know that a problem exists. You know that someone is unhappy and that an adjustment needs to be made. The person who makes the adjustment must do so with as much grace as possible. Try to satisfy as fully as possible the complaints of the distressed buyer.

**Illustration 13-4   Provide courteous attention to a customer's complaints.**

When the customer complains, give courteous attention and consideration and express genuine interest and concern. As much as possible, put yourself on the side of the customer to see what would be an equitable solution. A complaint may arise because the customer wants to "sound off." Do not stop the individual from talking until there is nothing further to say. The end result will be a relieved and calmed person. When you agree with the customer and make a proper adjustment, the situation clears up and the customer is happy because two rewards become clear: (1) The customer got the adjustment; (2) The customer convinced you that your original handling of the sale was done incorrectly. Many complaints are unjust. You will have customers who are constantly complaining and wanting adjustments. Keep in mind that you must deal with such individuals as part of your job. However, remember that you do an injustice to your firm by giving in completely to an unreasonable customer. Usually there is some middle ground that both sides will accept.

Complaints should be heard promptly and settlements made as soon as possible. When an adjustment must be made, do it pleasantly and at your earliest opportunity. Adjustments made grudgingly and slowly cause an unfavorable impression. You still have the inconvenience and expense, so why not be pleasant and win the customer's appreciation. Be careful not to make the customer feel that the concession had to be wrung out of you even though the adjustment was obviously the only fair thing to be done.

When your firm does not want to make a minor adjustment or replace a small part, make the adjustment on your own, and pay for it out of your own pocket to avoid dissatisfaction and possible loss of a customer. You are spending a small sum of your own money, but it is money spent well because of the trouble it saves, the disagreeable situation it prevents, and the possibility that it will preserve a valuable customer. If you are caught in a disagreement between your firm and a customer, you sometimes can salvage the situation by taking care of it discreetly without bothering your superiors. In doing so you must not criticize your own firm or boss even though the customer thinks ill of them.

## Remember Your Customers

In your work you may call on some customers so infrequently that weeks or months might pass between calls. Such lapses of time may cause your customer to forget you. It is inexcusable to let a customer forget you. Modern methods of communication enable you to hold the customer's attention in various ways without causing resentment. You might, for example, write. Perhaps you have uncovered some new idea or new item that is being featured and you send your customer a note with samples. Even though your subject matter might not have too great an appeal, at least the customer will remember you. A birthday or anniversary card is always acceptable. A congratulatory note on your customer's receipt of some honor is in order. You can also call on the telephone. After all, phone calls do not take much time, they are relatively inexpensive, and they are a gentle reminder of your presence.

**A Tickler File Is an Effective Reminder System.** This is nothing more than a file that brings information to your attention at designated intervals. Some salespeople use a reminder book to jot down information. Whatever method you use, be sure that the data are recorded to come to your attention at regular intervals.

Never forget a customer. If you forget, the customer will forget you and forget to give you orders. If you remember, you will serve your customer by seeing that goods are delivered as specified and on time. Remember to make special adjustments that have been agreed upon. Remember special packing. Remember color assortments. Remember special payment terms.

**Illustration 13–5** A reminder book or tickler file is useful in periodically checking on a customer's product needs and satisfaction.

*Tip* *Elva Potter sold various bulk dairy products for the Dalton Dairy Company. Elva was visiting one of her largest customers one day when a shipment of butterfat from Dalton arrived. Elva sold butterfat in bulk to this customer, for use in producing other dairy products, at the rate of a truckload or more a day. The butterfat was taken from separators in a semi-fluid state, put in sterilized 40-pound plastic bags, heat-sealed, and frozen to −15 degrees F. The frozen bags were then shipped to customers in refrigerated trucks.*

*Elva noticed that, on the customer's receiving docks, workers unloaded the frozen bags, one-at-a-time, from the truck onto pallets. When 40 bags were placed on a pallet, the pallet was moved by fork-lift truck into the customer's warehouse. Elva suggested that much time would be saved if the shipment arrived already on pallets for the customer. In this way, the bags could be moved immediately into the warehouse, eliminating the need for dock workers to lift all the bags onto pallets. It was just as easy for Dalton to load the bags onto pallets as onto the floor of its trucks, so this special arrangement presented no problems for Elva's company. Elva, however, received the benefit of a very pleased customer.*

## HUMAN RELATIONS AND THE CUSTOMER

Through careful attention to the principles of good human relations, over a period of time you can develop a firm bond of friendship with your customer. Being a genuine friend is important. The customer must know this and rely on you for assistance. Show that you will give sympathetic attention, the benefit of your experience, and your genuine interest.

Friendship gives a decided advantage to you; treat it with the greatest respect and care. With friendship comes trust, reliance, dependence, and many other conditions that you must treat with care. Never take advantage of other people; deal with them as you would like to have them deal with you in similar circumstances.

### Customer Consideration

Be considerate of your customer's feelings. Do not be critical of politics, religion, children, or backgrounds that would affect present relationships. In fact, be wary of any criticism, whatsoever, even that which might be said of a competitor.

Also be considerate of your customer's time. When you sell to an institution, such as a hospital or restaurant, the person whom you need to see may have very little time available for talking. Be considerate and make your call at the customer's convenience. This may be on particular days of the week and during odd hours of the day or night. Such thoughtfulness does much to foster a warm regard for the salesperson.

Be considerate of your customer's background. Whatever the level of education, try to fit your presentation to the needs of the listener. Never convey an impression of superiority. On the other hand, if you have a suitable product or service, you need not feel inferior, and the listener will not expect it of you. Neither talk up or down to a person. Talk directly to the person or persons making up the audience.

## Give Full Attention to Customers

If you are to maintain customer relations at their best, it is important to give full attention and respect to your customers. When a customer talks, you must listen. Do not interrupt, and be careful not to look bored. Think about people you enjoy. You like the way they listen to you and pay attention to you. Your customer is no different. When a customer talks, pay attention to what is said, laugh at the jokes, follow the customer's words with great interest; none of this will pass unnoticed.

## Do Favors for the Customer

Many times you have a choice of whether to do favors for your customer. Often, favors require additional effort. Maybe you bought that hard-to-get football ticket, introduced the customer to the right people at the country club, helped to move some old merchandise, suggested a way to help the children achieve certain goals, or aided in buying a special type of personal equipment at an attractive price. Your customer may never notice if you do not do these extra favors or give extra service but you will. Are you worthy of your customer?

Kind, thoughtful acts carried out without fanfare, without demand for recognition, and without expectation of reward bring the esteem of others. Your actions characterize your personality. Instinctively, your customer recognizes your qualities.

Do minor things for your customer. Each may be insignificant in itself; but accumulated, they soon have an effect. The customer may not warm up to you because you have done one or two small favors. Over a period of time, however, there will come a gradual change of attitude.

There is such a thing as showing too much kindness. Your helpful acts can become offensive. You can embarrass a customer. But your judgment should tell you how far to go. With some customers, you can be sycophantic and still be in good taste. A person genuinely motivated by a desire to help another probably will not go too far in extending help. But if one is motivated by a selfish desire to get ahead, selfishness may so cloud the vision that one is unable to detect the limit of propriety. The salesperson overdoes it—not because of anxiety to serve, but because of anxiety for the order. All efforts to serve the customer must be done with sincerity. Distinguish between sincere encouragement and flattery.

## Customer Appreciation

Each of us wants to be appreciated. When a youngster draws a picture of a dog and displays it proudly, parents say, "What a fine dog you drew," and the child goes away happy. Similar experiences can be repeated throughout life. Most of us have a pleasant feeling when others show their appreciation. This expression need not be particularly demonstrative as long as we know the other person recognizes and appreciates what we have done.

The customer craves appreciation. Ways of showing appreciation are numerous. Besides the verbal "Thank you," or the written note of appreciation, there are other forms that can be impressive. Entertain the customer and, perhaps, the customer's spouse and family at some activity that all enjoy. Send an appropriate gift. Visits to the hospital or flowers sent to the hospital during illness often are quite acceptable. If you discover a customer is having personal trouble, reassuring words over the telephone can be meaningful. In addition to sending a Christmas greeting, send a Thanksgiving greeting. This might be remembered even more forcibly because so few Thanksgiving greetings are received. If the customer is engaged in club activities, a door prize might prove to be most enjoyable. If the customer is to give a talk to a group, your attendance might demonstrate your interest. If a local paper features your customer, call and say how much you enjoyed reading the article.

## Gift-Giving

Insofar as possible, you should avoid giving gifts that might influence purchasing. Major gifts can be interpreted as bribes. However, small gifts, token gifts, are often appreciated and are not of sufficient value to influence the buyer except as an act of thoughtfulness. Certainly, a lunch or a dinner is not to be construed as bribery. A small token gift for an anniversary, a Christmas card, or a small Christmas present is not out of place.

**Tip** *Touchy sales situations sometimes arise when customers "ask" for certain gifts or favors as a condition to the sale, as Fred Hamernik discovered. Fred sells various types of fencing to industrial buyers. Fred was very close to a big sale with Lafayette Industrials when the purchasing agent, Mr. Karacostas, indicated a few additional "conditions" to the sale. The buyer wanted Fred's company to put a new mesh fence around his home and treat him to a weekend in Toronto.*

*To complete a big sale, many salespeople might give in to this request. Fred realized, however, that to give in once would put him in a vulnerable position in the future. Fred explained that company policy would not permit work at a private residence. He also explained that the Toronto trip was beyond his expense account, but he would be happy to treat the buyer to dinner. Fred then went on to summarize all the benefits to the buyer's company of dealing with Fred's firm.*

Although it is difficult to set an absolute limit between a major gift and a token gift, an item costing below $25 should evoke little criticism. Most buyers would not think of a minor gift of this nature as bribery; nor should you think of it in this way. A gift should be a genuine token of friendship, not a reward. Gift giving as a token of thoughtfulness is usually appropriate, and in good taste.

## Mistakes or Misunderstandings

In the course of business activities, errors crop up. Under normal circumstances, those errors may not be the result of mistakes on one side; they may result from misunderstandings or things done wrong by both. To blame an error on a customer is hardly prudent. When a problem arises and an investigation reveals the fault to be the customer's, the diplomatic salesperson smooths over the situation. When you or your firm makes an error, you must accept the blame even though you may try to mitigate it by indicating extenuating circumstances.

When you have surmised that a customer is to blame, tread a wary path. A customer who feels that giving you an order is a big favor does not like to be proven wrong. If little problems crop up, why should you blame your customer for them? Try to improve the situation, and go on from there to keep good customer relations. If you try to press your advantage by proving that the customer is wrong, you gain little. At best, you can only imply that the error might be the customer's; you never say it directly. Reasonable people will catch the drift of the conversation and recognize they are wrong. If they are willing to admit it, you should accept the explanation and take corrective action; if unwilling to admit it, make the best adjustment you can.

If an error is very costly, it may be necessary to assign the cost to the buyer. Although this may cause unhappiness, you hope that the justice of your position will be recognized. Even that does not leave a good taste, however. Neither of you are happy because the buyer has been saddled with additional cost and you have been given extra work because of a troublesome situation.

Errors must not be allowed to go uncorrected. Whether to meet them head on or wait to see what happens depends on present conditions. Often, time will correct the problem. A problem that looms dangerously large at the moment may be handled later by relatively minor adjustments. Do not get excited in the beginning. However, do not let the problem drag on indefinitely.

When you believe that a customer has committed an error, search your own operations to see how the error could have been prevented. Even though the customer may be at fault, the error might have been prevented if you or your firm had taken sufficient precautionary measures. It is not as important to assign blame as it is to prevent such an error in the future.

## IMPROVING SALES PERFORMANCE

A number of methods and approaches that may improve sales performance should be mentioned. The authors do not necessarily recommend any one of them. However, it appears that some people have used one or more of these techniques to produce an increased flow of thought, direction, or action.

## Transcendental Meditation

Every day we experience three states of consciousness— waking, sleeping, and dreaming. To this you can add a fourth state, *transcendental consciousness*. To achieve this state you relax in a comfortable chair for about 20 minutes, twice a day, allowing at least six hours between each session. You sit with eyes closed concentrating on an object less and less concretely until you are beyond all thoughts and feelings. You are unaware of your surroundings. You are still conscious; you are in a state that permits you to experience a level of pure creative intelligence. Here are two illustrations to make this state more understandable.

When you are watching a movie, you are seeing a rapidly moving series of pictures. By lowering the projected light, this series of pictures grows dim and finally all that remains is a white screen, which is the underlying reality. Electricity is carried from place to place by a conductor at normal temperatures. The atoms in this conductor are in a disordered state. This tends to impede the flow of electricity, which diminishes with increasing distance. In certain conductors when the temperature is lowered to –273 centigrade the atoms cease to be disordered and remain relatively quiet, and electric current flows with a minimum loss. The final result of both situations tend to show how, in pure consciousness, thoughts may flow from the brain rapidly and in great number.

In transcending, viewed subjectively "the mind becomes less active. Perception becomes more refined. The boundaries of experience expand. Eventually the attention transcends all activity and all experience, contacting the underlying universal field of pure consciousness."[1] Physically, the nervous system, which is at a high level of excitation, progressively becomes less excited, finally reaching minimum disturbance that permits a freer flow of transcendental consciousness.

---

[1] Phillip Goldberg, *The TM Program*, (New York: Holt, Rinehart and Winston, 1976), p. 38.

## Transactional Analysis

Transactional analysis is a communication approach that has been used for a number of years. The unit of social intercourse is a transaction. When two people meet, one may ask a question; the other replies, which completes the transaction. Transactional analysis uses a three-fold relationship, labeled *Parent, Adult,* and *Child* (P-A-C). These three states presumably exist in all people.

"The *Parent* is a huge collection of recordings in the brain of unquestioned or imposed external events perceived by a person in his early years, a period which we have designated roughly as the first five years of life. This is the period before the social birth of the individual before he leaves home in response to the demands of society and enters school."[2] This includes parental protection, demands, admonitions, and warnings. It includes words as well as nonverbal actions.

The *Child* represents the reaction of the child to the parent. In the earliest stages it becomes an inward reaction of the youngster to what he or she sees, hears, feels, and understands. Later the curiosity of youngsters enables them to detect changes and when they become mobile (crawl, walk) new experiences occur. This is the beginning of the *Adult.*

The *Adult* represents the period during which the child begins to assimilate *Parent* and *Child* to develop new perceptions that may vary from those during the original *Parent* and *Child* period.

Transactional analysis is frequently taught in groups. "The goal for each member of the P-A-C group is clear, concise and easily stated: to *cure* the patient by freeing-up his Adult from the troublemaking influences and demands of his Parent and Child. The goal is achieved by teaching each member of the group how to recognize, identify, and describe the Parent, Adult, and Child as each appears in transactions in the group."[3]

Characteristics of the *Parent* period that are readily identified in groups of people could be raised eyebrows, wagging a finger, or statements such as "It's clear to everyone," "It's common knowledge," and "Let's really find out the truth." The *Child* period shows in crying, sulking, withdrawal, and expressions

---

[2]Thomas A. Harris, M.D. *I'm O.K., You're O.K.,* (New York: Harper & Row, Publishers, 1969), pp. 18–19.
[3]*Ibid.,* p. 206.

such as, "Terrible, isn't it?" "Life is cruel, isn't it," or similar recriminating statements. At the *Adult* level, the individual applies thinking, examination, measurement of alternatives, and new information to reach solutions. Thinking individuals may take knowledge and experiences of others and come up with perspectives different from their predecessors.

To understand transactional analysis more fully, you should read the book cited here or other similar literature and perhaps find a therapy group within which you might participate. You must remember that the terms *Parent, Adult,* and *Child* have very precise meanings. Once this approach is clearly understood, you may find it useful in understanding and working with customers. It may help to develop greater empathy between you, the seller, and the buyer.

## Self-Assertiveness

The successful salesperson tries to control the selling situation. Salespeople try to direct interviews and presentations in their favor. Many interruptions may occur to upset a carefully planned situation. Handling prospects singly or in committees presents problems with individuals who range from unreceptive to antagonistic. These experiences are to be expected and preparations must include how to reach individuals irrespective of the immediate environmental conditions.

Beginning salespeople often are deficient in, or lack experience in, recognizing individual situations and proper responses to each situation. As rapidly as possible, the salesperson must learn personal reaction empathy with buyers, allay their suspicions, strengthen favorable conceptions, and secure responses that are favorable to the salesperson's suggestion. A beginning salesperson, however well-trained, will find difficulty in reacting to the many personalities encountered. Even the experienced salesperson will never completely understand individual buyer's idiosyncracies.

In every sale customers pay—financially, in time, in service, or in some other way. Customers must feel advantages in any transaction that overcome or at least equal their contribution. The salesperson likewise must present customer advantages that are greater than customer costs. In making adjustments in an unsatisfactory sales situation, the salesperson must try for an equitable compromise. This is the point where verbal skills are extremely important, particularly to satisfy and retain a customer.

Such skills are discussed and demonstrated under numerous conditions in assertiveness writings.

The salesperson should explore a number of self-assertiveness sources and choose those that meet specific needs. Much of the literature is inconsequential to the salesperson and can be ignored. The purpose here is to direct you to sources of information that will help you to succeed in selling. A number of books are available and more are appearing on the market. Each salesperson interested in exploring the topic of *self-assertiveness* should analyze and choose sources that will aid the most. To be useful, any printed source will require several readings to get the full impact.

## Overcome Yesterday's Negative with Today's Positive

The salesperson interested in developing a strong positive attitude can find a number of printed sources giving suggestions for developing self-positivism and thrusting away negative thoughts and actions still current from past experiences. To overcome self-defeating behavior requires individual effort, guided by correct action, which is reinforced by information developed by experts in particular areas. You must learn to take charge of yourself. "You are the sum total of your choices. . . . There is only one moment in which you can experience anything, and that is now."[4]

Among other topics, self-positivism stresses the importance of eliminating guilt that remains from past undesirable actions and worry for the future—both from possible repercussions of the past, and a fear of the future because of anticipated inability to meet coming situations and a host of other possible real or imagined events. The importance of controlling anger is a factor the salesperson cannot ignore. Usually it contributes nothing and often prevents making a sale. If possible, anticipate situations that could produce anger and avoid them.

Another important area is the power of belief. The areas of the subconscious reinforce and aid in bringing positive reactions in difficult periods. "Our fear thoughts are just as creative or just as magnetic in attracting troubles to us as are the constructive

---

[4]Wayne W. Dyer, *Your Erroneous Zones* (New York: Avon Books, 1977), p. 14.

and positive thoughts in attracting positive results."[5] Therefore, deliberately working to eliminate fear thoughts enhances the positive situation in a transaction.

Our power to use our subconscious mind multiplies many times our ability to develop positive approaches to successful selling. One might compare the use of the subconscious with the discussion of transcendental meditation. In both instances they draw on power and thought, which flow when inhibiting influences are removed. Being positive can be strengthened by techniques that sharpen individual acuity and belief to activate acceptable behavior in customer relationships. "One of the most outstanding insurance salesmen in America who early accepted the science of belief told me that he never called upon an important prospect without first giving his sales presentation in front of a mirror."[6] This permits you to visualize if your presentation is realistic enough to convince you—to sell you. Somewhat similar, but more scientific, are Paul Ekman's experiments with the face discussed in Chapter 5.

The authors of this text have briefly touched on some of the elements that promote the positive and put aside the negative. Possibly one of the more important books in this area is *The Power of Positive Thinking* by Norman Vincent Peale. The salesperson is urged to explore this positive approach in greater detail.

**Tip** *If you want to earn big money, you have to think positively and value your time. Russell Saberstein sells supplies to schools, hospitals, retirement homes and similar institutional customers. Russell, who was dissatisfied with his $18,000 per year income, improved his performance significantly with positive thinking and a goal geared to the value of his time.*

*Russell determined that he had about 2,000 hours per year to work with (250 working days at 8 hours per day). At a commission of $18,000 per year, Russell was earning $9 per hour. Since many people in unskilled jobs were earning more than this, Russell decided to set a goal in relation to what he felt his time was worth. Russell established $17 per hour as the value of his time and resolved to work hard enough to achieve this goal. Last year Russell earned $40,000 (about $20 per hour) through hard work, a clear goal, and positive thinking.*

---

[5]Claude M. Bristol, *The Magic of Believing* (New York: Pocket Book edition, Simon & Schuster, Inc., 1969), p. 29.
   [6]*Ibid.*, p. 105.

## Power—Position of Strength

You must maximize personal power and strength to serve customers effectively. You cannot expect to do your best for customers and prospects unless you are prepared to develop greater control of the sales situation. Greater control is achieved by positioning yourself as a source of power. You dominate as much as possible without offending the individuals involved. You gain their admiration and respect.

To achieve a position of strength entails great concentration on product knowledge both as to what can be accomplished by product use and specific benefits users gain. In a sales relationship there should be satisfaction to both seller and buyer as well as adequate compensation for the salesperson.

To hold a position of strength the salesperson must understand individual motivation and self-interest. People are inherently self-protective and are primarily interested in survival—not only basic survival but hopefully living an interesting, successful, and inspiring life at a comfortable economic level. The successful salesperson offers customers the chance to live and compete at increasingly higher levels.

An interesting approach to ways of gaining a position of strength is given in the book *Winning Through Intimidation* by Robert J. Ringer (Fawcett Publications, Inc., Greenwich, Conn., 1976). The title of the book may sound forbidding but its contents give the experiences of the author as a real estate broker. The authors of this text do not necessarily agree with all the contents of *Winning Through Intimidation* but feel it has merit in presenting some realities of selling that do exist. Salespeople have been observed demonstrating control by positioning themselves correctly. Additional books that you may want to consider reading are *How I Made the Sale That Did the Most for Me,* by J. Mel Hickerson (John Wiley & Sons, New York, 1981); *How to be a Successful Salesperson,* by Jack Wickett (Prentice-Hall, Inc., Englewood Cliffs, New Jersey, 1984); and *Increasing Your Sales Potential,* by Leslie J. Ades (Harper & Row, Publishers, New York, 1981).

## CREATIVITY IN CREATIVE SELLING

The basic structure of creative selling is dependent on individual ability to exercise *creativity*. Creativity may range from

"...simple problem-solving to conceiving it as the full realization and expression of all of an individual's unique personality . . . Creativity is, indeed, a multifaceted phenomenon."[7] Another way of identifying creativity is to indicate the characteristics that make up a creative individual.

## Characteristics of Creative People

Authors do not agree on the qualities and strengths that make a creative person. MacKinnon states that creative individuals are, in general, intelligent. They are independent in thought and action. They have curiosity and are discerning. They can concentrate attention and shift when it is appropriate. They are alert and able to isolate those thoughts that apply to the immediate problem.[8]

Flach states that creative people are flexible, stable, and in rather good balance in world relationships. They can evaluate and judge, and possess a high degree of self-sufficiency. They can remain free of the confusion and standards of the surrounding society. They appreciate approval and are not indifferent to the opinions of others. Creative people possess a high level of curiosity and a wide range of interests.[9]

Both authors stress the importance of intuition. Intuition is the added factor in decision making after a careful analysis and evaluation of facts and other pertinent criteria. Many successful business decisions are partially based on intuition. Some people have better intuition than others. Some sales executives prefer to govern their decisions solely on facts plus advice or suggestions from others, but some will take the same information and add their intuition to arrive at a decision.

## Creative Thinking

There is a process in creative thinking that may be divided into steps or may be considered as principles of creative thinking. Actually the creative process covers a complex set of factors involving recognition, motivation, and emotion that are involved in perceiving, imagining, thinking, planning, and deciding.

---

[7]Donald W. MacKinnon, "Creativity: A Multi-faceted Phenomenon," *Creativity*, edited by John D. Roslansky (Amsterdam: North-Holland Publishing Co., 1970), p. 19.
[8]*Ibid.*, pp. 28–29.
[9]Frederic F. Flach, M.D., *Choices; Coping Creatively with Personal Change* (Philadelphia: J. P. Lippincott Company, 1977), pp. 133–135.

The first step in the creative process is to isolate the specific problem. A salesperson may be asked to solve a particular problem by the sales supervisor but discovers that isn't the pertinent problem. The boss has not properly identified the real problem, may not recognize the real problem, or worse, may refuse to admit it exists when confronted with the facts. A failure to identify and solve a problem may be caused by insufficient information, or too much information that adds complexity to a relatively simple situation. A salesperson should avoid these hindrances and define the problem accurately.

One does not often arrive at a problem's solution rapidly. Withholding judgment by postponing immediate evaluation allows time for more new ideas and possible solutions to emerge. Your first thoughts may be governed by your past experience but reflection often brings other ideas into the solution pattern.

A quantity of ideas is essential to the creative process. Most of these ideas and suggestions will be discarded; but out of a large number either originating with you or suggested by others, a few will show merit. Redefining the problem may stimulate thinking and open new avenues of approach. Stating an issue in a number of ways can open new thought channels.

Submitting your problem to a group of salespeople in a sales meeting may generate a number of opinions and suggestions; one or two of these may be applicable.

Finally, before reaching a decision, it may be wise to distance yourself from the problem and its possible solution. You may have been too close to gain proper perspective. If you apply these methods, it is likely you will solve the problem, and aid your customer, your firm, and yourself.

## CREATIVE SELLING DEFINED

At this point you have covered in these 13 chapters what creative selling is and what to do to make it work. Now it is in order to summarize and bring this material into focus; to define the title. Perhaps each of you would word your definition differently. Your authors feel that the following sentence defines creative selling.

CREATIVE SELLING is the fullest utilization of your capacities to make a positive contribution to society by facilitating the transfer of goods and services and their satisfactions from the seller to buyers who, as a result of these transactions, experience happier and more worthwhile lives.

# QUESTIONS

1. The successful salesperson must keep analyzing sales efforts regularly. Why is this necessary and how can it be done advantageously?
2. Why is it common to think narrowly both in selling and in other facets in life? How can this limited thinking be overcome?
3. What is a valid reason for not meddling in a customer's personal problems?
4. Why is it important that you, the salesperson, help retail customers in their special sales efforts?
5. There are a number of ways to handle customer complaints. What are several approaches to specific complaints?
6. Why is it important to schedule regular calls on customers? What techniques will ensure that this is done?
7. In the area of gift giving, one encounters various problems that are vexing. What are some of these problems and how would you suggest they be solved?
8. Point out how to handle a customer error made by your firm. How does this procedure vary when the customer is at fault?
9. How can positive thinking ensure a successful interview with a prospective customer?
10. Is creative selling a result of positive thinking? Explain how this relationship works.

# SALES CHALLENGES

1. Ormand Simbrau goes from house to house selling vacuum cleaners. Sometimes he will make calls and demonstrations all day without making a sale. On other days he will make several sales. His best day produced five sales. Ormand receives a $75 commission on each complete sale, which includes accessories. An additional incentive is that once five sales have been made in one week, each additional sale that week earns a commission of $100. Ormand has been selling successfully and enjoys his job. After two years, Ormand has had his first $1000 week. He was elated and wondered what he should do to ensure more good weeks. Since $1000 was earned, why not try for $2000? What steps should Ormand take?
2. Niles Van Hellerman sells life insurance. During a sales call with Denise and Harry Bowman, who are new in town, Niles discovers that they have a 17-year-old daughter. To personal-

ize the conversation, Niles mentions that he has a 17-year-old son (actually his oldest child is ten). A policy is agreed to, with Niles to return in three days to pick up a check and have the policy signed. Upon returning, the Bowmans mention that their daughter does not know any boys in town and were wondering if Niles' son would take their daughter to an upcoming school dance so that she could start to get to know people of her age. What should Niles do now? Why is he in this situation?

3. Craig Ansley was extremely happy with his new car. He described the car to all of his friends and eagerly took anyone giving the slightest hint for a demonstration ride. Sandy Ogilvie, who had sold Craig the car, realizing that a satisfied customer is the best sales aid anyone could have, had personally inspected the car before turning it over to Craig.

A month later Craig took his car back to the dealership for its first inspection under its warranty. When picking his car up, Craig noticed that the mechanic who serviced his car had scratched the door and left a grease mark on the seat. Craig was annoyed and wished that the dealership took as good care of its customers after the sale as before. What can Sandy Ogilvie, who wants to maintain good customer relations, do about situations like this?

# CASES

## 13-1 International Insurance Company

Eric Galat, an insurance agent for International Insurance Company, arrives at the home of Marcus Hartjen at seven o'clock Tuesday evening to discuss Hartjen's insurance needs. The interview had been arranged in advance.

**Galat:** Good evening, Mr. Hartjen. I'm Eric Galat of International Insurance Company. It's about time to renew your fire insurance policy.

**Hartjen:** That's right. I knew it was coming up. Things have worked out pretty well so just keep it the same.

**Galat:** Yes, it's a good idea to take care of renewing early. But before we do that, let me show you our new homeowner's policy. I notice you have added a room to your house so we'll need to cover that. In addition, this new homeowner's policy covers some related features that have become increasingly important in the last two years.

**Hartjen:** I don't quite follow you. What do you mean?

**Galat:** If you increase your insurance to reflect today's higher values, that means you would keep even with higher home replacement costs. But our homeowner's policy gives you this coverage plus homeowner's liability, theft, hail, flooding, air disasters, and several other features listed here that are beneficial. Only the other day a homeowner collected for damage from the river overflow. Another collected damages from debris dropped from an airplane. Snow damage is another coverage that has proven useful to a number of our customers.

**Hartjen:** There was a lot of snow last winter. In last night's newspaper I read about pieces of metal that fell from an airplane. The chunks of metal punctured the roofs of several homes.

**Galat:** There are so many contingencies that one is responsible for as a property owner that it's almost impossible to think of them all.

**Hartjen:** Too bad, isn't it? But what can you do? I guess insurance is the best way to cover all these hazards, but how can I afford it?

**Galat:** You're right being covered for all possible dangers, Mr. Hartjen. Even though there are many different hazards, some of them occur so seldom in specific areas that the insurance cost is small. But in the event that any one of the unexpected events did occur, the cost could be catastrophic to anyone without insurance. Yet, from an insurance viewpoint, total costs are quite reasonable.

**Hartjen:** How can that be? Any major catastrophe could ruin me financially.

**Galat:** Well, before getting too worried, Mr. Hartjen, let's look at the total cost. Your home is currently insured for $90,000. This covers fire, extended coverage, lightning, and hail. A $10,000 increase would barely cover replacement costs. Also, if you are dislocated while your home is being rebuilt, we will pay up to $9,000 toward your rent expense. This is covered in section 1 of the policy. Section 2 covers the building in the back of your property where you have your workshop and where your boys do all their tinkering. Section 3 covers personal property. I note that you have some beautiful new bookcases and a fine collection of books. You must be proud of them.

**Hartjen:** Sure am. Always wanted room for my books. I have a few first editions. They are quite valuable.

**Galat:** We'll insure your personal property for $20,000. You have some very nice furniture, too, Mr. Hartjen.

**Hartjen:** Thank you. Much of it would be hard to replace. How about coverage on the car?

**Galat:** Your coverage on personal property covers fire, lightning, extended coverage, malicious mischief, and vandalism. Ten percent of your coverage, or $2,000, covers theft from your unlocked car and covers your children's belongings when away from home at school. Section 4 of the policy describes our coverage of personal hazards on your property such as your dog biting someone who is in your yard, or someone falling over some toys left on the path, and other accidents of that nature.

**Hartjen:** I wouldn't be responsible for such accidents, would I?

**Galat:** I'm afraid you would. Several court cases have been decided in favor of the trespasser. You are protected for up to $50,000 by our policy. Section 5 applies to outsiders on your property. For example, if a child is hurt and needs medical attention you have coverage up to $3,000. This applies to anyone who is your guest. Also, if you or any member of your family damages a guest's property, you are allowed up to $700 property damage.

**Hartjen:** I never knew I could be held responsible for all those things. Is there anything else you cover?

**Galat:** Here is a complete list of what the homeowner's policy covers. It includes glass breakage, debris removal, falling trees and tree branches, freezing water pipes, sporting accidents, boat liability— you can read the entire list.

**Hartjen:** I will, but can I afford such coverage? How much will it cost?

**Galat:** This new homeowner's policy with the increased coverage costs just a little more than your present policy; yet it offers far better coverage. We have been able to establish the low rates because of the volume; we sell these policies to hundreds of thousands of homeowners like yourself.

**Hartjen:** O.K. Let's write it up.

1. How are the principles of good customer service applied in this case?
2. Can both customer and salesperson achieve increased benefits? How?
3. Can the salesperson make a genuine contribution to the customer? Explain.

### 13-2  United Furniture and Fixtures, Inc.

Sarah Mocnik is district manager for United Furniture and Fixtures, Inc. Sarah's district covers Michigan and southern Ontario as far east as London, Ontario. Her office is in a suburb of Detroit.

Sarah achieved her position through her outstanding performance as a salesperson over a seven-year period. She is carrying out her job of district manager quite satisfactorily and sales are increasing throughout her district.

United Furniture and Fixtures is a major firm in the office furniture and related equipment field. It does not sell office supplies such as paper, pencils, and pens, nor does it sell office machinery. Its primary sales are in desks, tables, chairs, safes, files, dividers, lamps, and decorative features that make offices more pleasant. It is a well-known company, firmly entrenched with a good reputation.

Sarah hired three salespeople six months ago and they have gone through the regular training course. Part of this training included traveling with experienced salespeople in the district in both Michigan and Ontario to see how actual selling is conducted. Then, each was given a territory, two were placed in Canada and one in Michigan. They replaced three salespeople, one who retired and two who quit for personal reasons.

Each new salesperson set out, confident they would be happy and successful. Sales did not materialize as fast as expected, but Sarah realized this was common. However, when sales were unsatisfactory after six months, Sarah knew something was wrong, particularly when complaints began coming in from the territories about their brusque and sometimes irritating behavior. In an attempt to correct this situation, Sarah called in the three salespeople for a Saturday meeting in her office.

At this meeting, Sarah told them how far below a satisfactory performance they were. Also, she mentioned some of the complaints that had come in about them. She did not point out individual failures, rather, she spoke in general terms to all. She then gave them an encouraging sales talk about being positive, understanding, thoughtful, and helpful to customers. With this encouragement, she sent them away hoping for the best. She told her immediate superior, the sales manager, what she had done. He commended her and asked her to monitor closely the work of the three salespeople for the next three months.

Sarah followed instructions. She even spent two days with each one calling on customers. At the end of the three-month period, sales of all three improved somewhat but not enough. But now Sarah was prepared and called them in for another meeting. Sarah had noticed in her sales calls with each that they dwelt on the integrity and performance of United Furniture and Fixtures instead of working on the needs of their customers. They needed to spend less time on "How good our company is" and concentrate on "What they can do for the customers."

1. How should Sarah Mocnik conduct her next meeting? How could she change the thinking of the new salespeople from "What's in it for me?" to "What's in it for you?"

# 14

# ZEROING IN ON YOURSELF AND YOUR TERRITORY

Salespeople are on their own and must learn to manage themselves. In sales, there is no supervisor watching over you. Consequently, it is often easy to develop sloppy sales habits, take an afternoon off, or put off difficult tasks. The salesperson should be aware of self-management techniques to ensure that this does not happen.

## SELLING IS A 24-HOUR JOB

Successful people live their jobs. The teacher who teaches a few hours a day and then forgets teaching the rest of the time is not a teacher. The job is merely a way to earn some money by going through the motions of teaching. Farmers farm 24 hours a day. They work late at night to bring in that last load of hay. They stay up at night with a sick cow. If a piece of equipment breaks during the day, they stay up late that night repairing it. The doctor is subject to calls even after leaving the office. The minister is subject to calls at any hour of the day or night. In many instances, very little of a minister's work is done in the office or study.

You are a salesperson 24 hours a day, just as the teacher, the doctor, the minister, and the farmer are 24-hour-a-day workers. You cannot be a salesperson for 8 hours and someone else the other 16 hours. This is not to say that anyone should work 24 hours a day. But you should develop a total awareness of your functions as a salesperson and always be alert to opportunities that can help your sales career.

If you learn and practice what you have studied so far in this book, you should find success in selling. However, to avoid erratic selling, spotty performance, and insufficient sales volume, you must learn to manage yourself. Just as your car must receive proper care if it is to perform at its best, so must you pay attention to yourself, the human machine, if you expect to perform at a high level.

You learn to manage yourself by working at it. A baseball player learns to throw and to catch the ball, to bat, to run bases, and to be in the right position to field the ball. You can learn to manage yourself through self-discipline and creative selling principles that will teach you to prosper as a top-level salesperson. There is always room at the top for ambitious, well-trained salespeople who are willing to grow and expand their horizons.

## MANAGING YOUR TERRITORY

An essential part of self-management is managing your territory. Virtually all salespeople, other than those in retail selling, have their own territories. A territory is the geographical area that a salesperson is assigned to work. A territory may be a city, a county, a state, several states, or a specific trading area. Whatever the basic unit, your territory can become a gold mine. From it you must extract adequate sales to pay your salary and expenses and to contribute to your company's overhead. If you work your territory carefully, intelligently, and persistently, you will find the rewards greater than you ever dreamed. By using the most up-to-date methods, you can double or triple your productive capacity. You may be surprised at how much potential exists in your territory once you begin to uncover all the gold that lies there.

Through territory analysis, employers can tell how effectively a territory is being covered and how sales compare with potential. If your firm does not stress territory analysis, you have greater latitude to do your own study. If it makes partial studies, you still have the opportunity to explore areas that your superiors may be neglecting.

To determine how well a salesperson is handling a territory, many firms establish *quotas* for that salesperson and territory. Many salespeople are now working under quotas that require them to accomplish certain prescribed results. Thus, you may

**Illustration 14–1** Working your territory carefully and intelligently may benefit you greatly.

have a sales quota, a product quota, an expense quota, a product mix quota, and other quotas that fit your particular area.

A *sales quota* might be stated as a certain number of dollars or units of products expected to be sold each month, quarter, or year. An *expense quota* may be expressed as a percentage of sales but usually is given as a certain number of dollars per week or as specific daily allowances for food, lodging, and incidentals. A *product mix quota* is used when a salesperson handling several products is expected to sell each product in the line in certain quantities indicated by the quota plan. Some salespeople have quotas for collecting accounts, for setting up displays, and for training wholesale or retail salespeople. These are called *activity quotas*. In each case, your firm is introducing a measuring stick. You are evaluated by how well you perform against the standard.

*Tip Vivian Gearardo has a monthly sales quota divided into separate units for sales of different cosmetic products. Her employer wanted a balanced sales effort to promote the entire line. Vivian soon learned that she could not sell the entire line of cosmetics to every buyer. However, by skillful presentations and attention to the particular needs of each buyer, Vivian was able to balance one order against another so that monthly totals in each category were achieved by thoughtful and careful planning.*

Each year firms become more proficient in setting attainable quotas that have been developed scientifically. As these quotas become more realistic, salespeople are expected to fulfill them. Quotas are guidelines for performance; they are measuring devices that keep you and your boss informed about your progress. If you perform well, do not fear quotas. If you are a shirker, a quota will spotlight you. Whatever your present situation is, accept quotas as guidelines for a successful performance.

## PLANNING THE USE OF YOUR TIME

A second important area of self-management is planning the use of your time. Your time should be planned to spend the most valuable parts of the day with customers. Plan to cover your territory without wasting time and without repetitive backtracking. Plan to do your paperwork in the evening or at nonproductive sales hours. Personal activities should not be allowed to interfere with working hours.

As you go along you will find other important areas of planning, such as planning presentations, that are suitable for the needs of customers. Inevitably, when one develops a number of plans, some will interfere with others. It is up to you, the salesperson, to organize your routine so that plans dovetail rather than clash. Some plans must be modified to fit in with others. Some plans must be staggered for different time periods. Activities must be catalogued in order of urgency and time should be allotted in proportion to their importance.

To be meaningful, plans must be in writing. Merely thinking about them means that they can be forgotten easily or that sections of them can be omitted if time seems pressing. The fact that you write them down and try to arrange them in an orderly fashion will stress their significance. Arrange them in order of importance and weigh the value of each. If you faithfully follow a pattern, you will develop sound habits that become a part of you.

### Increase Your Selling Time

You have only a limited number of hours each day to meet customers. Capitalize on each hour. Studies reveal that many salespeople spend only about two hours a day actually in contact with customers. If this could be increased by 30 minutes, or one more effective call per day, that would amount to 250 extra calls a year. Selling costs are rising so rapidly that more selling time is

**Illustration 14–2    Plan your time in writing at the start of each sales week.**

required of each salesperson. If more work cannot be obtained from the sales force, alternative sales approaches—such as heavy advertising with direct catalog selling—are adopted. Salespeople are eliminated when costs become excessive.

A written schedule is a great help to most salespeople in budgeting their selling time. The schedule lists all the activities a salesperson hopes to accomplish in a day and the time allotted to each activity. Many salespeople tentatively schedule all their activities for the coming week, then each night make a detailed schedule for the following day. The schedule may be determined by the number of hours they plan to work, the number of calls they hope to make, or the sales volume they hope to obtain.

Each day should have a definite starting time and a tentative stopping time. The most important calls of the day should be planned for the salesperson's best selling hours, usually early in the day; salespeople and customers alike tend to lose enthusiasm as the day wears on. However, appointments should be scheduled for the customer's convenience as much as possible. It is important to allow adequate time for interviews. It is also important to schedule secondary selling activities, such as telephoning prospects or writing reports, in case an appointment is unexpectedly canceled or takes less time than anticipated. For this reason, most salespeople schedule more work than they can accomplish in a given day.

## Budget Your Travel Time

Many salespeople spend too much time traveling. When you use precious selling time for travel, you are wasting one of your most valuable assets. Excess travel time can be eliminated by proper routing; that is, making a formal plan for covering a territory. A salesperson must know the territory thoroughly before making an effective routing plan. The calls made each day should be planned so that they are in a relatively compact area. This avoids needless driving back and forth between calls.

Plan your travel in advance. Instead of jumping from customer to customer without regard for distance, plan to go in as direct a route as possible from one customer to the next. Avoid retracing and zigzagging. Sometimes your territory permits you to go directly from one customer to another and you end up near your starting point. If your customers are in a more or less straight line, it might be well to start with the one farthest away early in the morning and work your way back to the customer nearest your office or home. In this way, if you don't make it to your last call, the missed customer is close to home and can easily be contacted the next day. Do your distance driving before or after selling hours. If you have a long distance between two customers, try to travel during noon hours.

**Tip** In some situations, even well-planned travel schedules can be disrupted by customer emergencies. When this happens to Lucy Ihad, she makes the best of the situation. Lucy's territory covers a wide geographic area. From time to time, she will receive a call from a key customer in a distant location who requires immediate servicing. Before leaving to service the customer, Lucy checks her customer files for other prospects along the way, or in the area, who she can also call on. This way, Lucy maximizes the use of her travel time.

## Arrange Your Report Time

You may be one of those salespeople who is flooded with report writing. Most companies insist on some reports. Some firms ask salespeople to write innumerable reports that are rarely used. With other firms, sales reports are very important and must be complete, informative, and written on time. One salesperson was required to fly from Detroit to Pittsburgh to deliver a weekly report that had not been sent to the home office on time.

Seldom do you write a report immediately after an interview. Your selling hours are too valuable to be devoted to report writing. When you are told to write your reports as soon as possible, that usually means to write them in the evening of the day of the interviews. If you have time during the day while waiting for an interview, you might use that time for report writing. As a rule, complete your day's reports before you go to bed. You should not let report writing wait beyond a weekend or the backlog of work will catch up with you.

When you neglect writing your reports for several days, your memory becomes hazy. Details important at the time of the interview are forgotten or improperly reported. Delaying report writing is one way to lose your job. Many a salesperson, otherwise adequate, has foundered on report writing.

## Reserve Time for Sales Preparation

Of all your many duties as a salesperson, your primary job is to sell. A careful review of activities prepares you for the important minutes you spend selling your product to the customer. Time spent in preparation is time well spent. Preparation implies readiness, which in turn implies studying your product, organizing your presentation, and assembling the necessary props to ensure success when you talk to a prospect. You prepare yourself, you prepare the environment for your presentation, and you prepare your demonstration. Try to think of every contingency; attempt to eliminate every chance for error.

Preparation gives you the confidence you need when you face a prospect. Since this contact time is brief, be ready. Often secondary data may be needed to make a sale. Don't be caught without relevant information; the prospect has the right to learn everything and anything about the product or service provided by the company you represent.

## Keep Small Talk at a Minimum

Too many salespeople waste their time and their buyer's time in "visiting" or in "small talk." You do not need to spend much time in idle chatter with the customer. One of the best wholesale drug salespeople in Ohio does not waste time discussing weather, gossip, or anecdotes. The selling time is spent discussing the customer's business needs. Some customers like to spend time chatting; however, most customers are usually more interested in hearing you tell how to improve business than listening to jokes. Surveys show that weak salespeople spend a lot of time chatting; strong salespeople spend their time on the purpose of the sales call. Some salespeople chat idly because they think it is required; they are like those speakers who think that every talk must be introduced with a story or joke. Time spent in small talk, like preparation time and presentation time, should have a purpose. No one of these is an end in itself; however, each one should contribute to the sale.

Occasionally, after you have closed a sale and finished your business, you find a buyer who wishes to relax and chat. Do not hurry away if you sense that the buyer wants to talk. This is a particularly good time to get better acquainted because the buyer is asking you to get better acquainted. Never pass up this opportunity to cement a friendship. Everything you do in the presence of a buyer should contribute to selling. Keep visiting to a minimum unless you are sure that you need the chit-chat to make the sale.

## Time Is Too Important to Waste

There are innumerable ways to fritter away time. Some salespeople are slow getting started in the morning. Precious hours are lost through procrastination, uncertainty, and indecision. What shall I wear? What equipment will I need today? Which customer shall I see first? Would it be better to wait until tomorrow? These and other questions can arise in the morning. Most could have been resolved the night before.

Much time is wasted while waiting to see buyers. While waiting in an office lobby you can either work or waste time reading newspapers, current magazines, or chatting idly. Through careful scheduling, however, you can reduce the time wasted in lobbies or outer waiting rooms. Calling on buyers at inopportune periods of the day is an inexcusable waste of time. To make this mistake once with a buyer is understandable; to continue making the same mistake is not.

Do not waste time at lunch. If you eat alone, adjust your schedule to avoid using selling time. If you take buyers to lunch, they can spend only a limited time with you. Be observant and be guided by their wishes. If they are receptive, discuss selling at lunch. Adjust your lunch period differently each day, if necessary, so that you maximize selling time.

Do not waste time waiting in the office lobby after lunch if you are not the first on the afternoon schedule. During the day, coffee breaks can waste much valuable time. You cannot afford such periods unless the buyers want them. Make your closing hours in the afternoon flexible. You need not stop selling at 5 p.m. if buyers work later. Tailor your hours to fit theirs.

You do not forget your job at 5 p.m. In the hotel in the evening you can waste your time by doing nothing of importance, or you can use it efficiently. You can either daydream or think. Some salespeople confuse the two. You do not have to forget your work on weekends, either. Even subconsciously thinking about selling helps to fix thoughts and ideas. Instead of letting your mind go blank, apply it to some knotty problem. Many salespeople feel that if they give their employer 40 hours a week, they have done their duty; but selling is not a 40-hour-a-week job. If you choose to forget selling after hours, you are wasting time; a scarce and valuable commodity.

## CONTINUE YOUR LEARNING ACTIVITIES

As a beginning salesperson, you will probably be involved in some training activities sponsored by your firm. These may be in the form of classroom training given by the sales manager or on-the-job training with an experienced salesperson. Such topics as selling duties and techniques, nonselling duties, company policies and procedures, markets, buyers, and products may be covered in these training sessions.

A salesperson's training, however, should not stop when the formal training sessions are over. Books, magazines, and newspapers can improve a creative salesperson's knowledge. The successful salesperson is always learning something new. Training continues in a two-pronged fashion. One prong follows those activities that increase knowledge, broaden perspectives, and develop creativity. The other prong is the retaining one. It is

**Illustration 14–3    Continue your learning through training programs.**

refresher training, going over material once learned but now forgotten through disuse or misuse. Valuable information can easily be forgotten in the press of everyday activities.

*Tip   Harvey Smigelski realizes he cannot remain static if he is to be alert and aggressive in his selling. Continuous training and study are necessary. Therefore, he reads a daily newspaper, skims through current issues of magazines in his line of business, and buys at least one new sales book every year. He carefully reads all literature and directives from the home office and uses this information in his selling. During his travels, he visits with salespeople from other sales areas to see if he can transfer some of their strengths to his work. Knowing that his product area is constantly changing, he tries to keep abreast of new competing products. These diligent study habits help Harvey remain one of the leading salespeople in his firm.*

Most firms have sales conferences at certain intervals to retrain and refresh their salespeople and give them new ideas. Every year you will probably attend one or more of your firm's conferences. Some salespeople consider this a waste of time or a recreation period. Salespeople attend far too many conferences with the idea that nothing will be gained; they enter with a defeatist attitude. With this attitude it is impossible to gain anything. Until such attitudes are changed, employers will be throwing away money on sales personnel.

Firms set up conferences for well-established objectives. They may want to train or retrain salespeople or to introduce new products and new methods. Often, a conference is used to recharge the batteries of enthusiasm.

Some conferences include not only company salespeople but also dealer salespeople, and other sales representatives. In such a group it is not uncommon to have some participants who cause difficulties—heckling, resentful, griping, talkative, stubborn people who may be satisfactory in selling even though each may have a definite weakness. In selling you also have such customers. Whether in a one-to-one situation or leading a meeting, here is a valuable tip: "In dealing with problem people, resist that clever remark, that sarcastic retort, or embarrassing humor. . . . Ridicule, acid wit, and talking down to individuals leave deep and lasting wounds."[1]

Carefully planned and executed conferences are rewarding for alert salespeople. Creative salespeople gain a keener perspective of their firm, get better acquainted with executives, and learn more about the other salespeople. They gather knowledge of new sales tools and techniques. They have a chance to improve their knowledge, to find answers to perplexing problems, and to develop better sales strategies.

If you participate eagerly in a conference, if you actively try to develop your techniques, learn more about your products and

---

[1]Homer Smith, "Meet Bored Boris and 14 Other Gremlins Who May Show Up at Your Next Session," *Sales and Marketing Management* (September 17, 1979), pp. 100, 102, 104, 106.

how to handle questions and problems more intelligently, the conference will be a rare opportunity. Here, in one group, are many people who daily meet and overcome obstacles that may be serious hindrances to you. Use the conference as a positive sales builder to stimulate you to greater success.

## MAINTAINING YOUR PHYSICAL RESOURCES

Your body is a machine that must be given proper attention if you are to sell effectively. When this machine malfunctions, sales suffer.

Exercise moderation in food and beverages; eat and drink sensibly and avoid excesses. If you know you may have to drink one or more cups of coffee with customers during the morning, go easy on coffee for breakfast. If you have a buyer for lunch, avoid too much food or drink even if the buyer eats much more than you. The buyer will not be offended by what you do as long as you eat a sensible meal.

Improper eating habits may have little effect on young people, but age takes its toll and soon you begin to pay greater attention to what you eat. By giving careful attention to your diet, you will be better able to meet the requirements of your job.

Each day you should start out fresh and optimistic. This is impossible, though, if you spend a sleepless night. Unless you recoup your energies at night, your next day's work will be listless. Do not cut into your sleep by staying up late in the evening. Do not try to drive home at night when you ought to stay in a hotel. Many salespeople waste valuable selling time driving home, when they ought to stay in their territories overnight and on occasional weekends.

Refrain from long tiresome drives at night if you are permitted to take a plane; public transportation is faster and less tiring than being your own chauffeur. Do not travel Sunday night if you have an important meeting Monday morning. Do not crowd your appointments so that you must rush from one to another. At the same time, do not be afraid of a 4:30 p.m. appointment. Many a buyer may be willing to stay after 5:00 if your presentation is interesting.

Rest means not only proper night comfort but also proper day comfort. If your day has been hectic, by four o'clock in the afternoon you will be in no condition to meet another buyer. An irritable salesperson is not very efficient. Determine how much rest you need, and discipline yourself to get enough.

Relaxation is an important part of managing your physical resources. Learn to relax. You do not use all parts of your mind and body at the same rate. If your selling requires little movement but much mental attention, your mind tires, but your body does not. Physical exercise in the evening may be relaxing. If your day is both physically and mentally exhausting, a quiet evening may be what you need to relax.

Do not overlook entertainment—movies, plays, concerts—as a means of relaxation. Such activities can be not only relaxing but also stimulating because you acquire new ideas as you listen and observe. Relaxation should relieve tension, loosen muscles, and induce a restful attitude. It should relieve you so that you have a chance to recharge yourself physically, mentally, and emotionally.

Any machine develops weak spots in time. Our bodies, like machines, are not immune to weaknesses. Although the body constantly rebuilds itself, there is always the chance that certain parts will weaken. To avoid physical breakdown, have medical checkups at regular intervals. Your physician can determine how often you need a checkup. Many minor illnesses, caught early, can be overcome with proper attention. If neglected, minor illnesses become major problems.

## CONTROLLING YOUR MENTAL RESOURCES

In a recent medical experiment a group of professional actors were wired to equipment to check on their automatic (involuntary) nervous system activity. They were directed to move various facial muscles to express fear, disgust, happiness, and several other feelings. "With just the different emotions-mimicking facial expressions, the researchers found wide variations in heart rate and skin temperature. They also discovered *that each emotion led to a different nervous system pattern.*"[2] Apparently, emotions cause physical disorders and physical disorders affect emotions. This indicates that there are mind/body relationships that must be understood by salespeople.

---

[2]"Emotions and the Body," *Executive Health Report,* Vol. XXI, Number 10 (July 1985).

Your physical self is being replaced constantly. New cells replace old ones. Your hair and nails grow. Your body changes shape. Aches and pains come and go. You are changing each minute.

Mental changes go on like physical changes. We may not be aware of mental changes because they may be hard to detect. Mentally, you can become a better salesperson or a worse one. You can improve mentally to some extent through desirable associations; merely being with some people may prove beneficial. It is not likely, however, that you will improve yourself much unless you consciously strive to improve.

Plan a pattern of activity to improve yourself mentally. Set aside a "thinking" period each day when you concentrate on specific problems or subject matter. Address your thoughts to chosen areas and do not let thoughts drift aimlessly. Jot down some of your thoughts and ideas and rearrange them in a number of ways to see if you can establish new relationships. Think creatively!

When difficult sales problems crop up, take time to work out solutions and test them in sales situations. Revise and rework them. See if you can improve solutions that you now consider satisfactory. Do not be content to solve a problem in a careless way if you can approach it with painstaking care or watchful attention. Do not be satisfied with the status quo. Who knows, you may improve so much that you will be promoted to an executive position, or you may change to a more difficult selling job with another firm. If you are doing well at your present selling job, continue to look for more challenging opportunities and goals. This attitude may impel you to greater achievement, a more difficult job, and a more rewarding life.

The possibilities of improving yourself mentally are so enormous that you should work at it all your life. You will never reach the pinnacle of your mental development. Most salespeople settle for a mental plateau that is below their potential achievement level. No matter how far you push your mental abilities, you still possess unused capacity. What you consider a peak achievement at one period in your life may later look feeble. Many a salesperson, immensely proud of the success of ten years ago, looks today at that period with amused tolerance. Little did this person think then how much future growth there would be.

# BALANCING YOUR FINANCIAL RESOURCES

An area that gives many salespeople difficulty is that of managing their earnings. You may be paid in one of several ways. You might be paid a straight salary, such as $2,000 a month, no matter what sales volume you achieve. You might be paid a straight commission, such as 6 percent of your net sales volume. Or you might be paid a salary plus commission or bonus, which is a set salary per week or month plus a certain percentage of your sales volume over that set amount.

However you are paid, in the long run your salary comes from a percentage of sales. Your firm allows a budgeted amount for sales expenses, and your total earnings and expenses cannot exceed this amount. Small variations do occur, but such amounts do not long exceed the budget.

## Budget Your Spending

If your earnings are a predictable amount each period, plan your spending accordingly. Often, salary fluctuations necessitate a different type of planning. When you begin selling, your earnings may be small. As your selling ability grows, your earnings should grow. There is nothing magic about how much you earn. Except for a beginning or training period during which you are a financial liability, your earnings will reflect your worth to your employer. Your performance is balanced against your cost. As your performance improves, your employer willingly contributes a greater amount to your earnings. You register your worth on a scale of values for which the pay is commensurate.

Beware of earnings that increase dramatically. Do not spend them all. You may be lucky. If your earnings increase rapidly, be cautious in spending until time demonstrates whether you can maintain such earnings. A slow but steady increase in earning power is usually more typical of selling. Such progress is fairly dependable if you are creative and work hard.

Very often the beginning salesperson with a family may find earnings inadequate. It is so easy to buy beyond your means. This is the time to exercise prudence in spending. Early in your selling career you may change jobs. There can be periods of unemployment. This is no time to incur long-term obligations. You are in a period of adjustment—a new job, perhaps a new place to live, and many things to buy—when you should not spend much money.

Budget your income. List essential expenditures and then those expenditures that you would like to make but that are not essential. As income increases, expenditures for nonessential items can increase. Although certain expenditures such as food, clothing, and perhaps a car might head your list of essentials, there can be major deviations in each category. For example, although a car may be essential to a salesperson, a Cadillac is not.

Many times you may be tempted to buy high quality when a lesser quality would be suitable. Think of your income as a limited resource that can decrease, increase, or even disappear temporarily. Wise salespeople give themselves a savings cushion. They do not spend all their money nor mortgage their future indefinitely with onerous payments.

## Should You Use Credit?

One important matter to consider in the managing of financial resources is whether to use credit. Interest is paid for the use of money. Whether you borrow money outright or borrow by having a purchase financed, you pay interest. After all, the individual or institution that makes loans must earn a profit to stay in business.

Whenever you buy and do not pay cash, you are borrowing someone else's money. Somebody pays cash, either you or the person lending money. Consequently, when you buy on credit, you pay two costs—the merchandise cost and the money cost. Because of the high merchandise cost of some items, you will buy on credit because it will be impossible to pay cash. To enjoy owning a house and car today, you buy on credit. You have committed yourself to give a specified amount of your income to credit payments each month. This is what is meant by "mortgaging your future."

Credit is an admirable way to finance purchases; but like other good things, it can be used wisely or abused. Judiciously used, it permits you to enjoy a fuller life. Improperly used, credit can bring worry, suffering, and ruin. Do not borrow with the hope of paying back with higher future earnings. Plan to pay back on your present earnings scale. Wait until future increased earnings materialize before you borrow against them.

## Emergency Plans

The prudent salesperson restricts spending. Life consists of a series of financial advances and reverses. Unexpected expenditures such as exceptional medical costs and repairs are inevitable. It is wise to restrict spending so that you can accumulate a reserve to meet the unknown. Just as machinery, equipment, and bridges are built with a generous margin for safety, so should you order your life to provide for emergencies.

Many unexpected contingencies can be handled through insurance. Examine your insurance portfolio to see how well you and your family are protected. Substantial immediate protection for your family can be secured through life insurance at a moderate cost. Is your car liability insurance adequate? You cannot protect against all contingencies, but you can save yourself much possible grief by a savings account that can handle minor emergencies and assist in handling major emergencies.

## IMPROVE YOUR RELATIONSHIP WITH YOUR FIRM AND YOUR SUPERVISOR

No discussion of self-management would be complete without looking at the management of your relationship with your firm and your immediate supervisor. Although a salesperson's primary job is to please and serve the customer, it is also essential to please and serve your firm and supervisor.

### Serve Your Firm with Maximum Effort

Just as you make an extra effort to be of maximum service to your customer, you must be willing to make an extra effort to be of maximum service to your firm. You must try to ensure success to everyone connected with the enterprise; success for one must be measured by success for all. At times you will be asked to do things that do not please you. You may feel that supervisors are infringing on your rights, asking you to do what should be done by other people, or giving you extra work when you are ill-prepared. Nevertheless, try as much as possible to fulfill the wishes of your firm.

Some salespeople have too many negative thoughts. They do not realize that some parts of a business may suffer temporarily so that more important parts succeed. What you must consider is how other members of the firm look at your job. What do they think your job is? How do they think it should be done? What do they consider a poor job as contrasted with a good one?

Treat your employer as you would like to be treated if you were the employer and you were reviewing the work of a salesperson. Do not begrudge your employer extra effort, additional time, and more concentrated attention. Do your part well, and the firm's management will be pleased. In doing your part, supply that little extra, that activity beyond the call of duty that will show how earnestly you are devoted to your task.

### Serve Your Supervisor with Maximum Effort

Perhaps even more important than the relationship with your firm is your relationship with your supervisor. You must deal frequently with your supervisor, and your supervisor knows more about you than does anyone else in the firm.

Many people fail to realize that the sales manager has personal worries in relation to the firm. Although each salesperson has responsibility for sales in only one territory, the top sales executive has responsibility for total company sales. The sales manager tries to understand each salesperson. But do you as a salesperson try to understand the problems of the manager—problems pertaining to the position; problems of responsibilities to top management and to each individual salesperson; problems to avoid sagging sales and profits? If you fail, your superior will have to help you to improve your selling or replace you. It is expensive to replace you, and one never knows if a new salesperson will do better. Therefore, it probably is preferable to give extra effort to try to positively change your performance. Not only is your success monitored but also the success of all other salespeople. When you think of your supervisor under these circumstances, you may become sympathetic to the efforts directed toward improvement. Devices and procedures seemingly harsh may then reveal themselves as steps in firmness and direction to increase productivity.

Are you willing to make the extra effort with your supervisor that you do with your customers and your firm? Are your reports clear, understandable, and on time? Do you treat your customers as your sales manager would like to have them treated? Do you put in extra hours of selling time to do a better job? Do you plan your work? Do you keep your superior informed of all matters that are important in your territory? Do you go to your field supervisor soon enough when you feel problems are too hard for you to handle alone? Or do you let them drag until you get so hopelessly involved that no one can pull you out?

Making the extra effort certainly means more than talking—it means action that will benefit both of you. It means selling successfully against price competition, product competition, delivery competition, and many other kinds of competitive effort. If your job were simple, you would not have it. Your firm would not need you. It could substitute some mechanical device for you or get someone cheaper. If your job has difficult aspects, accept them. You are employed to handle difficult situations.

Learn to be a well-rounded individual who can cope with problems as they arise. Study your work to see where improvements are feasible. As long as you are content to go along in your usual fashion, you are not effectively cooperating with your boss. If you think up new ways of doing things, or attempt to do things better, or make friendly suggestions that have definite value, you are on the right track; you are giving liberally of yourself.

Share in the responsibilities of your territory, or take more of the burden carried by your supervisor. Willingly accept your duty of furthering mutual interests. Become a standby, a dependable person, a confident person who can be entrusted with difficult tasks, a loyal person who executes orders, an adventurous person with original thinking, a thoughtful person for consultation. Be watchful, not careless; thoughtful, not indifferent; aggressive, not lazy. You have a position to fill, an example to set, and your behavior should impress people. Be level-headed and prudent when you talk to your superior. Show respect without implying or exhibiting a weakness in your position. Do not nurse grudges against your boss; do not expect extra attention. Realize that your boss has many duties to perform.

*Tip    Flora Boersema was an effective salesperson. She prided herself on being self-reliant, depending little on her boss for help in her territory. At sales meetings she had observed some salespeople repeatedly asking the boss how to handle their sales problems. She also knew that some of her colleagues bothered the boss with personal problems. Flora had her personal problems but handled them without recourse to her superior. Her sales problems were handled without help and without fanfare or complaint. Occasionally, she might ask the boss a question at a sales meeting, but mostly, she complimented her superior for being effective. At performance review time, given that Flora handles her territory well, doesn't complain, and earns money for her firm, is it any wonder why Flora is rated so favorably?*

# FIRMING YOUR RELATIONSHIP WITH OTHERS

Your life has many facets. You cannot isolate yourself, nor can you live a narrow, compartmentalized life. If you are sincerely interested in your work and those connected with it, you should also develop equally good family and community relations. One element of life inevitably carries over into another. Make your whole life one unit; become a living example of the fine qualities that are displayed by every successful salesperson.

The importance of each segment of your life can vary from year to year. One year you might tutor; the next year you could work with the Boy Scouts; during the next several years you might follow high school athletics; finally, your interests are directed to college or elsewhere. As you become established in a community, civic duties grow. Imperceptibly, life becomes more complex, time becomes more important, and requests for help increase. Unless you recognize the demands of a well-developed pattern of living and allocate your time for each essential segment, you will discover that progress becomes difficult. You may not improve each part of your life at the same time, but eventually each part must be given its proper attention.

Life is a totality. Either you are optimistic, cheerful, helpful, kind with unrestrained enthusiasm and the ability to get ahead—or, conversely, you are disappointed, chagrined, unhappy, upset. The latter characteristics prevent proper application to your daily work. Just as it is important to take care of your body, it is also important to take care of your mental health, your spiritual health, and your attitude toward others. Blended in a positive way, your traits will give you the courage to forge ahead to a goal marked "success." To reach it, put forth the effort. To enjoy future success, think positively.

# YOUR COMMITMENT TO THE JOB

Some salespeople may carry on most of the activities discussed in this chapter and yet be average performers when they ought to be superior. They may fulfill all training requirements, carry out their duties as outlined by the sales manager, and in every way seem to be ideal salespeople, yet fail to be top producers. Why? Perhaps because they fail in commitment.

A committed student does not ask how many times to read an assignment but continues to work until the assignment has been mastered. A committed artisan does not guess the work is satis-factory but rather uses definite tests or checkpoints until satisfied that the work is of the proper quality and meets specifications. Perhaps the measure of a salesperson is not activity, following orders, or attention to customers—although these are all essential and expected—but intellectual commitment to a superior per-formance.

Intellectual commitment may not call for harder work, for more time on the job, or for more and better attention to details, although all of these are important. Rather, it will call for a direction of attitude and a sense of willingness to concentrate more effectively on your job. If this spirit can be generated inwardly, you will be transformed mentally. This is not an appeal to sentiment. It is an attempt to reach within yourself and bring forth those traits that will create greater customer empathy.

**Illustration 14–4  Com-mitted salespeople ap-proach their duties enthus-iastically.**

*The Prudential*

Many salespeople fail to grow because they view their jobs too narrowly. They fail to see their need for commitment, the necessity to view their work as it fits the buyer and the environ-ment, and the desirability of seeing their selling job in new dimensions. Even as they gain experience and learn to sell better, they still fall short of superlative performances until they have developed the inner self to be sensitive to buyers' requirements. Once you have gained this inward appreciation, you will see innumerable opportunities to improve your work by paying attention to areas previously neglected. You will begin to pick up loose ends you used to skip; you will pay attention to factors you used to consider unimportant; you will sharpen your sensitivity to conditions you used to dismiss as pointless.

Committed salespeople do not look forward to the end of the day or week, do not long for retirement, do not become restless under daily demands. They enjoy their work and willingly give the time and effort the job deserves. Committed salespeople do not slight duties to family, community, school, and other activities, but approach each with zest because all these duties make up a satisfying, useful, activity-oriented life.

## MY IMPROVEMENT SCHEDULE

**I EITHER GO FORWARD**
**OR**
**I SLIDE BACKWARD**
**I CANNOT STAND STILL**

**DAILY**—Time: 1 to 2 hours
1. Follow current events in daily newspapers, on the radio, and television.
2. Read some worthwhile literature that may improve, educate, and develop me.
3. Spend some time in real thinking.
4. Plan tomorrow's work.

**WEEKLY**—Time: 2 to 4 hours
1. Read weekly business magazines.
2. Clean up unfinished work.
3. Make sure all reports are finished or kept current.
4. Plan next week's work.

**MONTHLY**—Time: 2 to 4 hours
1. Read monthly business magazines.
2. Evaluate month's activities.
3. Participate in some activity with the family or friends.
Monthly activities can be accomplished both during and at the end of the month.

**QUARTERLY**—Time: 8 hours
1. Analyze quarter's activities.
2. Plan definite improvement steps for the next quarter.
3. Assess current economic conditions.

Quarterly activities tend to be concentrated at the end of the quarter.

**YEARLY**—Time: 3 weeks
1. Attend conventions or special meetings.
2. Take vacation.
3. Analyze year's performance and compare with some standard or quota.
4. Develop goals for the coming year.

Yearly activities may be done during the year as well as at the end of the year. Your year does not have to be identical with a calendar year.

**FIVE YEAR**—Time: as needed
1. Refresher training.
2. Realignment of goals.
3. Long-range planning.
4. Monitor career development and goals.

## QUESTIONS

1. Is there a relationship between self-management and non-performance? Explain.
2. Why does a so-called 24-hour job not fit the traditional 40-hour week? Why would "clock watchers" have difficulty fitting into the 24-hour jobs?
3. How does a salesperson's territory compare with a gold mine?
4. Are quotas important to a salesperson? If so, provide several reasons why.
5. Are there advantages to refresher training? What are they?
6. Are conferences useful in disseminating certain types of information? In what way?
7. How does a mature salesperson meet responsibilities to the community and society?
8. What are successful relationships between salespeople and supervisors? Between salespeople and the firm?
9. What are some of the features of a salesperson's life relating to job, community, and personal satisfaction?
10. What is creative selling?

# SALES CHALLENGES

1.  Patty Gilson has been a salesperson for Collier, Inc. for the past year. She sells drugs and medical supplies for animals. She travels the states of Iowa and Nebraska. She calls on hospitals, pharmacies, and stores that regularly handle her products, and also on some large farms where they employ a veterinarian. She covers major accounts every quarter, and smaller accounts every half-year. Whenever she calls on a customer, Patty provides background information on new products, business trends in the area, and other information of interest to veterinarians and pharmacists. Any order she receives she forwards that same evening to her firm. Most orders are received directly by the company by telephone over a toll-free line reserved for customers. Patty also has a toll-free telephone service for customers to her home where she can be reached every weekend. Patty has competition from smaller suppliers in local districts but most of these lack the flexibility of Collier and usually have higher prices. Patty is doing well but her sales manager receives too many complaints from customers about Patty. It appears Patty is careless at times, too lazy to do certain things, and often forgets some of her promises to customers. The sales manager feels that Patty is capable of doing better work and will respond favorably to closer home office direction.

    You are assigned by the sales manager to develop a guidance outline for Patty to follow. This outline should be detailed, not sketchy. We might say the sales manager wants a guide to "lay down the law" to Patty in a firm manner.

2.  Fern Mensch is having financial problems. Her commissions vary greatly from one month to the next. She cannot seem to budget her finances so that she has money to cover her needs on a consistent basis. Some months her base pay amounts to about half of her commissions; some months the base pay is about all she makes; while other months, the base pay represents only a small part of what she earns. Not knowing what she will be getting from one month to the next, there are times she is desperate for cash because she has not spent wisely. Her total yearly income is quite adequate—even generous. It is a personal problem, but one that needs an answer.

    Draw up a financial schedule for Fern that shows her what she must do every day in the month. She covers her territory once every four weeks and returns home each weekend. All of her territory is less than 100 miles from her home base. Her car and car expenses are covered separately by her employer.

3. You are a salesperson for Electro-Vac vacuum cleaners, which are sold on a house-to-house basis. You are about to begin making calls on certain qualified customers in a 12-block area, as shown below. The houses you will be calling on are identified by a ★. Identify a route patten to cover these homes while minimizing travel distance.

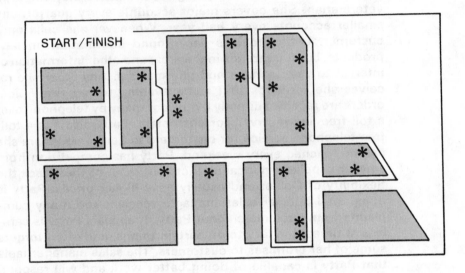

START/FINISH

## CASES

### 14-1 The Kline Company

The Kline Company of Wilmington, Delaware sells sports and leisure clothing throughout the eastern states. A vacancy occurred through the retirement of one of the salespeople and Amy Jordan, a sister of one of the company's current salespeople, was hired. Amy had previously sold clothing in a department store.

Amy felt that her new job with Kline would allow her to develop her sales abilities. Because of her previous selling experience, Amy was assigned to a territory after a very short training program.

Amy spent her first month on the job becoming acquainted with her territory, her customers, and the clothing lines she was selling. It did not take long for Amy to reach an acceptable sales level, about the same as had been achieved by her predecessor in the territory.

Amy routinely called on her current accounts and contacted new prospects as she found out about them. Amy often found when she called on new retail outlets that competitive salespeople had already been there and had secured large orders and valuable display space. Amy was often able to secure small orders and less desirable space in these situations.

On days when Amy stopped at the district office to pick up samples and talk to her sales manager, she would often remain in the office and contact her customers by phone rather than make personal visits to their stores. If the buyer wasn't in, Amy would leave a message that she had called and ask that the buyer return her call if any merchandise were needed. And in bad weather Amy would often call rather than drive through her territory. After missing a few sales calls, Amy would often find that a competitor had gotten some of the display space previously occupied by her products. Amy could not understand this since the Kline items sold very well.

When customer problems arose and were brought to Amy's attention, she would suggest that the customer contact the Kline complaint department at a toll-free number that Amy would provide. After all, Amy reasoned, that's why there is a complaint department.

It has been a year since Amy joined the Kline Company. Amy feels that she is doing a very good job. Amy's sales manager has reviewed her performance and, although Amy's sales have remained constant, competitors' sales are increasing substantially in Amy's territory. The sales manager informs Amy that unless her performance improves substantially, the company will start looking for a replacement.

1. What is the danger in being content with just maintaining past performance?
2. Identify all of the areas where Amy has been weak in her performance.
3. Outline a program for Amy to use to improve her performance.

## 14–2 Hometown Sales Territory Planning

You have been covering the Hometown sales territory for the Pacific Supply Company for the past three years. You live in Hometown and all of your customers are within a two-hour drive of Hometown. It is a Saturday afternoon and you are drawing up your territory travel plans for the coming month.

Over the past year, your sales have been averaging $30,000 per month. This coming month is important because your company has just announced a sales contest. A cash prize of $5,000 will be awarded to the salesperson achieving the highest sales over the next four weeks. You would really like to win this prize.

*Your goal is to plan your travel and sales calls for the next four weeks to generate the maximum total sales.*

A list of your customers, where they are located, their monthly sales potential, and the appropriate person(s) to contact is shown in Exhibit 1. A map of the Hometown sales territory is shown in Exhibit 2.

Your customers can be contacted between 8:30 a.m. and 5:00 p.m. from Monday through Friday. They are not available at other times. This means that you have approximately 170 hours in which to generate sales during the contest period (8.5 hours per day $\times$ five days per week $\times$ four weeks). Your actual time available to sell is reduced by travel time, waiting time, and lunch, as will be described in the following paragraphs.

All travel through your territory is by car. Travel times from town to town in your territory are shown in Exhibit 2. Driving to your first call can be done prior to 8:30 a.m. and driving home can be done after 5:00 p.m. If you are traveling from one town to another during the day, make sure that you account for the travel time. For example, it takes one hour to drive from Middleton to Northville. If you are calling on two customers in the same town, allow 30 minutes for travel and some waiting time to see the buyer. For example, assume that you wish to call on Westown Fabricating to be followed by a call on Wallace Brass. Both of these customers are located in Westown. If your sales call on Westown Fabricating ends at 10:30 a.m., your call on Wallace Brass could not begin until 11:00 a.m.

It is important that you maintain proper nourishment, therefore you must allow 60 minutes each day for lunch. You can schedule your lunch at any time between 11:30 a.m. and 1:30 p.m. each day. You may take a buyer to lunch but this represents only a social contact, not a sales call.

You can schedule your sales calls with each buying contact at your customer firms for periods of 30, 60, or 90 minutes. No sales call with an individual buying contact can exceed 90 minutes. Each 30 minutes of selling time with a buying contact has some value. These values are shown in Exhibit 3.

## Exhibit 1

### LIST OF CUSTOMERS

| Customer Number/Location | Monthly Sales Potential | Buying Contacts |
|---|---|---|
| **Hometown** | | |
| 1. Hometown Steel | $3,500 | Design Engineer Foreman |

| | | |
|---|---|---|
| 2. Howard Electric | $2,500 | Purchasing Agent |
| 3. Harris Products | $3,500 | Purchasing Agent |
| | | General Foreman |
| 4. Harley Tools | $1,500 | Purchasing Agent |

**Middleton**

| | | |
|---|---|---|
| 5. Middleton Motors | $3,500 | Design Engineer |
| | | Purchasing Agent |
| | | Foreman |
| 6. Maple Plastics | $2,200 | Purchasing Agent |
| 7. Marvin Copper | $3,500 | Purchasing Agent |
| | | Foreman |
| 8. Millard Coil & Tube | $1,500 | Foreman |

**Westown**

| | | |
|---|---|---|
| 9. Westown Fabricating | $4,000 | Design Engineer |
| | | Purchasing Agent |
| | | Foreman |
| 10. Wallace Brass | $1,750 | Foreman |
| 11. Windsor Electric | $3,500 | Purchasing Agent |
| | | Foreman |
| 12. Winter Works | $1,500 | General Foreman |

**Northville**

| | | |
|---|---|---|
| 13. Northville Knots | $2,500 | Purchasing Agent |
| 14. Norris Stampings | $3,500 | Purchasing Agent |
| | | Foreman |
| 15. Newton Forgings | $5,500 | Design Engineer |
| | | Purchasing Agent |
| | | Foreman |
| 16. Nester Containers | $1,500 | Foreman |

**Eastown**

| | | |
|---|---|---|
| 17. Eastown Electric | $2,500 | Purchasing Agent |
| | | Foreman |
| 18. Eastern Machinery | $3,500 | Purchasing Agent |
| | | Foreman |
| 19. Everly Pottery | $2,500 | Foreman |
| 20. Easter Sealings | $3,000 | Purchasing Agent |
| | | Foreman |

**Southboro**

| | | |
|---|---|---|
| 21. Southboro Tools | $5,500 | Design Engineer |
| | | Purchasing Agent |
| | | Foreman |
| 22. Selleck Solvents | $3,500 | Purchasing Agent |
| | | Foreman |
| 23. Southern Sockets | $1,000 | Foreman |
| 24. Sherman Shelving | $3,500 | Purchasing Agent |
| | | Foreman |

**Exhibit 2**

**HOMETOWN SALES TERRITORY**

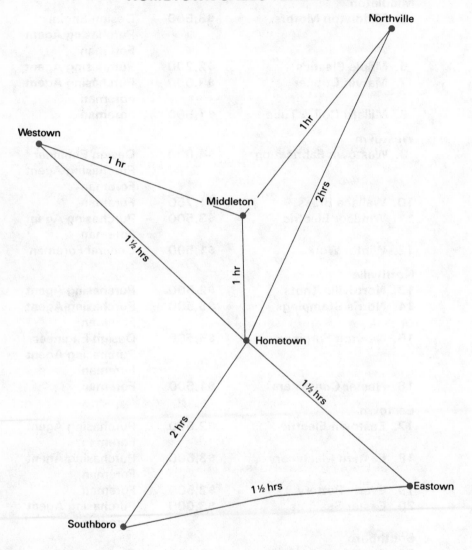

# Exhibit 3

## SALES CALL VALUE

| | First Call | | | Second Call | | | Third and Later Calls | | |
|---|---|---|---|---|---|---|---|---|---|
| | 1st 30 min | 2nd 30 min | 3rd 30 min | 1st 30 min | 2nd 30 min | 3rd 30 min | 1st 30 min | 2nd 30 min | 3rd 30 min |
| Decision Maker | 9 | 7 | 5 | 4 | 5 | 2 | 3 | 4 | 2 |
| Key Influence | 6 | 4 | 2 | 4 | 4 | 3 | 4 | 2 | 1 |

The top name shown for each of your customers in Exhibit 1 is the decision maker (such as the design engineer for Hometown Steel); any following names represent key influences (such as the foreman for Hometown Steel). For some customers there is only one name shown. This means that there is only a decision maker for that customer and no other key influences.

The numbers in Exhibit 3 represent probabilities of making a sale. That is, if you schedule a 60-minute call on the design engineer at Hometown Steel at 8:30 a.m. on Monday morning, followed by a 60-minute call on the foreman of Hometown Steel at 9:30 a.m., you would have generated a 26-percent probability of making a sale to Hometown Steel (9 + 7 + 6 + 4 = 26). This represents the probabilities of 9 and 7 for the decision maker (the design engineer) plus the probabilities of 6 and 4 for the key influence (the foreman). Note that there was no travel or waiting time between calls since they were both at Hometown Steel. If your next call is on another customer in Hometown, you must allow 30 minutes travel and waiting time, meaning that your call could start no earlier than 11:00 a.m. If you next call is on a customer in Middleton (for example), you must allow one hour for travel from Hometown to Middleton (see Exhibit 2). Therefore, your call could start no earlier than 11:30 a.m. Keep in mind that lunch and travel time *cannot* be combined.

Each customer can be contacted only once a week; customers become annoyed if contacted by the same salesperson more often than this. If you are contacting a customer for the second, third, or fourth time in the month, be sure you use the appropriate value from Exhibit 3.

You are now ready to develop your territory travel plans. The following (Exhibit 4) is an example of a completed territory planning form for one day. To develop your territory travel plans for the next four weeks, you should use the planning form in Exhibit 5. You will need four copies of this form, one for each week.

The sample one-day travel plan in Exhibit 4 should be interpreted in the following manner. The day began with a trip to Middleton to visit Middleton Motors (customer number 5) at 8:30 a.m. The design engineer (DE) was contacted for 60 minutes followed by a 60-minute call on the purchasing agent (PA). The next customer visited was Marvin Copper where the purchasing agent was contacted for 90 minutes. Note that the appropriate 30-minute travel and wait period for customers in the same town was accounted for. Lunch was scheduled from 12:30 to 1:30 with another 30-minute travel and wait preceding the 60-minute sales contact with the foreman (F) at Millard Coil & Tube. Finally, one hour of travel to Hometown resulted in the last call of the day at

## Exhibit 4

## TERRITORY PLANNING FORM

| Hours | Monday | | |
|---|---|---|---|
| | Customer Number | Contact | % |
| 8:30 - 9:00 | 5 | DE | 9 |
| 9:00 - 9:30 | | DE | 7 |
| 9:30 - 10:00 | | PA | 6 |
| 10:00 - 10:30 | | PA | 4 |
| 10:30 - 11:00 | | WAIT | — |
| 11:00 - 11:30 | 7 | PA | 9 |
| 11:30 - 12:00 | | PA | 7 |
| 12:00 - 12:30 | | PA | 5 |
| 12:30 - 1:00 | | LUNCH | — |
| 1:00 - 1:30 | | LUNCH | — |
| 1:30 - 2:00 | | WAIT | — |
| 2:00 - 2:30 | 8 | F | 9 |
| 2:30 - 3:00 | | F | 7 |
| 3:00 - 3:30 | | TRAVEL | — |
| 3:30 - 4:00 | | TRAVEL | — |
| 4:00 - 4:30 | 1 | DE | 9 |
| 4:30 - 5:00 | | DE | 7 |
| Summary | Customer 5 = 26% Customer 7 = 21% Customer 8 = 16% Customer 1 = 16% | | |

**Exhibit 5**

## TERRITORY PLANNING FORM

| HOURS | MONDAY | | | TUESDAY | | | WEDNESDAY | | | THURSDAY | | | FRIDAY | | |
|---|---|---|---|---|---|---|---|---|---|---|---|---|---|---|---|
| | Customer Number | Contact | % | Customer Number | Contact | % | Customer Number | Contact | % | Customer Number | Contact | % | Customer Number | Contact | % |
| 8:30 - 9:00 | | | | | | | | | | | | | | | |
| 9:00 - 9:30 | | | | | | | | | | | | | | | |
| 9:30 - 10:00 | | | | | | | | | | | | | | | |
| 10:00 - 10:30 | | | | | | | | | | | | | | | |
| 10:30 - 11:00 | | | | | | | | | | | | | | | |
| 11:00 - 11:30 | | | | | | | | | | | | | | | |
| 11:30 - 12:00 | | | | | | | | | | | | | | | |
| 12:00 - 12:30 | | | | | | | | | | | | | | | |
| 12:30 - 1:00 | | | | | | | | | | | | | | | |
| 1:00 - 1:30 | | | | | | | | | | | | | | | |
| 1:30 - 2:00 | | | | | | | | | | | | | | | |
| 2:00 - 2:30 | | | | | | | | | | | | | | | |
| 2:30 - 3:00 | | | | | | | | | | | | | | | |
| 3:00 - 3:30 | | | | | | | | | | | | | | | |
| 3:30 - 4:00 | | | | | | | | | | | | | | | |
| 4:00 - 4:30 | | | | | | | | | | | | | | | |
| 4:30 - 5:00 | | | | | | | | | | | | | | | |
| Summary | | | | | | | | | | | | | | | |

Hometown Steel with the design engineer. The percentages shown are taken from Exhibit 3. They represent the first calls of the month and are taken from the rows for the decision maker and key influence.

To score your performance for the month, use the scoring form shown in Exhibit 6. Your percent probability of making the sale multiplied by the customer potential represents your sales income. Remember: Your objective is to achieve the highest possible sales volume.

## Exhibit 6

### SALES SCORING FORM

| Customer | Monthly Potential | X | Probability | = | Sales |
|----------|------------------|---|-------------|---|-------|
| 1. Hometown Steel | $3,500 | X | | = | $ |
| 2. Howard Electric | 2,500 | X | | = | |
| 3. Harris Products | 3,500 | X | | = | |
| 4. Harley Tools | 1,500 | X | | = | |
| 5. Middleton Motors | 3,500 | X | | = | |
| 6. Maple Plastics | 2,200 | X | | = | |
| 7. Marvin Copper | 3,500 | X | | = | |
| 8. Millard Coil & Tube | 1,500 | X | | = | |
| 9. Westown Fabricating | 4,000 | X | | = | |
| 10. Wallace Brass | 1,750 | X | | = | |
| 11. Windsor Electric | 3,500 | X | | = | |
| 12. Winter Works | 1,500 | X | | = | |
| 13. Northville Knots | 2,500 | X | | = | |
| 14. Norris Stampings | 3,500 | X | | = | |
| 15. Newton Forgings | 5,500 | X | | = | |
| 16. Nester Containers | 1,500 | X | | = | |
| 17. Eastown Electric | 2,500 | X | | = | |
| 18. Eastern Machinery | 3,500 | X | | = | |
| 19. Everly Pottery | 2,500 | X | | = | |
| 20. Easter Sealings | 3,000 | X | | = | |
| 21. Southboro Tools | 5,500 | X | | = | |
| 22. Selleck Solvents | 3,500 | X | | = | |
| 23. Southern Sockets | 1,000 | X | | = | |
| 24. Sherman Shelving | 3,500 | X | | = | _____ |
| | | | Total Sales | = | $_____ |

# INDEX

## A

accomplishment, tree of, 322
activity quota, defined, 366
appearance:
    and sales presentations, 200
    and sales success, 32-37
appointment for sales presentations:
    arranging by mail, 195
    making, 192-198
    telephoning for, 193-194
approach:
    defined, 213
    types of, 213-216
assumption close, 308-309
attitudes:
    changing, 129-130
    nature of, 128-129
    and sales presentation, 200
    and sales success, 44-46
    understanding, 128-130
audiovisual aids, and sales
    demonstrations, 247
audiovisual sales presentations, 211

## B

behavior, as part of learning
    process, 127-128
behavioral sciences:
    applying knowledge of, 157-158
    knowledge of as aid to effective
    selling, 111-112
behavior norms, and society, 142
behavior patterns, looking for,
    335-336
beliefs:
    nature of, 130
    understanding, 128-130
bird dogs, defined, 175

boomerang technique, for handling
    objections, 272
business firm, and selling, 13-14
buying behavior:
    influence of groups on, 143-148
    and communication, 150-157
buying motives:
    of customers, 73-75
    emotional, 75
    rational, 74

## C

call-backs, paving the way for, 228
canvassing, cold, 173
catalogs, and sales demonstrations,
    246
charts, and sales demonstrations,
    244-245
choice close, 311-312
close:
    assumption, 308-309
    attitudes toward the, 298-299
    choice, 311-312
    deciding when to, 303-307
    direct, 309-310
    dispose of the obstacle, 310-311
    early, 303-304
    emotional, 312-313
    at end of presentation, 304-305
    final detail, 312
    how many times to try to, 305
    looking for signs to, 306
    managing the, 300-303
    part-way through, 304
    special concession, 314-315
    standing-room-only, 313-314

## S

sale:
  analyzing each, 334-335
  closing the, 298-324
sales appeals, types of, 76-77
sales demonstrations:
  and audiovisual aids, 247
  and catalogs, 246
  and charts, 244-245
  developing a positive, 248-253
  and display boards, 244
  effective, 233-254
  and graphs, 245
  group, 241
  ingredients of, 242-248
  of intangibles, 242
  and kits, 245-246
  and overlays, 244
  and plant tours, 240
  and portfolios, 246
  and posters, 245
  preparation of, 234-236
  and product, 243
  and product testing, 237-238
  and prospect involvement,
    238-240
  and samples, 247
  and sense appeal, 237
  and showmanship, 240-241
  techniques of, 237-242
sales efforts, examining, 334-336
sales information, sources of, 97-100
sales knowledge:
  of your company, 88-92
  converting to customer benefits,
    100-102
  importance of, 83-84
  of your industry, 84-88
  of your products, 92-97
sales performance, improving,
    350-356
  and self-assertiveness, 353-354
  and transactional analysis, 352-353
  and transcendental meditation,
    351
salesperson:
  complete, and sales success, 31-32
  the "thinking," 336-337

sales positions, types of, 16-22
sales preparation, reserving time for,
    370
sales presentations:
  adjusting for different customer
    types, 223-224
  and appearance, 200
  appointments for, 192-198
  and attitude, 200
  audiovisual, 211
  characteristics of good, 226-227
  and equipment, 200-201
  guidelines for, 216-221
  length of, 223
  memorized, 208-209
  need analysis, 211
  need identification, 210-211
  outlined, 210
  planning, 198
  preparing for, 187-202
  and showmanship, 221-223
  types of, 208-212
sales profile:
  developing, 46-48
  setting goals for, 48
sales promotion, geared to
    customer, 341-343
sales quota, defined, 366
sales success:
  and appearance, 32-37
  and attitude, 44-46
  and complete salesperson, 31-32
  and health, 36
  and mannerisms, 35-36
  and manners, 36
  personality traits to cultivate for,
    37-42
  personality traits to overcome for,
    43-44
  and voice and speech habits, 35
samples, and sales demonstrations,
    247
segments, market, 57-60
self-assertiveness, to improve sales
    performance, 353-354
self-image, 131-135
  nature of, 134-135